Cryptodemocracy

Polycentricity: Studies in Institutional Diversity and Voluntary Governance

Series Editors: Lenore T. Ealy & Paul Dragos Aligica

This interdisciplinary series explores the varieties of social institutions, processes, and patterns of governance that emerge through individuals' coordination, cooperation, and competition in governance systems based on freedom of choice, freedom of exchange, and freedom of association. Under conditions of relative freedom of association, human diversity leads to institutional diversity and polycentric structures. In contrast to monocentric, unitary, and hierarchical command and control systems, polycentric social systems comprise many decision centers interacting freely under an overarching set of common rules. First introduced by Michael Polanyi as a descriptive and normative feature of free societies and further elaborated by Nobel Prize in Economics recipient Elinor Ostrom and public choice political economy co-founder Vincent Ostrom, the notion of polycentricity has proven itself able to offer a powerful analytical framework for expanding our understanding of the operation of governance regimes, constitutional federalism, law, public administration, private ordering, civics and citizenship, subsidiarity, nonprofit organization, cultural pluralism, civil society, and entrepreneurship. Studies in this series will refine the conceptual framework of polycentricity and its governance theory implications, while expanding their application in the study of what Alexis de Tocqueville called the art and science of association. These studies should be of interest to scholars, policymakers, executives, social entrepreneurs, and citizens working to devise ways of living together harmoniously in civil societies.

Recent titles in the series:

Cryptodemocracy: How Blockchain Can Radically Expand Democratic Choice, by Darcy W.E. Allen, Chris Berg, and Aaron M. Lane

Cryptodemocracy

How Blockchain Can Radically Expand Democratic Choice

Darcy W.E. Allen, Chris Berg,
and Aaron M. Lane

LEXINGTON BOOKS
Lanham • Boulder • New York • London

Published by Lexington Books
An imprint of The Rowman & Littlefield Publishing Group, Inc.
4501 Forbes Boulevard, Suite 200, Lanham, Maryland 20706
www.rowman.com

6 Tinworth Street, London SE11 5AL

British Library Cataloguing in Publication Information Available

Library of Congress Cataloging-in-Publication Data Available

ISBN 978-1-4985-7963-6 (cloth)
ISBN 978-1-4985-7964-3 (electronic)

Contents

Preface   vii

1   Introduction   1
2   Technologies of Choosing   19
3   A Framework for Institutional Collective Choice   35
4   Delegating the Vote   49
5   Bargaining and Exchange in a Cryptodemocracy   69
6   Cryptodemocratic Corporate Governance   89
7   Cryptodemocratic Labor Unions   111
8   The Future of a Cryptodemocracy   133

Bibliography   141
Index   155
About the Authors   163

Preface

Democracy is a technology with which we control government. Not all governments are democratic and not all democratic governments are equally democratic, but for the most part the world's ideas of what a democracy looks like are relatively fixed. Each person gets a vote to elect a representative legislature and/or an executive leader (such as a president) that implements existing laws and in some way passes new ones. Constitutional change comes from either formal mechanisms (like a referendum or convention or supermajority vote in the legislature) or political violence (such as a revolution).

Not only do these requirements make it hard to innovate in political structure—revolutions and referendums are costly and rare—but the rules by which democracies are governed are necessarily monopolistic. If "we" as a community decide that we should organize ourselves as a first-past-the-post presidential system with three-year fixed terms, then "we" all have to abide by that decision as a community, even those individuals who would prefer a Westminster system or four-year terms.

In Australia in 2017 there was a national vote on whether the Commonwealth government should legislate for same-sex marriage. (The vote was technically a postal survey, and unlike other political votes in Australia was voluntary, rather than compulsory, but these details need not detain us.) Popular opinion suggested that a large majority of Australian voters supported same-sex marriage. And a headcount on how parliament would have voted if it was presented as legislation suggested that same-sex marriage would pass. Yet at the same time a similarly large majority of voters supported the idea of a national vote. It seemed that many voters both wanted same-sex marriage to be legalized and the right to choose whether same-sex marriage would be legalized.

These two preferences in some apparent tension with each other suggest that we are not entirely and always happy with the basic feature of representative democracy: that we ought to delegate our equal stake in the policy decisions of government to representatives nominated and elected ahead of time.

But like the taco ad says: why not both? It is the argument of this book that the structure that gave us this tension is not a necessary permanent feature of democratic orders. As we explore here, blockchains, the distributed ledger technology underpinning cryptocurrencies such as Bitcoin and Ethereum, provide an infrastructure on which we can make new choices not just about how to vote, but about what it means to have an individual, sovereign stake in the political choices of the societies in which we live. Many Australians wanted to have a personal say on the question of same-sex marriage. Many Australians were happy to delegate that decision to their political representative. Each could—should—be able to choose how he or she exercises his or her shared democratic stake.

We are three economists—Darcy is an innovation economist, Chris is an economic historian, and Aaron works at the juncture of law and economics—interested in the institutions that structure our exchanges, and how those institutions shift as ideas and technologies evolve. The study of the democratic applications of blockchain is obviously productive and, we think, a surprisingly rich vein to mine. We call the resulting framework *cryptodemocracy*—a democratic framework that exploits cryptographically secure distributed ledgers and enables for the decentralized construction of a political system. We cannot answer the question of what a democratic system would look like if voters were given the power to delegate their voting power on their own terms, including the ability to variably compensate delegates for doing so (what would under most democratic systems be described as vote trading). But the reason we cannot answer that is because it is an entrepreneurial question. Just as the market framework results in a spontaneous order that no analyst could predict ahead of time, we make no claims as to what voters want, or what services delegates will offer—just that the move from a "planned" democracy to a cryptodemocracy offers a vast new space for innovation and entrepreneurship.

There is of course a major caveat. As we write in 2019, there are many technical and sociological problems with the use of blockchains as a tool by which electoral authorities can manage elections. While there is an obvious appeal there, and a great deal of work being done in this area, distributed ledger technology is not a silver bullet that can resolve the myriad challenges around security, auditability, and openness that plague all digital voting systems.

But this book is not really about blockchain as a technology of voting. It is about blockchain as an institution. We are less interested in the act of voting and more in voting as a tool for the coordination of human activity—whether that activity is economic, political, or social, broadly defined. Distributed ledgers allow democracy to operate differently—to give us new ways to exercise the one-person, one-vote principle in more complex, subtle, responsive, and dare we say Hayekian ways.

There is no reason to believe that the structures of democracy cannot be subject to the same institutional and entrepreneurial innovation that characterizes market coordination. This book is the working out of some of the implications of putting democracy on a blockchain, exploiting some of the tools and opportunities that this strange new technology affords us.

This book is a product of the RMIT Blockchain Innovation Hub, the world's first science research center into blockchain technology, founded in 2017. The Hub was an initiative of its now director, Jason Potts, who was a co-author of the first paper we wrote on cryptodemocracy in the *Review of Austrian Economics* and is a great supporter of this project, and supported by Calum Drummond, Ian Palmer, Geoff Stokes, and Tim Fry, all of whom this book would not have been possible without. We would also like to thank our colleagues Sinclair Davidson, Mikayla Novak, Alastair Berg, Brendan Markey-Towler, and Ana Pochesneva, and the many others who are affiliated and work with the Hub.

This book and some of the papers which fed into it have been presented in various forums. We would like to thank the participants at the Mont Pelerin Society Young Scholars session in Stockholm in 2017, and particularly Keith Hankins and Pavel Kuchar, for their extremely valuable comments. We would like to thank those who attended presentations of earlier versions of this work including at the Linked Democracy: AI for Democratic Innovation Conference in Melbourne, particularly Marta Poblet, and the RMIT Blockchain Innovation Hub Proof of Work Seminar series. We would also like to thank the members of the International Society for the Study of Decentralised Governance and the Worldwide Blockchain Innovation Association, with whom many of the ideas in this book have been canvassed.

Chris would like to thank his indulgent and forgiving family. Darcy would like to thank his wife, Klara, for her patience. Aaron would like to thank his wife, Jess, for her loving impatience.

—Darcy W.E. Allen,
Chris Berg,
and Aaron M. Lane,
Melbourne, April 2019

Chapter One

Introduction

This book applies institutional economics, political philosophy, and democratic theory to analyze the use of blockchain as an institutional technology for collective choice. New technologies open up the institutional possibilities of the decision-making process by lowering the costs of coordination, collaboration, and contract. When technologies change so too do the possible structures of democratic decision making. Language and writing enabled more elaborate voting procedures. Transportation technologies and the printing press facilitated representative democracy over greater distances and ballots. The internet might facilitate more frequent referenda in a direct democracy through electronic voting. In this book we develop and apply a new theoretical framework to analyze how blockchain technology—a technology for creating and maintaining distributed ledgers of information, including voting rights—might change the way we make collective choices.

As a governance technology, blockchain technology opens new possibilities for democratic coordination in what we call a *cryptodemocracy*. A cryptodemocracy is a democratic framework that allows vote-holders such as citizens to allocate and exchange their voting power as they see fit. We treat the vote as a form of property right, secured as a digital asset on a blockchain. Where in a representative democracy voters vote to choose a representative in a parliament every few years, in a cryptodemocracy voters delegate their vote to a delegate—on contractual terms which they have agreed with the delegate. This means that they can withdraw their delegation at any time (subject to the terms of the contract), retain their vote on issues that are important to them personally (allowing for direct democratic engagement on issues they care about, and delegative democracy on those they are less interested), and make compensatory exchanges around those delegations (vote trading). Voters are free to delegate their vote to any person (or algorithm) they like, whether that delegate is a neighbor, someone in their same suburb, or on the other side of the continent.

The result is a complex, evolutionary, unplanned democratic order—or, to adopt the term developed by Friedrich Hayek, a democratic *catallaxy*.[1] We explore the dynamics of various voting rights in a cryptodemocracy—including decomposing, delegating, and selling votes—and apply these understandings to lower-level collective choice examples of union governance and corporate governance. The structure that any cryptodemocracy takes emerges from the individual contracts between voting right holders as they seek to minimize their agency costs and decision-making costs of engaging in collective choice. Through a constitution, any cryptodemocratic system could reverse engineer some of the democratic features we are familiar with such as a formal parliament with a fixed number of seats, formal election cycles, and even geographic electorates. But these are neither a necessary nor inherent feature of cryptodemocracy. We argue that a cryptodemocracy is a new type of collective choice infrastructure on which more polycentric and dynamic structures of democracy may emerge, with the potential to radically change how individuals interact, learn, and discover.

This introductory chapter proceeds as follows. In the second section we introduce the problem of social choice in the twenty-first century through the lens of political parties and representation, motivating an analysis of a cryptodemocracy. Blockchain technology is introduced in the third section as a governance technology, demonstrating how it may ameliorate some of the challenges of collective choice under uncertainty. We lack a generalized framework to analyze how cryptodemocratic infrastructure—collective choice decision making facilitated through blockchain—changes the way we choose. Both developing and applying that framework is the task of this book. In the fourth section we outline the concept of democracy and its relationship to the evolution of a cryptodemocracy. In the fifth section we review our approach and structure of the book before providing a preview of our main findings.

THE PROBLEM OF SOCIAL CHOICE IN
THE TWENTY-FIRST CENTURY

Why this book, and why now? The first and simplest answer is because it is only now that we have technologies that make dynamic and polycentric cryptodemocratic structures possible. While blockchain technology was first invented in 2008, the blockchains that allow for the complex contracting and exchange that we see as central to a cryptodemocratic system only date from 2015. Furthermore, scholarship on the institutional possibilities of blockchain technology began in earnest only after the creation of those systems.[2]

While many of the ideas of democratic form that we explore predate block-chain technology, with this new generation of blockchains we can see how those ideas could be implemented.

The second reason relates to the form and institutions of democracy at the end of the second decade of the twenty-first century. It is widely believed that we are living through an age of democratic crisis, or popular dissatisfaction with democratic outcomes. In 2008, a group of political scientists, Marty Cohen, David Carol, Hans Noel, and John Zaller, published *The Party Decides: Presidential Nominations Before and After Reform*.[3] This book documented the success of party insiders in steering presidential nominations in the United States after the apparently "democratizing" reforms to party structure in the 1970s. Central to their argument was the existence of what they called the "invisible primary"—the period before the start of primary voting in Iowa and New Hampshire—where prospective candidates compete to lock down support from the party's top consultants and fund-raisers, political influencers, interest groups, and donors. The cover of the book features wisps of smoke, symbolizing the smoke-filled rooms where insiders coordinate to choose an elite-friendly, coalition-satisfying candidate.

Eight years later the nomination of Donald Trump at the top of the Republican Party presidential ticket seemed to be a big mark against their thesis. Trump defeated sixteen other candidates who provided to a greater or lesser degree a more insider-friendly policy platform. As the authors of *The Party Decides* reflected, they had underestimated the attention given by the press to the "invisible" primary—it was not so invisible anymore—and the strength of factions within the Republican Party itself.[4] Trump attracted a faction in the party who were strongly anti-immigration and anti–free trade, going significantly further in rhetoric and policy proposals than his competitors.[5] And, critically, Trump ran as a "populist."

Populism is a rhetorical and ideological stance, rather than a set of policy prescriptions.[6] Populists, argues Jan-Werner Müller, are anti-elites (the same insiders that had locked up previous presidential nominations), claim to represent "the people" against those elites, and are exclusive (that is, they draw boundaries between genuine members of the "people" and others, such as elites or outsiders).[7] Trump embodied this populist stance, appealing to a "real" America, whipping up anti-migrant sentiment, and promising to "drain the swamp" of Washington, DC, against the insiders—including the Republican insiders ("never-Trumpers") that opposed his candidacy. To be sure, factions within the Republican Party were not the only populist, anti-insider surge. The "Brexit" vote in the United Kingdom was a populist reaction against insider support for the European Union. There have been other variously successful swings across Europe, including Sweden—long seen as an exceptional state for its absence of a radical right-wing party.[8] Nor is populism in the developed world limited to the right side of politics. The Democratic Party nominated a classic insider candidate in Hillary Clinton but only after defeating a strong insurgent candidacy in the form of Bernie Sanders. Jeremy Corbyn's leadership of the British Labour Party also represents a factional takeover of a governing party by the left.

How should we understand the rise of these new populist movements? Political scientists and economists working on the economics of politics have long emphasized the role that parties play in directing, organizing, responding to, and sometimes resisting the wishes of the electorate. Edmund Burke described political parties as groups of people organizationally united in the pursuit of shared ideological interests.[9] In spatial models of political choice, political parties coordinate around policy stances. In his seminal work on the public choice of voting, Anthony Downs argued that parties tended to compete for the "median" voter.[10] The platforms of political parties as a result would coalesce around the center of a linear left-right ideological spectrum. Later elaborations of these spatial models have relaxed Downs's uni-dimensionality by arranging voter preferences around an *n*-dimensional space.[11] To the extent that voter preferences are not symmetrically arranged, it is mathematically trivial to demonstrate that there are many situations where there is no median voter for parties to coalesce around.[12] Downs also recognized that relaxing the assumption of single peaked preferences meant that parties might spatially locate apart from each other and rely on ideological claims to distinguish themselves. A further problem with the Downsian spatial model is that elections do not occur as a series of constant events—which facilitate an equilibration around toward the median voter—but as discrete events separated by a number of years.[13]

Political parties are both bottom-up and top-down. Many have questioned whether political parties (often in concert or competition with media outlets) follow or lead voter policy preferences.[14] For the most part, spatial models depict parties following voter preferences, rather than leading them. The empirical claim of the *Party Decides* was that party insiders have a great deal of leeway in determining not only the preferred presidential candidate but also the party's policy positions. Giovanni Sartori describes political parties as two-way "transmission belts" for the communication of policy preferences between the public and political insiders: parties "aggregate, select, and, eventually, deviate and distort."[15] Institutional analysts have emphasized how bottom-up communications channels are mediated by political institutions—the processes by which policies are considered through committees, rules, and other constraints.[16] Other agents in the political contest pursue different ends to satisficing the median voter. Regulatory state theorists have emphasized the increasingly large policy domain controlled by bureaucratic agencies deliberately separated from the lines of democratic accountability.[17] And a group of scholars working on the "cartel party" thesis offer an argument that seeks to limit political competition by exercising influence over the funding and entry rules for political parties themselves.[18] These generations of political scientists and economists paint a picture of a democratic political system that is unlikely to aggregate preferences in a stable or reliable way. Charles R. Plott, writing of developments in social choice theory up to 1976, concluded that

> What they now appear to have been uncovering is a gigantic cavern into which fall almost all of our ideas about social actions. Almost anything we say and/or anyone has ever said about what society wants or should get is threatened with internal inconsistency. It is as though people have been talking for years about a thing that cannot, in principle, exist, and a major effort now is needed to see what objectively remains from the conversation.[19]

The way that political preferences are aggregated or formed—whether pushed through voters or pulled through parties—is in part a function of the technologies available. As we will see in chapter 1, new technological developments shape the possible ways that voters interact in the political process. Technologies change the potential institutional procedures and structures that coordinate millions of people to make a decision. From this perspective, political parties are just one potential solution to this challenge and their relevance or efficiency will change as new technologies become available. Indeed, parties can be considered just one mechanism through which voters economize on the decision costs of voting under uncertainty. The argument of this book is that a new technology—distributed, decentralized ledgers— opens up the possibility for a large number of alternative mechanisms.

BLOCKCHAIN AS A GOVERNANCE TECHNOLOGY

First invented by the pseudonymous Satoshi Nakamoto in the Bitcoin White Paper in 2008, blockchains consist of an immutable digital ledger of transactions chained together into blocks and validated by a decentralized network of nodes.[20] Nakamoto's innovation was to develop a distributed ledger that did not rely on a trusted central authority to maintain and enforce consensus over the state of the shared ledger. To achieve this goal, Nakamoto combined public key cryptography (to ensure that only the holders of a private key to an amount of cryptocurrency can spend it) and game-theoretic economic incentives. In Bitcoin, a group of users called "miners" compete to solve a computationally difficult cryptographic ("hashing") puzzle. The winner of this game has the right to group new transactions that have been announced to the network into blocks, and claim a reward in Bitcoin for doing so (as of 2019, 12.5 Bitcoin). This "proof of work" consensus mechanism provides the security for the network by making it more expensive to attack the network rather than defend it.

This design gives the Bitcoin blockchain a number of economically relevant features. It is *censorship resistant*: under the normal operation of the Bitcoin blockchain, no single entity is able to rewrite the shared ledger. One possible exception to this is a "51 percent attack," in which a single entity gains control of 51 percent of the hashing power. While a successful 51 percent attack would not allow that entity to rewrite the history of the blockchain, it would allow it to "double spend" Bitcoin—effectively the cryptocurrency version of counterfeiting. The possibility of such an attack has focused much attention on the effective decentralization of Bitcoin mining. The Bitcoin network is also *byzantine fault tolerant*: it is able to come to a consensus over facts even in the presence of non-cooperative agents or communications problems.

Bitcoin was conceptualized as a form of "electronic cash." However in Bitcoin, the cryptocurrency functions as a valued token within the blockchain network to incentivize good behavior. Bitcoin contains a scripting language which allows users to build basic functions into the Bitcoin blockchain itself, such as freezing funds until a given time. Since 2011 a large ecosystem of new blockchains have been "forked" from the Bitcoin network or created from scratch, varying (for example) the purpose of the cryptocurrency and its features (such as the inflation rate), the consensus mechanism, the scripting language, how publicly accessible the network is, and the degree of decentralization. Alternative cryptocurrencies such as Litecoin, Dash, Dogecoin, Monero, and ZCash vary the proof-of-work rules, block size, and privacy features of Bitcoin respectively. "Private" or "permissioned" blockchains such as IBM's Hyperledger Fabric and R3's Corda limit who can write and read the shared ledger. Alternative consensus mechanisms also provide a dimension on which cryptocurrencies have been developed—such as proof-of-stake, and distributed or practical byzantine fault tolerance. These institutional constitutional experimentations are being driven by a constant process of entrepreneurial discovery.[21]

A new generation of blockchains offer significantly more complex scripting languages, and open up a space for more complex economic transactions. Ethereum, which launched in 2015, boasts a "Turing complete" programming language that can store and execute scripts across the Ethereum Virtual Machine. This language allows for complete computer programs to be included on the distributed ledger, making Ethereum a censorship-resistant, byzantine fault–tolerant distributed platform for executing any program. A class of these programs are described as "smart contracts": algorithmic contracts that execute exactly as programmed across the network when the contract's conditions are met.[22] Users of smart contracts are assured that the contract will execute as written automatically, without the need for external authorities to enforce the contract terms. A simple example of a smart contract is an escrow function, which remits funds when a certain event (either an event internal to the blockchain, or external using an "oracle" to trigger the contract) occurs. More complex programs on Turing complete blockchains are called distributed applications (DApps).[23] More complex again are distributed autonomous organizations (DAOs) which organize human and machine activity through smart contract system. A DAO is effectively a decentralized version of the firm. A range of alternative public blockchains are in development that offer similar or comparable features (such as NEM, NEO, and EOS).

At time of writing (early 2019) blockchains are an early stage innovation. Many of the most common and popular blockchain implementations currently have limitations that might preclude them from the sort of uses we explore in this book. The first- and second-generation blockchains suffer from scaling problems, meaning that they can only propogate a limited number of transactions per second. Where the VISA payments network boasts of being able to handle 24,000 transactions per second, the Bitcoin network can process between 3.3 to 7 transactions per second.[24] In late 2017 the Ethereum network was "clogged" by the release of a blockchain game called Cryptokitties. The popularity of the game caused significant delays to transactions across the network. Software upgrades to these blockchains, as well as "second-layer" solutions such as Bitcoin's Lightning Network, offer a potential solution to these scaling problems, although at the time of writing they remain a significant constraint. Storage space may be a limitation on blockchain scalability. Immutability means that the transaction ledger continuously grows (although again there are potential solutions to this problem, including sharding or reducing the amount of data that each node stores). Other technical limitations of blockchains include their user experience—as managing private keys can be unwieldy it is asking a lot of blockchain users to do that themselves. There are also concerns over the proof-of-work consensus mechanism used by Bitcoin and many other blockchains being electricity intensive. One estimate suggests that the Bitcoin blockchain alone consumes 2.55 gigawatts, comparable with the electricity consumption of Ireland.[25] There are alternative consensus mechanisms which are in part being designed to reduce this electricity consumption, and any discussion of the cost of consensus must be compared to existing governance structures seeking to build and enforce trust.[26]

It is of course possible that "blockchains" (as a specific instance of a decentralized ledger that groups transactions into blocks and chains them together) will not in the future be the dominant form of decentralized ledger. Alternative distributed ledgers, such as those powered by directed acyclic graphs, which come to a consensus on transactions by focusing on how the network "gossips" about new transactions, promise to resolve many of the current problems with blockchains (scalability, energy consumption, and so forth).[27] But these alternatives are in an even earlier stage of development.

Consequentially, in this book we refer to *blockchains* as a stand in for all decentralized, distributed, digital ledger technologies, taking the risk that future technological developments might make this terminology anachronistic. We are not interested in specific blockchain implementations. Just as we are institutionally neutral over the eventual structure of collective decision making that emerges, our argument is intended to be neutral to any particular distributed ledger technology, provided it offers the features of smart contracting and can be deployed for the use of voting mechanisms. Blockchains are a proof-of-concept technology that demonstrates the viability of consensus around shared ledgers without the need for a trusted central authority.

This book offers a contribution to the study of blockchains through the lens of *institutional cryptoeconomics*.[28] Conventional cryptoeconomics draws on game theory and mechanism design and focuses on the protocols of distributed ledger technology. In contrast, *institutional* cryptoeconomics draws primarily on institutional economics to examine the role that ledgers play in structuring property rights, the nature of the firm, public goods provision, supply chains, and business processes. Blockchains are a self-enclosed space for economic coordination, with mechanisms to facilitate the exchange of value (tokens), property rights protection and security (cryptography), information provision (the public immutable ledger), and contracting (smart contracts). Applying the conjoined schema of Friedrich Hayek, Ronald Coase, Oliver Williamson, Douglass North, and Elinor Ostrom—what can broadly be termed in the mainline of economic thought—blockchains are an institutionally distinct coordination mechanism, competing with firms, markets, commons, clubs, relational contracting, and governments.[29] In this view blockchains are a technology of governance that provide for the protection, verification, and exchange of property rights. Given that blockchains, at least theoretically, significantly reduce the search and coordination costs of exchange, how will they shift the governance of property rights and the nature of economic organization? Just as blockchain has been applied to applications in law, supply chains, charities, and identity management, in this book we apply the potential of blockchain technology to the problem of collective choice in a democracy.[30]

THE DEMOCRATIC NATURE OF CRYPTODEMOCRACY

Current attempts to build voting systems using blockchain technology are not grounded in an understanding of democracy as an economic coordination problem. In this book we apply blockchain technology to the problem of collective choice to create a democratic collective choice infrastructure we call *cryptodemocracy*. Our analysis works at the unusual intersection between economics, computer science, and democratic theory. We expect that the last is likely to be the most uncomfortable. An extremely diverse range of political systems describe themselves (and are recognized) as being in some way *democratic*. The mechanisms by which these systems make collective choices vary considerably. Common—but not constant—features are a representative body (the legislature), an executive (which may be drawn from that representative body or may be elected separately), a head of state (sometimes from the executive, sometimes a hereditary position), a judiciary (sometimes appointed by the executive, sometimes directly elected, sometimes subject to approval by the representative body), a bureaucracy (with a mixture of appointed, elected, approved, and permanent "non-political" positions), some form of adult suffrage, and majority (sometimes supermajority) voting rules. A cryptodemocracy may enable new structures to emerge through a dynamic process of contracting over voting rights.

This multiplicity of democratic features is the result of two and a half thousand years of experimentation and democratic innovation. Casting our net wider across historical space we can see an even greater diversity of features described as democratic: variously limited franchises, voting rules that require unanimous consent (such as the Polish-Lithuanian Commonwealth's *liberum veto*), selection by randomization (sortition) rather than by election, vote buying, and government-by-plebiscite. Some elements of these approaches remain in modern democratic systems (Switzerland's referendum system, for instance), and others have been abandoned to historical curiosity. In this sense, the democratic form has evolved through time.

What makes cryptodemocracy democratic? Dictionary definitions of democracy tend to be vague or smuggle in normative organizational arguments. Merriam-Webster gives us two such definitions: "government by the people; *especially*: rule of the majority," degrading the role of supermajorities or unanimity rules, and "a government in which the supreme power is vested in the people and exercised by them directly or indirectly through a system of representation usually involving periodically held free elections," again tying democracy to specific institutional features. But we are looking for an approach that encompasses not just direct and representative democracy but more exotic models, such as democracy-by-sortition—or some other framework that is yet to be discovered—that could emerge under the framework we explore. In effect we wish to define and develop a system that can be considered democratic while remaining as institutionally neutral as possible.

A more fruitful approach is to specify ahead of time a normative criteria for democratic organization. The fundamental democratic claim is that of political equality. Political equality, or egalitarianism, is a widely accepted and shared requirement for democratic legitimacy. Equality is not sufficient for democratic legitimacy but it is necessary. As Charles Beitz has written, political equality "serves as the chief regulative principle of democratic political competition by defining fair terms of participation in it."[31] Each individual member of the society has an equal claim to decision-making power about the governing arrangements of his or her society.[32] Political equality manifests itself differently across separate domains. In liberal societies, political equality has been understood to grant each member of the society the equal right to speak, but not the equal right to be heard. Capability theorists and critics of liberalism have responded that formal institutional political equality may privilege media owners and disadvantage minority voices (who may experience barriers to effective participation). In a voting system, formal political equality is reflected at the first instance by the "one-person, one-vote" (1p1v) rule, which determines how votes are weighted against each other. Andrew Rehfeld describes this as an institutional initial position, and points out that many features of real-world democracies violate the 1p1v criteria. For example, while a vote for a legislator in an electoral division may be weighted equally against other members of that electoral division, differences in the population size of those divisions make any given individuals vote more or less "powerful" when compared against a member of a neighboring division. We start from the criteria of 1p1v, and derive the institutions of cryptodemocracy from that normative principle.

One additional normative criteria commonly placed on democratic systems is majority rule—a decision rule that determines under what circumstances a question should be seen to have been "agreed" to by the group. By contrast with 1p1v, majority rule is less well attested in principle and practice. Methods of electing representatives differ considerably around the world (first-past-the-post, preferential voting, Hare-Clark, etc.) and sometimes only tangentially relate, or are judged by, a straight majority rule principle. Further, as Knut Wicksell and James Buchanan demonstrated, for many questions of collective choice supermajorities are desirable because the normative basis for majority rule is unstable.[33] Placing majority rule as a democratic criteria—rather than a common democratic feature—would exclude both unanimity systems and sortition systems from the pantheon of democracies. We consider majority rule one of a set of constitutional choices that a democratic society can make, without forfeiting its claim to be democratic.

As this suggests, the cryptodemocratic framework we describe in this book is best understood not as a specific system of government (with particular organizational features around suffrage, representation, parliaments, and heads of state) but as a base layer of economic and political infrastructure on which a variety of systems of government can *emerge*. Rather than a centrally planned democracy—through restrictions such as electorates and parliaments—a cryptodemocracy lets these institutions emerge over time, drawing on the local contextual knowledge of voters and their choice of how they wish to selectively engage in the political process. The determinant of what features emerge is the institutional preferences of the voters themselves. Cryptodemocracy empowers voters not only to vote for specific public policy questions (as in a plebiscite) or for delegates to do so on their behalf (as representatives) but to individually tailor how their vote is delegated or reserved according to their preferences about policy and circumstance. For example, it is possible under a cryptodemocratic framework for a voter to delegate her vote to a representative but reserve her vote on certain policy issues (such as moral questions regarding same-sex marriage or foreign policy, for example, or tax rules that might affect her personal finances) to be exercised directly. The resulting cryptodemocratic system is a hybrid of both representative and direct democracy. How representative or direct the system is would depend on how voters chose to reserve or delegate their votes. This is a relatively simple example. More complex contracts around the conditions on which delegates exercise their votes, the circumstances under which those contracts are voided or renegotiated (the parallel here is with elections), and how voters choose to divide political power among their delegates, division of political power would lead to complex, evolutionary, and adaptive structures of collective choice.

STRUCTURE AND APPROACH

Our approach to analyzing a cryptodemocracy is interdisciplinary, drawing variously on new institutional economics, entrepreneurial theory, and political philosophy. Our approach is to develop a theoretical framework of democracy that begins from the perspective of votes as bundles of property rights, and the institutions governing those votes as having to operate both under uncertainty and with positive transaction costs. In this way our analysis of a cryptodemocracy is contract-theoretic, drawing on the mainline of economic theory.[34]

The book proceeds as follows. In chapter 2, "Technologies of Choosing," we contextualize our analysis of a cryptodemocracy through a historical analysis of the relationship between technology and collective choice. We explore the historical links between democracy and technology in both directions. How have new technologies shifted the way we collectively organize? What does it mean to treat voting as a bundle of property rights? What are the lessons from democratic history and democratic political philosophy? The evolution of democratic structures has been propelled through institutional experimentation. We show that the structure that collective choice infrastructure takes is in part a response to the technologies available. From Ancient Athens to the twenty-first century, technologies have been developed to ameliorate the transaction costs of collective decision making under uncertainty. Technologies not only change the choices that are made, but the processes and institutions that are possible. This understanding lays the foundations for our new framework for the institutions of democratic choice (the task of the following chapter), and ultimately allows us to explore how blockchain shifts the process of democratic institutional evolution.

In chapter 3, "A Framework for Institutional Collective Choice," we develop a new theoretical framework to understand institutional choice. Collective choices must take place under uncertainty, with positive transaction costs, and utilizing subjective and distributed knowledge. Our new Democratic Institutional Possibility Frontier (DIPF) shows that we can view different democratic institutions as trading-off the costs of coordination of bundles of voting property rights (the most basic of which is the right to or not to vote) into a collective choice. Agency costs are those costs incurred in making and enforcing agreements over representatives while decision costs are those incurred while formulating positions on collective choice issues. From dictatorships to direct democracies, institutions ameliorate these costs by governing constellations of voting rights in comparatively effective ways. The institutional set, however, is bounded by prevailing technologies. We propose that blockchain technology opens up new institutional possibilities within the DIPF space—including vote delegation and exchange in a cryptodemocracy—through more secure and effective governance of voting rights. This positions us to explore the nature of some of those rights in the following chapters.

In chapter 4, "Delegating the Vote," we examine how in a cryptodemocracy voters could exercise their right to delegate voting rights to others. In a pure cryptodemocracy voters are free to contract away their voting property rights through delegative contracts—conducted through blockchain-based smart contracts—including conditions with those contracts. This raises interesting questions over the structure and nature of democratic governance. For instance, rather than the democratic procedural structure being defined—for instance as a chain of delegation from voter to representative to the executive and so on—in a cryptodemocracy that procedural structure emerges as the function of the preferences of the franchise. Delegation in cryptodemocracy uniquely comes from a contract-theoretic approach to voting property rights because each delegation is entered into as a voluntary agreement. Compared to a representative democracy, in a cryptodemocracy voters can delegate to any other voter and tailor that contract with conditions attached ("conditional decomposition" of votes). This is a much more nuanced and bespoke space of political action, with emergent polycentric characteristics. From here it follows that individuals might want to enter into delegative contracts not just with conditions attached, but also exchange their voting rights in a marketplace.

In chapter 5, "Bargaining and Exchange in a Cryptodemocracy," we explore how voters might exchange and bargain for compensation over voting property rights. This introduces deeper market-based processes into the political process—the cryptodemocratic parallel to voting markets—and theoretically incorporates more intensity of political preferences. We outline some of the objections to voting markets—such as mapping economic inequality onto political inequality—and the reasons why they might be desirable. Blockchain overcomes one of the fundamental problems of voting markets—the cost of enforcing vote exchanges—by reducing the potential for *ex post* opportunistic behavior. Voters could code conditions into automatically executing contracts that remain attached to a vote as it is delegated to others. By comparing a cryptodemocracy to another attempt to integrate prices into voting, we propose that a cryptodemocracy is more conducive to coordinating the uncertain, distributed, and subjective knowledge necessary to form and to express political opinions. We also suggest that monetary compensation could flow in either direction: voters might pay delegates to act on their behalf, or delegates might pay voters for their voting rights. Allowing voters to receive or pay for votes incentivizes democratic discourse and exchange across the political spectrum, rather than only delegating votes to likeminded delegates. At the same time a cryptodemocracy maintains the fundamental democratic principle of 1p1v. We do not make a claim of efficiency or optimality in a cryptodemocracy. Rather we propose it as an institutional structure conducive to the dynamic process of democratic governance. In the following chapters we apply these cryptodemocratic principles to lower levels of collective action—corporate governance and labor union governance.

In chapter 6, "Cryptodemocratic Corporate Governance," we provide a case study of a cryptodemocracy examining shareholder voting in public companies. In the corporate context, voting rights are a key part of the bundle of property rights that go along with share ownership. Decision making in the company is polycentric as power is divided between directors and shareholders. Although directors are responsible for most day-to-day business and capital decisions of the company, shareholders retain power over important decisions including electing directors, approving major mergers and acquisitions, having a "say on pay," and changing constitutional rules. However, it is often impractical for shareholders to attend company meetings and exercise these votes directly. This chapter examines how shareholders are contracting, delegating, and exchanging voting power to economize on the decision costs of exercising voting rights. These range from contracts for the provision of information, to delegating votes to a proxy solicitor seeking an outcome in a "proxy contest," through to outright corporate vote buying, among others. Our focus then turns to the system for recording share ownership. Current share settlement systems are complex, and this has caused several problems of "pathologies" that undermine the important role of shareholder voting in corporate governance. In this chapter we address how a corporate cryptodemocracy would change the corporate voting landscape and strengthen proprietary voting rights.

In chapter 7, "Cryptodemocratic Labor Unions," we move on to considering collective decision making within the employment bargaining context. We proceed on the basis that every worker has an individual property right in his or her own labor but faces a fundamental trade-off between decision costs and agency costs in seeking to strike a bargain with an employer. This means that every worker should have input into his or her own wages and conditions. Collective bargaining economizes decision costs. One of the key differences between corporate governance and trade union governance is coercion—unhappy shareholders can sell their shares, but rarely can unhappy employees in unionized industries exit to another labor union. This means that corporate shareholders face relatively high decision costs, but unionized employees face relatively higher agency costs. In this chapter we present a case study on a recent Australian Royal Commission into Trade Union Governance to highlight the real agency costs faced by union members. Applying cryptodemocratic principles to these problems, we argue that trade union governance could be strengthened and that a new polycentric collective action could emerge in the modern economy.

In chapter 8, "The Future of a Cryptodemocracy," we make speculative predictions over how the cryptodemocratic process might eventuate. A cryptodemocracy is the foundational collective choice infrastructure where bundles of voting rights are governed through blockchain, and on which the structures of democratic decision making emerge through the preferences of contracting voters. This infrastructure enables new institutional possibilities within the DIPF space outlined in chapter 3. While we cannot predict precisely what a cryptodemocracy might look like in practice, we can make claims over the behavior of voters and delegates based on the incentives they face. For instance, what will delegates do? The delegate is a new type of political entrepreneur who is incentivized to further reduce the transaction costs of mutually beneficial exchange and to coordinate voter preferences. These entrepreneurial activities will include developing new governance technologies—such as standardized open source delegative contracts—that reduce the frictions in discovering and forming the preferences of voters. Eventually we suspect that delegates will begin to offer goods and services in return for voting rights: creating new polycentric states within the democratic system. And how might voters behave? Voters might deploy other new complementary technologies—such as artificial intelligence (AI)—to seek mutually beneficial exchanges on their behalf. Voters might utilize a combination of machine learning and AI to fully express their political rights and autonomously seek mutually beneficial exchanges. This is effectively a disintermediation and decentralization of lobbying, and is a natural progression from providing property rights to voters where that property has some value.

NOTES

1. Friedrich A Hayek, *Law, Legislation and Liberty: A New Statement of the Liberal Principles of Justice and Political Economy* (United Kingdom: Routledge, 2012).
2. For example, see Trent J. MacDonald, "Theory of Non-Territorial Internal Exit," *available at SSRN 2661226* (2015); Christian Catalini and Joshua S. Gans, "Some Simple Economics of the Blockchain" (National Bureau of Economic Research, 2016); Sinclair Davidson, Primavera De Filippi, and Jason Potts, "Blockchains and the Economic Institutions of Capitalism," *Journal of Institutional Economics* (2018).
3. Marty Cohen et al., *The Party Decides: Presidential Nominations Before and After Reform* (University of Chicago Press, 2009).
4. Marty Cohen et al., "Party Versus Faction in the Reformed Presidential Nominating System," *Political Science and Politics* 49, no. 4 (2016).
5. For the difference between faction and party, see Giovanni Sartori, *Parties and Party Systems: A Framework for Analysis* (ECPR Press, 2005).
6. Cas Mudde and Cristóbal Rovira Kaltwasser, *Populism: A Very Short Introduction* (Oxford University Press, 2017).
7. Jan-Werner Müller, *What Is Populism?* (Penguin UK, 2017). See those in France (the National Front), the Netherlands (the Party for Freedom), Australia (One Nation), Germany (Alternative for Germany), the Czech Republic (ANO Party), Austria (the Freedom Party), Italy (5 Star Movement), Hungary (Fidesz), Poland (Law and Justice Party), and Sweden (Sweden Democrats).
8. Jens Rydgren, "Radical Right Populism in Sweden: Still a Failure, but for How Long?" *Scandinavian Political Studies* 25, no. 1 (2002); Jens Rydgren and Sara Van der Meiden, "Sweden, Now a Country Like All the Others? The Radical Right and the End of Swedish Exceptionalism," *SU Department of Sociology Working Paper Series* (2016).
9. Edmund Burke, *Select Works of Edmund Burke, Vol. 1 (Thoughts on the Cause of the Present Discontents; Two Speeches on America)* (Indianapolis: Liberty Fund, 1770).
10. Anthony Downs, "An Economic Theory of Political Action in a Democracy," *Journal of Political Economy* 65, no. 2 (1957).
11. However, this comes at the expense of their predictive power. See Charles R. Plott, "A Notion of Equilibrium and Its Possibility under Majority Rule," *The American Economic Review* 57, no. 4 (1967); Otto A. Davis, Melvin J. Hinich, and Peter C. Ordeshook, "An Expository Development of a Mathematical Model of the Electoral Process," *American Political Science Review* 64, no. 2 (1970); Gerald H. Kramer, "On a Class of Equilibrium Conditions for Majority Rule," *Econometrica: Journal of the Econometric Society* 41, no. 2 (1973); Richard D. McKelvey, "Intransitivities in Multidimensional Voting Models and Some Implications for Agenda Control," *Journal of Economic Theory* 12, no. 3 (1976).
12. See the discussion in Christopher H. Achen and Larry M. Bartels, *Democracy for Realists: Why Elections Do Not Produce Responsive Government*, vol. 4 (Princeton University Press, 2017), 24–26.
13. See discussion in Charles K. Rowley, "The Relevance of the Median Voter Theorem," *Journal of Institutional and Theoretical Economics*, no. H. 1 (1984).
14. Edward James Fagan, "Marching Orders? US Party Platforms and Legislative Agenda Setting 1948–2014," *Political Research Quarterly* (2018); Jeffery A. Jenkins and Nathan W. Monroe, "On Measuring Legislative Agenda-Setting Power," *American Journal of Political Science* 60, no. 1 (2016).
15. Sartori, *Parties and Party Systems: A Framework for Analysis*, 25.
16. Kenneth A. Shepsle, "Institutional Arrangements and Equilibrium in Multidimensional Voting Models," *American Journal of Political Science* 23, no. 1 (1979); William H. Riker, "Implications from the Disequilibrium of Majority Rule for the Study of Institutions," *American Political Science Review* 74, no. 2 (1980).
17. Giandomenico Majone, "Nonmajoritarian Institutions and the Limits of Democratic Governance: A Political Transaction-Cost Approach," *Journal of Institutional and Theoretical Economics* 157, no. 1 (2001); Majone, "The Rise of the Regulatory State in Europe," *West European Politics* 17, no. 3 (1994); Chris Berg, *The Growth of Australia's Regulatory State:*

Ideology, Accountability and the Mega-Regulators (Melbourne, Australia: Institute of Public Affairs, 2008); Edward L. Glaeser and Andrei Shleifer, "The Rise of the Regulatory State," *Journal of Economic Literature* 41, no. 2 (2003); John Braithwaite, "Accountability and Governance under the New Regulatory State," *Australian Journal of Public Administration* 58, no. 1 (1999); Andrei Shleifer, *The Failure of Judges and the Rise of Regulators* (Cambridge, MA: MIT Press, 2012).

18. Richard S. Katz and Peter Mair, "Changing Models of Party Organization and Party Democracy: The Emergence of the Cartel Party," *Party Politics* 1, no. 1 (1995); Katz and Mair, "The Cartel Party Thesis: A Restatement," *Perspectives on Politics* 7, no. 4 (2009). See also Samuel Issacharoff and Richard H. Pildes, "Politics as Markets: Partisan Lockups of the Democratic Process," *Stanford Law Review* 50, no. 3 (1998).

19. Charles R. Plott, "Axiomatic Social Choice Theory: An Overview and Interpretation," *American Journal of Political Science* 20, no. 3 (1976).

20. Satoshi Nakamoto, "Bitcoin: A Peer-to-Peer Electronic Cash System," (2008).

21. See Darcy W.E. Allen, "Entrepreneurial Exit: Developing the Cryptoeconomy," in *Blockchain Economics*, ed. Melanie Swan et al. (World Scientific, 2019); Alastair Berg and Chris Berg, "Exit, Voice, and Forking," *RMIT University Working Paper* (2017); Darcy W.E. Allen, "The Private Governance of Entrepreneurship: An Institutional Approach to Entrepreneurial Discovery" (RMIT University, 2017).

22. Also see Nick Szabo, "The Idea of Smart Contracts," *Nick Szabo's Papers and Concise Tutorials* (1997).

23. See Siraj Raval, *Decentralized Applications: Harnessing Bitcoin's Blockchain Technology*, 1st edition (United States of America: O'Reilly, 2016); Melanie Swan, *Blockchain: Blueprint for a New Economy* (O'Reilly Media, Inc., 2015).

24. Kyle Croman et al., "On Scaling Decentralized Blockchains" (paper presented at the International Conference on Financial Cryptography and Data Security, 2016); Visa, "Visa Acceptance for Retailers," https://usa.visa.com/run-your-business/small-business-tools/retail.html.

25. Alex de Vries, "Bitcoin's Growing Energy Problem," *Joule* 2, no. 5 (2018).

26. On the cost of trust, see Mikayla Novak, Sinclair Davidson, and Jason Potts, "The Cost of Trust: A Pilot Study," *Journal of the British Blockchain Association* 1, no. 2 (forthcoming).

27. For a discussion, see Federico Matteo Benčić and Ivana Podnar Žarko, "Distributed Ledger Technology: Blockchain Compared to Directed Acyclic Graph," *arXiv preprint arXiv:1804.10013* (2018).

28. See Trent J. MacDonald, Darcy W.E. Allen, and Jason Potts, "Blockchains and the Boundaries of Self-Organized Economies: Predictions for the Future of Banking," in *Banking Beyond Banks and Money: A Guide to Banking Services in the Twenty-First Century*, ed. Paolo Tasca et al. (Cham: Springer International Publishing, 2016); Davidson, De Filippi, and Potts, "Blockchains and the Economic Institutions of Capitalism"; Chris Berg, Sinclair Davidson, and Jason Potts, "Ledgers," *available at SSRN 3157421* (2018); Chris Berg, "What Diplomacy in the Ancient Near East Can Tell Us About Blockchain Technology," *Ledger* 2 (2017); Darcy W.E. Allen et al., "Blockchain Tradetech," in *APEC Study Centres Consortium Conference (ASCCC)* (Port Moresby, Papua New Guinea, 2018); Chris Berg, Sinclair Davidson, and Jason Potts, *How to Understand the Blockchain Economy: An Introduction to Institutional Cryptoeconomics* (Edward Elgar, 2019); Darcy W.E. Allen, Alastair Berg, and Brendan Markey-Towler, "Blockchain and Supply Chains: V-Form Organisations, Value Redistributions, De-Commoditisation and Quality Proxies," *The Journal of the British Blockchain Association* 2, no. 1 (2019).

29. Institutional cryptoeconomics draws in particular on Oliver E Williamson, *The Economic Institutions of Capitalism* (New York: Free Press, 1985); Ronald H. Coase, "The Nature of the Firm," *Economica* 4, no. 16 (1937); Friedrich A. Hayek, "The Use of Knowledge in Society," *The American Economic Review* 35, no. 4 (1945); Elinor Ostrom, *Governing the Commons: The Evolution of Institutions for Collective Action* (Cambridge University Press, 1990); Douglass C. North, *Institutions, Institutional Change and Economic Performance* (Cambridge University Press, 1990).

For a summary, see Chris Berg, Sinclair Davidson, and Jason Potts to Cryptoeconomics Australia, September 27, 2017, https://medium.com/cryptoeconomics-australia/the-blockchain-economy-a-beginners-guide-to-institutional-cryptoeconomics-64bf2f2beec4.

30. For instance, for an application to law, see Aaron Wright and Primavera De Filippi, "Decentralized Blockchain Technology and the Rise of Lex Cryptographia," *Available at SSRN 2580664* (2015); Wright and De Filippi, *Blockchain and the Law: The Rule of Code* (Harvard University Press, 2018).

31. Charles R. Beitz, *Political Equality: An Essay in Democratic Theory* (Princeton University Press, 1989).

32. Chris Berg, *Liberty, Equality and Democracy* (Connor Court Publishing Pty Ltd., 2015).

33. Knut Wicksell, "A New Principle of Just Taxation," in *Classics in the Theory of Public Finance* (Springer, 1958); James M. Buchanan and Gordon Tullock, *The Calculus of Consent*, vol. 3 (Ann Arbor: University of Michigan Press, 1962).

34. See Peter J. Boettke, "Liberty vs. Power in Economic Policy in the 20th and 21st Centuries," *The Journal of Private Enterprise* 22, no. 2 (2007); Peter J. Boettke and Matthew Mitchell, *Applied Mainline Economics: Bridging the Gap between Theory and Public Policy* (Arlington, VA: Mercatus Center at George Mason University, 2017).

Chapter Two

Technologies of Choosing

INTRODUCTION

There are a number of institutional mechanisms to both support and enable a collective choice. Some of those technologies have been invented precisely to facilitate collective action, while others have been applied to facilitate collective choice after the fact. By examining the connections between technological innovation and the structures of collective choice, this chapter contextualizes the application of blockchain in a cryptodemocracy. From observing the history of democratic choice we see that when technologies change democracies change. Furthermore, new technologies don't just make existing democratic structures more efficient—lowering the costs of democracy while maintaining the same structure—but rather open up entirely new institutional possibilities. This leaves open the question of how democracies will change through blockchain technology, which is the task of the remainder of the book. In this chapter we proceed as follows. In the second section we examine pre-democratic technologies including language and communication, which are foundational technologies for collective decision making. In the third section we examine Athenian democratic technologies that prevented forgery, including the *kleroterion*. In the fourth section we see how the printing press enabled the emergence of ballots, and in the fifth section we outline how modern voting machines and information technology have shaped the way we vote. This chapter acts as the foundational motivation for developing and applying a new analytical framework for democratic institutional choice.

PRE-DEMOCRATIC COLLECTIVE ORGANIZATION

Social animals make collective decisions. They coordinate movement, share resources, and defend against predators. A flock of birds, for example, moves together as a coherent whole, making sometimes sharp, consistent changes in direction. Often this is in response to external shocks (such as the detection of predators) but it has been shown that these movements can occur without external influence. Information about a turn is propagated through the flock from birds on the outermost sides of the formation. Collective decision making is led by the position of the birds in the flock, and the rest of the birds follow an "align-with-your-neighbor" coordination rule.[1] Similar localized coordination rules are observable in large groups of ants, fishm and locusts.[2] Small group primates also organize collectively. Decision making can be driven by the behavior of leaders (such as the mountain gorillas that follow a silverback male to maintain the cohesion of the group) or distributed between the group or a subgroup of leaders. Non-vocal signals (such as a posture or a movement in an intended direction) or vocal signals (grunts) can coordinate collective action.[3]

The first major technology of collective choice was language. The famous dispute between Noam Chomsky and Stephen Pinker as to whether the language instinct can be explained on the basis of Darwinian natural selection (Chomsky: no, Pinker: yes) hinges on whether language was an evolutionarily unique "special creation."[4] Pinker's view emphasizes the use of language for social adaptation and survival. While tackling this fraught question is beyond our scope, supporting Pinker's position is evidence from primatologists that primates learn rudimentary language through the needs of communication rather than as a discovery of internal cognition.[5] Language allowed for social coordination around complex tasks. Some archaeologists have argued that we can observe the development of language by proxy through the study of pre-historic human behavior that would have required minimum language skills. It is probable that the earliest human migration was imitative (like that of the mountain gorillas). Yet the indigenous settlement of Australia (possibly 65,000 years ago) required the sort of coordination to make water vessels, and may therefore be the first evidence we have for modern human language and social groups.[6] Other small-scale cooperative behavior and division of labor becomes apparent around 50,000 years ago and may also be evidence for the use of language for collective action.[7]

Collective organization and decision making was a feature of much premodern human political organization. While there is a long tradition depicting human society (particularly since the agricultural revolution) as autocratic and hierarchical, recent anthropological and archaeological evidence has shifted this picture considerably.[8] Richard Blanton and Lane Fargher have documented the wide variety of collectivity around decision making in pre-modern states.[9] Rather than the single autocratic chieftain or kingship model, they uncover a multiplicity of political forms in the pre-modern world, from kings, to governing councils, to heterarchies, to democracies. While monarchies were common, power was frequently shared with other institutions such as councils or bureaucracies. Likewise, other institutions facilitated participation in political decision making by non-elites, such as petitioning and complaints, or the direct recruitment of non-elites into positions of power.

One key historical region about which the debate about autocracy and hierarchy has played out has been Mesopotamia. It was suggested as early as 1943 that the ancient Near East featured some instances of "primitive democracy," where major decisions were made collectively, rather than autocratically.[10] Certainly the region's written records and literary texts are replete with references to assemblies that often selected kings and judicial authorities that are distributed rather than concentrated, and councils of elders to which proposals have to be presented for deliberation.[11] In a detailed study of a large cache of cuneiform texts from the city of Mari (located in modern Syria), Daniel Fleming draws out the complex two-way relationship between rulers and those they ruled.[12] While rejecting the description of the ancient Near East as "democratic," Fleming's close reading of language in the Mari archives shows how the population—of Mari and the many other societies Mari took an interest in—was often seen as holding its own collective agency, which the king needed to either manipulate or acquiesce to. While remaining hierarchically superior, kings would rely on the support of (limited representation) assemblies of the town. Egyptian pharaohs, who have a historical reputation for autocratic rule, were also supported by councils of leaders that presented them with proposals for legitimation or rejection.[13]

How were these collective decisions made? While the Mari archives sometimes reveal the result of the decisions—recording the "towns" that came out to support the king—the procedure by which towns chose who to support is less clear. But we do have some evidence for Mesopotamian voting procedures thanks, in part, to mythology. The Babylonian creation story has a council of gods dividing up responsibility by casting lots, and Sumerian and Egyptian flood stories describe the gods deliberating before a flood.[14] Surveying the literary and administrative documentary evidence, Yves Schemeil writes that group decision processes tended to be facilitated by speeches from among the group, voting on motions through symbolic acts ("kneeling, or walking to the speaker, to approve; sitting, to disapprove"), and that a meeting chair could end deliberation ("let it be!").[15] Sometimes when a decision could not be made the "franchise" would be expanded by bringing in new participants to a meeting. While these collective decisions were never absolute—as far as we can tell, they always existed as one of a plurality of different hierarchical governing structures—they were surprisingly sophisticated.

CHOOSING IN ATHENS

Where our understanding of Mesopotamian collective choice in the ancient world is vague, we are in a much better position to understand the remarkable democracy of classical Athens during the fourth and fifth centuries BCE. The peculiarity of that system and the flourishing culture of the period has left us with enormous detail not only about the institutions of collective choice but the technologies used to arrive at those choices. Athenian democracy was distinct in that it not only sought to make decisions collectively but had an ideology that valorized the individual (male) citizen's right (and obligation) to participate in those decisions.[16] With this democratic philosophy, the Athenians needed more formal—and more reliable—mechanisms of aggregating political preferences than the informal assemblies and councils of the ancient Near East. An ideology of political equality and participation required new tools.

The basic elements of Athenian democracy are well known. The three key institutions were the Assembly of the People, the Council of the 500 (*boule*), and the People's Court.[17] Along with ad hoc boards of lawmakers, these institutions formed the legislative, executive, and judicial branches of Athenian government. The Assembly was open to all male citizens over the age of eighteen, subject to having completed two years' service as a military cadet. Quorum for the Assembly seems to have been 6,000 people, while decisions were made by majority vote. Membership of the 500-member *boule*, the People's Court (usually 200–500 people in size, but could be up to 1,500 members for serious cases), and the approximately 700 other offices and committee positions were chosen by sortition (that is, by random lot).

These broad outlines are easy to describe but the Athenians faced a number of practical challenges to implement them. Attendance and votes needed to be counted, and some scheme of randomization needed to be implemented. For example, one problem was how to both ensure and verify that a quorum for the Assembly was reached. Lower rates of participation led to the introduction of payments for attendance after the Peloponnesian War.[18] The method for assessing whether a quorum had been reached was crude but effective: the Pynx (the hill on which the Assembly met) had enough space for 6,000 people and no more. After the introduction of paid attendance, a red painted rope prevented Athenians from crowding in further.[19]

Votes in Athenian democratic institutions were conducted one of two ways.[20] The first was a show of hands. At the Assembly, the nine members of the presiding committee (chosen by lot that morning) would estimate the proportion of hands raised for and against a motion. This procedure was imperfect. Any member of the Assembly could challenge that estimation on oath, necessitating a re-vote. Xenophon records an instance where it was too late in the day to see hands clearly.[21] The alternative to this crude reckoning was the use of ballots to register and count votes. Seashells were first used as ballot tokens.[22] A sophisticated ballot method of voting is described in great detail by Aristotle in the context of the People's Court.[23] Voters were given two tokens. A token with a hole in it represented a vote for the first speaker (the prosecutor) and a solid token represented a vote for the second speaker (the defendant). Voters placed their desired token in a copper urn with a hole on the lid just large enough for one token at a time (to prevent double voting). They discarded their unused token in a wooden jar. The tokens were designed to allow for a secret ballot: voters could hide their tokens between their fingers, determining by touch which token was which. The procedure for counting votes was similarly refined. The contents of the copper urn were poured out onto a reckoning board that had holes for each token, allowing rapid counting. Even so, voting by ballot would have been time consuming. Only when a precise count of quorum was needed was it used in the Assembly.

Appointment by lot presented its own practical challenges. The *boule* and most offices and committees were chosen by lot (with the exception of senior military positions, which were filled through election).[24] Random allocation served a number of functions: preventing demagoguery (by reducing the prestige of holding office), limiting the growth of factions, reducing rent seeking, and limiting bribery and corruption.[25] Reforms to random allocation procedure (such as reallocating jurors to different courts each day) were targeted at reducing these sorts of problems.[26] Nonetheless, it is the nature of randomness that it is hard for outsiders to verify that the draw has not been rigged. It is virtually impossible to prove that a selection was not truly random after the fact. Sortition requires a great deal of trust in those who perform the draw.[27]

The Athenians were well aware of the trust problem in sortition. Early selection by lot was done through the drawing of tokens from a container, but more transparent randomization was brought about by machine.[28] In his *Athenian Constitution*, Aristotle described a complex system for allocating members of juries. How exactly this procedure worked was obscure until the published discovery in 1937 of the *kleroterion*—the first instance of a dedicated device for facilitating democratic choice.[29] The *kleroterion* consists of a large stone or marble machine with columns of slots designed to hold jurors' tickets made of bronze or wood.[30] A set of black and white balls would be poured down a tube on the side of the machine—the number of black balls corresponding to the number of jury allocations needed. As the balls were removed rows of citizens would be allocated or withdrawn. This allocation was a public ceremony. Aristotle notes how the officials called the color of the balls aloud. The officials who conducted the procedure were themselves chosen by sortition. One downside was that this procedure, like voting, was time consuming.[31] With this public ceremony and the *kleroterion* machine, the Athenians were able to assure each other that each allocation had been made fairly—that is, randomly—preventing jury tampering, bribery, and reducing the possibility of political capture.

VOICES AND BALLOTS

Athenian democracy shows that the ballot box was invented at least 2,300 years ago. But informal voting either by hand, or more commonly by voice, remained a dominant electoral technique well into the early modern era. To understand why societies choose technologies of choosing we need to understand how they thought about choosing. The Athenian emphasis on democratic randomness was not unique: the use of sortition appears in medieval Italian city-states, early modern Switzerland, and of course remains a predominant way of choosing modern juries.[32] Nonetheless, Athens' particularity was the political philosophy it built around sortition as a means of making collective choices. Classical scholars tend to argue that the Athenians distinguished between voting by a show of hands and by ballot according to an efficiency-accuracy trade off. By contrast, scholars of early modern England observing the informality of voting by voice have emphasized the purpose of quasi-democratic selection.

It is easy to be anachronistic when looking at early English parliaments, particularly before the seventeenth century. The first recognizable "parliaments" in England appear in the thirteenth century, although they emerge as part of a longer tradition of great councils and assemblies dating from the tenth century. Parliaments grew out of a need for the court to gather information about the status of the king's dominions.[33] The need to have attendees come from all corners of a kingdom shaped the principle of parliamentary representatives chosen according to geographic location ("territorial representation").[34] The selection of representatives in pre-modern elections were not understood as elections in the same sense as today, despite some familiarity with proceedings. It is better to understand elections as opportunities to affirm and celebrate prior choices made informally than discrete systems of choice by themselves. The jockeying for position occurred before the "vote" was held.[35]

Collective decisions were *viva voce* because they were literally voices agreeing, rather than choosing.[36] This does not mean elections were not sometimes competitive. But contested votes were rare enough for courts weighing in on disputed elections to argue that it was unnecessary to give a precise count of the numbers, and that a vote by voices or hands should be sufficient.[37] Voice voting need not be completely arbitrary or subjective, and various techniques have been used to reduce possible corruption or encourage truthful preference revelation. A simple example of the latter appears in early Indian collective choice procedures. The Buddhist canon gives some suggestion of the methods of collective decision making in India. The *Mahavagga* describes the application of a unanimity rule to admit a candidate for an *upasampadā* ordination: a full assembly would be convened and would be asked three times if there was any objection.[38] Plutarch describes the method of election for Sparta's council of elders designed to reduce opportunistic or corrupt behavior on the part of election officials.[39] When the voters were assembled, a small group of officials were placed in a separate room where they could hear the assembly but not see it. As each candidate passed through the assembly one by one in random order, the officials recorded the loudness of voices in support. With this blind method, the officials were prevented from favoring their preferred candidate.

Any open voting system has downsides. External agents can exploit the fact that open voting allows them to verify how an individual has voted to influence their choice. William Hogarth's four painting series *The Humours of an Election*, depicting a parliamentary election in 1754, emphasize the rioting and intimidation that could accompany representative selection. Party officials would open hotels, bribe voters with free beer, police the hustings with hired thugs, and encourage disorder against the supporters of their opponents.[40] Even when they were relatively free of violence or corruption, pre-universal suffrage elections in Britain (and its colonial offshoots, Australia, Canada, and the United States) were akin to festivals.[41] Openness had its supporters. Cicero argued that the ballot was a "cover for corrupt and hypocritical votes."[42] John Stuart Mill believed that public voting encouraged better votes—away from "malice, from pique, from personal rivalry, from the interests of prejudices of class or sect."[43] The novelist Anthony Trollope, who ran for a House of Commons seat in 1868, believed that the secret ballot was "unmanly."[44] Electioneering in this environment was as much about demonstrating courage, masculinity, and communal feeling as it was about free selection.[45]

Attempts to reduce voter intimidation through changes to the mechanisms and technologies of elections long predate the formal introduction of the secret ballot in the nineteenth century. Voting by voice need not be open voting—one can declare one's choice quietly and privately to an official who marks it down. A 1362 vote for the mayor of Lancaster was arranged to "give their voices privily and secretly every one by himself," and a 1416 vote for the mayor of Bishop's Lynn instructed officials to "secretly write down the wishes" of each voter.[46] Although not widely used, secret ballots are found throughout the pre-modern and early modern period. London aldermen in 1532 voted by placing black or white peas into a box. In an election in 1689 in Barnstaple, two pots with the names of candidates were placed side by side. Voters were given one ball each, and, placing a hand in each pot, secretly dropped the ball into the preferred candidate's pot. Even written ballots, where voters wrote their name on a scroll and dropped it in a box or bag, existed as early as 1607. Once counted, the ballots were then burned to prevent reidentification.[47]

These experiments notwithstanding, the first recognizably modern secret ballot system was developed in the Australian colony of Victoria in 1856.[48] As a newly independent colony, Victoria had less of the bribery and intimidation than England but more of a utilitarian reforming zeal.[49] Early Australian elections were open votes. The Victorian reform of 1856 had two core innovations. The first was the existence of individual booths—inspired by the private compartments of pawnbrokers' shops and confessionals—within a quiet voting room where voters could make their choice without external observation. But the core of the "Australian ballot" was the use of an official ballot paper with a list of candidates printed at government expense. Earlier written ballot systems lacked this, giving voters (or candidates) that responsibility. Printed ballots solved a number of practical problems with written ballots. Not all voters were literate, and for those voters printed ballots made candidate identification easier. Voters were asked to cross out names until only their preferred candidates were unmarked; in 1858 South Australia developed the idea of marking a cross next to chosen candidates. Printed ballots were also intended to reduce fraud. Election officials signed the back of each ballot paper, to prevent fake ballots from being introduced between the vote and counting, and to reduce the possibility of voter impersonation wrote a unique voter number corresponding to their position on the electoral role. Voters then folded their ballot paper and dropped it into a locked ballot box.[50] In this form, the Australian ballot might be seen as conditionally secret—anonymous in normal use, but allowing for possible reidentification in the case of controversy.[51]

Victoria's printed ballot system was adopted rapidly throughout the Australian colonies, spread to Britain in 1872 and throughout the United States between the 1880s and 1900s.[52] One American consideration of the Australian ballot was titled "The Feasibility of printing and distributing ballots at the Government's Expense."[53] The pivotal technological change that facilitated adoption of the Australian ballot was the decline in printing costs throughout the second half of the nineteenth century.[54] From a political party's perspective, government-supplied ballots defrayed the often significant cost of producing tickets at the party expense.[55] In his model of democratic reform, Roger Congleton emphasizes the impact that cheaper communications technologies had on the ability of political entrepreneurs to form new organizations.[56] Here we can see how cheaper printing also helped clean up voting procedures.

Nonetheless, secret ballots are no panacea against voter intimidation. When the ballot was introduced in the Roman republic, the elevated walkways to the ballot box had to be narrowed to prevent continued harassment of the voters.[57] A number of historians have been skeptical that secret ballots did much to reduce bribery.[58] In England, for instance, it is possible that other legislation—such as the 1883 Corrupt Practices Act—were more effective at cleaning up elections than the secret ballot.[59] The printed ballot in Victoria was also accompanied by enhanced laws against electoral bribery and undue influence.[60] However, in an analysis of bribe prices and election expenditure in nineteenth-century Britain, Christopher Kam finds that candidates after the introduction of the secret ballot shifted their spending from vote buying to encouraging voter turnout.[61]

INFORMATION TECHNOLOGY OF DEMOCRACY

In their 1838 *People's Charter*, the British Chartist movement not only called for a secret ballot but described a machine which would record the vote.[62] In this scheme, voters would be given a brass ball which would be dropped into a box with holes corresponding to each candidate. As the ball went through the machine, it would trigger a switch adding another vote to the preferred candidate's total on a dial. When the ball dropped out, it would then be given to the next voter. Compared to the later Australian ballot—or even other written ballots—this vote was not entirely secret: while it was to be done in an enclosed room, the process was to be observed by a deputy returning officer.[63] Yet that officer was unable to observe the results of the vote as it proceeded. Once the ballot had concluded, a door on the machine would be ceremonially opened, and candidates would be able to observe the results. The Chartists' proposed machine may never have been built.[64] But it underlines how this working-class movement for democratic expansion saw procedural and technological change as a vehicle for reform.

The mechanical innovation in the second half of the nineteenth century was no less applied to elections. New techniques and technologies of registering and counting the vote were developed simultaneously with demands for political reform. In the United States, the fact that the Australian ballot shifted a financial burden onto the government accelerated political interest in reducing that cost through machinery.[65] Douglas Jones identifies the desirable engineering requirements that early voting machines tried to satisfy: (1) the ballot should be secret; (2) voting should be transparent (allowing voters to see that the ballot box was empty before voting began); (3) voters should be able to verify that their vote had been registered; (4) the system should allow for a recount to be made if necessary; and (5) the machine should have a way to ensure only valid votes were registered (rejecting, for instance, repeated voting).[66] Very few of the early voting machines could satisfy these requirements.

Voting machines in the twentieth century can be divided into two categories: document and non-document-based systems. The relevant question is whether they record a vote on a physical document which can then be counted, whether manually or electronically. Lever voting machines, which were first introduced in the United States with the Myers Automatic Booth, were the heirs of the Chartist system. In the most typical system, voters entered a mechanical booth and pulled a large lever to close a curtain behind themselves. They then flicked down small levers corresponding to each race and candidate they preferred. The machines were programmed so that each vote was compliant with the rules of the election (a voter could not vote for more candidates than allowed in a single session, for instance). Opening the curtain again flicks all the levers upward, registering the votes and resetting the machine for the next voter. The votes were recorded on an odometer inside the machine, a form of automatic counting. Like in the Chartist model, one significant weakness of this system is that it records no independent record of each vote. The complexity of the machines meant that they could register votes imperfectly if they were worn out, and the technicians who maintained the machines could also potentially tamper with them. [67]

An alternative approach was a document-based voting machine. Here we see the first integration of computer and proto-computer technology into election processes and counting. The punch card was invented by Herman Hollerith to process data for the United States census in 1890. [68] The Votomatic, a punch card voting system at one time owned by IBM, was widely used for American elections between 1965 and 2000. These record votes on a punch card with a fixed number of pre-scored voting positions. Voters then punch through the card to create a hole next to their preferred candidate(s). Problems with the Votomatic are now legendary, thanks to the disputed 2000 presidential election. [69] Nonetheless, the Votomatic (and other twentieth-century punch card systems) offered election officials both a documentary record allowing for recounts and vote verification, as well as a system for automatic vote counting—the punch cards could be collected and put through a computer.

While there is now a great deal of discussion about "digital democracy," in fact digital democracy has a long history. Punch card systems are a digital voting system, where votes are registered as a binary question of whether a hole has been punched or not. Their failure in 2000 pivoted around the fact that not all holes had been cleanly or clearly punched—rather than registering a yes/no vote, voter intent was too often unclear. Punch card systems are also electronic insofar as they are counted by electronic computers. Optical scan machines have long been used to count marked ballots. Experiments in electric or electronic democracy date back to the nineteenth century. One such voting machine was invented by Thomas Edison, not for use in public elections but as a mechanism for recording votes within a legislature. His

"Electrographic Vote-Recorder and Register" registered yes and no votes against each legislators name by connecting circuits from a battery. [70]

The confusions of the 2000 presidential election sparked a great deal of interest in fully electronic voting—known as direct-recording electronic (DRE) voting machines, that record votes in digital memory and (often) transmits those votes to a central authority for counting. Early DRE machines registered votes through a push-button mechanism—the first were introduced in the mid-1970s—but now DRE can be offered through touch screens. [71] DRE is used currently in countries such as Brazil and India. However, DRE voting has significant security problems that have not been overcome. The security specialist Bruce Schneier has argued that the complexity needed to make DRE machines user-friendly also creates risks for errors and opportunities for tampering. [72] Software bugs have often produced inaccurate tallies in elections where DRE machines have been used, and the difficulty of third parties reading code can make it hard to detect when the software has been programmed poorly—or maliciously. Security problems compound when DRE voting is connected to the internet—or where votes are conducted over the internet—exposing the system to potential hackers. These concerns have meant that the introduction of DRE voting has not been widespread, and some countries which had expressed interest in "e-voting" have held back.

CONCLUSION

In this chapter we examined the relationship between new technologies and collective choice. The technologies that human societies have used to make choices shape the choices that are made. Vote technique and technology can also affect the process by which voters come to make a decision. [73] One of the objections raised by legislators when Thomas Edison was trying to market his electronic voting machine was that it would eliminate the vocal roll-call, a key method by which legislators deliberated. [74] And finally, new technologies offer the possibility of new forms of collective decision making. Language gave humans the power for complex coordination. Technological advances reduced the monetary cost of collective choice and increased trust in those choices. The *kleroterion* gave more reliable, public verification that selection was truly random. Cheap printing reduced the cost to government of printing ballots and allowed for the Australian ballot.

What do these dynamics mean for our understanding of blockchain as applied to collective choice? Since the nineteenth century we have seen a rapid change in information technologies, yet the adoption of new technology for collective choice has been relatively slow compared to how those technologies have been adopted elsewhere in the economy. In part this is because the institutional structure around voting has changed little since the information revolution. While voting systems are more or less complex—for instance compare the first-past-the-post system in the United States with the Hare-Clark system in New Zealand and Tasmania—the act of voting remains the selection of a representative to make decisions by proxy in a legislature or executive.

Each collective choice system analyzed in this chapter has been fundamentally planned in an economic sense: each represents a deliberatively designed mechanism whereby preferences are collected, aggregated, and made ready for implementation. Representative democracy doesn't allow individuals to create their own centers of decision making based on their own local and contextual knowledge. While a representative democracy might appear polycentric, those multiple centers are by design, not by emergence. In the following chapter we introduce a framework for understanding the impact of blockchain on the structure of collective choice, and, as we will see throughout the book, this creates a new infrastructure on which polycentric democratic institutions can emerge from the interactions of contracting voters.

NOTES

1. Alessandro Attanasi et al., "Emergence of Collective Changes in Travel Direction of Starling Flocks from Individual Birds' Fluctuations," *Journal of The Royal Society Interface* 12, no. 108 (2015). See also William Bialek et al., "Statistical Mechanics for Natural Flocks of Birds," *Proceedings of the National Academy of Sciences* (2012); Andrea Cavagna et al., "Physical Constraints in Biological Collective Behaviour," *Current Opinion in Systems Biology* 9 (2018).

2. Sepideh Bazazi et al., "Collective Motion and Cannibalism in Locust Migratory Bands," *Current Biology* 18, no. 10 (2008); Iain D. Couzin and Jens Krause, "Self-Organization and Collective Behavior in Vertebrates," (2003); Iain D. Couzin et al., "Effective Leadership and Decision-Making in Animal Groups on the Move," *Nature* 433, no. 7025 (2005); Shay Gueron, Simon A. Levin, and Daniel I. Rubenstein, "The Dynamics of Herds: From Individuals to Aggregations," *Journal of Theoretical Biology* 182, no. 1 (1996).

3. Julia Fischer and Dietmar Zinner, "Communication and Cognition in Primate Group Movement," *International Journal of Primatology* 32, no. 6 (2011); Sabine Stueckle and Dietmar Zinner, "To Follow or Not to Follow: Decision Making and Leadership During the Morning Departure in Chacma Baboons," *Animal Behaviour* 75, no. 6 (2008); Cédric Sueur and Jean-Louis Deneubourg, "Self-Organization in Primates: Understanding the Rules Underlying Collective Movements," *International Journal of Primatology* 32, no. 6 (2011).

4. Steven Pinker, *The Language Instinct: How the Mind Creates Language* (Penguin UK, 2003); Noam Chomsky, *On Nature and Language* (Cambridge University Press, 2002); Chomsky, "Three Factors in Language Design," *Linguistic Inquiry* 36, no. 1 (2005).

Also see discussions in Julie Tetel Andresen, *Linguistics and Evolution: A Developmental Approach* (Cambridge University Press, 2013); Alan Barnard, *Language in Prehistory* (Cambridge University Press, 2016).

5. Klaus Zuberbühler and Alban Lemasson, "Primate Communication: Meaning from Strings of Calls," in *Language and Recursion*, ed. Francis Lowenthal and Laurent Lefebvre (New York: Springer, 2014).

6. Iain Davidson and William Noble, "Why the First Colonisation of the Australian Region Is the Earliest Evidence of Modern Human Behaviour," *Archaeology in Oceania* 27, no. 3

(1992); Chris Clarkson et al., "Human Occupation of Northern Australia by 65,000 Years Ago," *Nature* 547, no. 7663 (2017).

7. Eric Reuland, "Language: Symbolization and Beyond," in *The Prehistory of Language*, ed. Rudolf Botha and Chris Knight (Oxford University Press, 2009); Steven L. Kuhn et al., "What's a Mother to Do? The Division of Labor among Neandertals and Modern Humans in Eurasia," *Current Anthropology* 47, no. 6 (2006).

8. See Richard E. Blanton and Lane F. Fargher, *How Humans Cooperate: Confronting the Challenges of Collective Action* (University Press of Colorado, 2016). Blanton and Fargher attribute this to Karl Marx, who developed a quasi-evolutionary theory of staged social orders that led from herd-like behavior under autocrats to individualization under commercial society. For a more recent example of this reasoning, see Paul Shankman, "Kent Flannery and Joyce Marcus, the Creation of Inequality: How Our Prehistoric Ancestors Set the Stage for Monarchy, Slavery, and Empire," *Asian Ethnology* 73 (2014).

9. Blanton and Fargher, *How Humans Cooperate: Confronting the Challenges of Collective Action*.

10. Thorkild Jacobsen, "Primitive Democracy in Ancient Mesopotamia," *Journal of Near Eastern Studies* 2, no. 3 (1943).

11. Norman Yoffee, *Myths of the Archaic State: Evolution of the Earliest Cities, States, and Civilizations* (Cambridge University Press, 2005).

12. Daniel E. Fleming, *Democracy's Ancient Ancestors: Mari and Early Collective Governance* (Cambridge University Press, 2004).

13. Yves Schemeil, "Democracy before Democracy?" *International Political Science Review* 21, no. 2 (2000); William F. Edgerton, "The Government and the Governed in the Egyptian Empire," *Journal of Near Eastern Studies* 6, no. 3 (1947).

14. Wilfred G. Lambert, Alan Ralph Millard, and Miguel Civil, *Atra-Ḥasīs: The Babylonian Story of the Flood* (Eisenbrauns, 1999), 43; Schemeil, "Democracy before Democracy?"

15. Schemeil, "Democracy before Democracy?" 104.

16. Fleming, *Democracy's Ancient Ancestors: Mari and Early Collective Governance*.

17. Some details of the description below depend on the period which is being considered, but we have endeavored to describe Athenian democracy at its height and peak of institutional maturity. For an overview of Athenian democratic institutions, see Mogens Herman Hansen, *The Athenian Democracy in the Age of Demosthenes: Structure, Principles, and Ideology* (University of Oklahoma Press, 1999); Christopher W. Blackwell, *Dēmos: Classical Athenian Democracy* (Stoa: A Consortium for Electronic Publication in the Humanities, 2003); Robert K. Sinclair, *Democracy and Participation in Athens* (Cambridge University Press, 1991).

18. Hansen, *The Athenian Democracy in the Age of Demosthenes: Structure, Principles, and Ideology*, 130–31. See Aristot. Const. Ath. 41.3. Another explanation for this, as Josiah Ober points out, could be that the lower classes of Athens were seeking to prevent dominance by the upper, wealthier classes. See Josiah Ober, *The Athenian Revolution: Essays on Ancient Greek Democracy and Political Theory* (Princeton University Press, 1996).

19. Hansen, *The Athenian Democracy in the Age of Demosthenes: Structure, Principles, and Ideology*, 131.

20. A detailed exploration of this is *The Athenian Ecclesia II: A Collection of Articles, 1983–1989*, vol. 2 (Museum Tusculanum Press, 1989).

21. "It was decided, however, that the matter should be postponed to another meeting of the Assembly (for by that time it was late in the day and they could not have distinguished the hands in the voting)" —Xen. Hell. 1.7.

22. Alan L. Boegehold et al., "The Lawcourts at Athens Sites, Buildings, Equipment, Procedure, and Testimonia," *The Athenian Agora* 28 (2009).

23. Aristot. Const. Ath. 68–69.

24. For general overviews of selection by lot, see James Wycliffe Headlam, *Election by Lot at Athens* (The University Press, 1891); Hansen, *The Athenian Democracy in the Age of Demosthenes: Structure, Principles, and Ideology*; Fredrik Engelstad, "The Assignment of Political Office by Lot," *Information (International Social Science Council)* 28, no. 1 (1989). Aristot. Const. Ath.

25. Defenses of the democratic nature of random allocation appear in Berg, *Liberty, Equality and Democracy*; Jacques Rancière, *Hatred of Democracy* (London: Verso Books, 2009); George Tridimas, "Constitutional Choice in Ancient Athens: The Rationality of Selection to Office by Lot," *Constitutional Political Economy* 23, no. 1 (2012); Alan A. Lockard, "Decision by Sortition: A Means to Reduce Rent-Seeking," *Public Choice* 116, no. 3–4 (2003); Peter Stone, *The Luck of the Draw: The Role of Lotteries in Decision Making* (Oxford University Press, 2011), chapter 6.

Skepticism about sortition is of course too widespread to summarize, but Socrates was accused of teaching "his companions to despise the established laws by insisting on the folly of appointing public officials by lot, when none would choose a pilot or builder or flautist by lot, nor any other craftsman for work in which mistakes are far less disastrous than mistakes in statecraft," Xen. Mem. 1.2.9.

26. Larry Patriquin, *Economic Equality and Direct Democracy in Ancient Athens* (Springer, 2015), 28–29.

27. See the discussion in G.E.M. de Ste. Croix, *Athenian Democratic Origins and Other Essays* (Oxford University Press, 2004), 99–100.

28. Sinclair, *Democracy and Participation in Athens*, 18.

29. Sterling Dow, "Aristotle, the Kleroteria, and the Courts," *Harvard Studies in Classical Philology* 50 (1939); J. David Bishop, "The Cleroterium," *The Journal of Hellenic Studies* 90 (1970); Boegehold et al., "The Lawcourts at Athens Sites, Buildings, Equipment, Procedure, and Testimonia."

30. John H. Kroll, *Athenian Bronze Allotment Plates* (Harvard University Press, 1972). Aristot. Const. Ath. 63;

31. One recent simulation suggests the process for empaneling a jury of 2,000 (spread across a number of courts as multiple cases were tried each day) could take around thirty minutes. See Alessandro Orlandini, "Kleroterion: Simulation of the Allotment of Dikastai," (Academia.edu).

32. Engelstad, "The Assignment of Political Office by Lot."

33. John Robert Maddicott, *The Origins of the English Parliament, 924–1327* (Oxford University Press, 2010).

34. Although as Andrew Rehfeld points out, it might be better to think of early territorial representation as "town" or "county" representation. Andrew Rehfeld, *The Concept of Constituency: Political Representation, Democratic Legitimacy, and Institutional Design* (Cambridge University Press, 2005).

35. Derek Hirst, *The Representative of the People? Voters and Voting in England under the Early Stuarts* (Cambridge University Press, 2005).

36. Mark A. Kishlansky, *Parliamentary Selection: Social and Political Choice in Early Modern England* (Cambridge University Press, 1986).

37. Hirst, *The Representative of the People? Voters and Voting in England under the Early Stuarts*, 14.

38. Mv (*Mahavagga*) 1.28, https://dhammawiki.com/index.php/Mv_1.28.

For a defense of early Indian democratic and republican tradition, see Steven Muhlberger, "Republics and Quasi-Democratic Institutions in Ancient India," in *The Secret History of Democracy*, ed. Benjamin Isakhan and Stephen Stockwell (Springer, 2011).

39. Plut. Lyc. 26.

40. Marian Sawer, "Inventing the Nation through the Ballot Box," in *From Subjects to Citizens: A Hundred Years of Citizenship in Australia and Canada* (University of Ottawa Press, 2004); Jon Lawrence, *Electing Our Masters: The Hustings in British Politics from Hogarth to Blair* (Oxford University Press, 2009).

41. Frank O'Gorman, "Campaign Rituals and Ceremonies: The Social Meaning of Elections in England 1780–1860," *Past and Present*, no. 135 (1992); O'Gorman, "The Culture of Elections in England: From the Glorious Revolution to the First World War, 1688–1914," in *Elections before Democracy: The History of Elections in Europe and Latin America*, ed. Eduardo Posada-Carbó (Palgrave, 1996).

42. Marcus Tullius Cicero, *The Political Works of Marcus Tullius Cicero, Vol. 2 (Treatise on the Laws) [-51]* (London: Edmund Spettigue, 1842).

43. John Stuart Mill, *The Collected Works of John Stuart Mill, Volume XIX—Essays on Politics and Society Part 2 (Considerations on Rep. Govt.)* (Toronto: University of Toronto Press, 1977), 336.

See also Timur Kuran, *Private Truths, Public Lies: The Social Consequences of Preference Falsification* (Harvard University Press, 1997), 91–97.

Philip Pettit and Geoffrey Brennan offer a defense of ballot openness: Geoffrey Brennan and Philip Pettit, *The Economy of Esteem: An Essay on Civil and Political Society* (Oxford University Press, 2004).

44. Anthony Trollope, *An Autobiography. 1883* (New York: Oxford University Press, 1999).

45. Lawrence, *Electing Our Masters: The Hustings in British Politics from Hogarth to Blair*, 19–21.

See also the discussion in Elaine Hadley, *Living Liberalism: Practical Citizenship in Mid-Victorian Britain* (University of Chicago Press, 2010).

46. Charles Gross, "The Early History of the Ballot in England," *The American Historical Review* 3, no. 3 (1898): 457.

47. Ibid., 460.

48. John Hirst has a detailed history of its introduction in John Hirst, *Making Voting Secret* (Victorian Electoral Commission, 2006). See also Mark McKenna, "Building 'A Closet of Prayer' in the New World: The Story of the Australian Ballot," in *Elections: Full, Free and Fair*, ed. Marian Sawer (Federation Press, 2001). William Coleman, "Australia's Electoral Idiosyncracies," in *Only in Australia: The History, Politics, and Economics of Australian Exceptionalism*, ed. William Coleman (Oxford University Press, 2016); Peter Brent, "The Australian Ballot: Not the Secret Ballot," *Australian Journal of Political Science* 41, no. 1 (2006).

49. Hirst, like a number of writers, identifies the influence of Jeremy Bentham on the introduction of the secret ballot (p. 44). Bentham had argued for the secret ballot since 1789; see Jeremy Bentham, "Rights, Representation, and Reform: Nonsense Upon Stilts and Other Writings on the French Revolution by Jeremy Bentham," (2002). It is often argued that Bentham had a significant influence on Australian institutions, the secret ballot being the archetypal case.

See David Geoffrey Matthew Llewellyn, "Australia Felix: Jeremy Bentham and Australian Colonial Democracy" (University of Melbourne, 2016); Matthew Lesh, "A Regulatory Culture?" in *Australia's Red Tape Crisis: The Causes and Costs of Over-Regulation*, ed. Darcy W.E. Allen and Chris Berg (Australia: Connor Court, 2018); Hugh Collins, "Political Ideology in Australia: The Distinctiveness of a Benthamite Society," *Daedalus* (1985). By contrast, one of us has argued that Bentham's influence is more asserted rather than demonstrated, and Bentham seems to have been little read in the colonies (see Chris Berg, "Adam Smith and Jeremy Bentham in the Australian Colonies," *History of Economics Review* 68, no. 1 [2017])

50. Hirst has valuable instructions printed in the *Geelong Advertiser* guiding voters in this new method. See Hirst, *Making Voting Secret*, 35.

51. For a discussion of conditional secrecy, see Douglas W. Jones, "Early Requirements for Mechanical Voting Systems" (paper presented at the Requirements Engineering for e-Voting Systems [RE-VOTE], 2009 First International Workshop on, 2010).

52. For the United States, see L. E. Fredman, "The Introduction of the Australian Ballot in the United States," *Australian Journal of Politics and History* 13, no. 2 (1967).

53. Hirst, *Making Voting Secret*, 43.

54. There were still some thorny technological limitations. Folding a paper with freshly drawn ink risked blotting out the cross on the opposite side, leaving some votes disputed. While electors were supposed to be supplied with blotting paper, this was not always available. See John Thrasher and Gerald Gaus, "James Buchanan and Gordon Tullock, the Calculus of Consent," in *The Oxford Handbook of Classics in Contemporary Political Theory*, ed. Jacob T. Levy (Oxford University Press, 2015).

55. A discussion of the high cost of party tickets is in Fredman, "The Introduction of the Australian Ballot in the United States."

56. Roger D. Congleton, *Perfecting Parliament: Constitutional Reform, Liberalism, and the Rise of Western Democracy* (Cambridge University Press, 2010).

57. Cic. Leg. 3.38; see also Howard Troxler, "Electoral Abuse in the Late Roman Republic" (University of South Florida, 2008).

58. Bruce L. Kinzer, *The Ballot Question in Nineteenth Century English Politics*, vol. 9 (New York: Garland Pub., 1982); Harold John Hanham, *Elections and Party Management: Politics in the Time of Disraeli and Gladstone* (Shoe String Pr Inc, 1959).

59. Cornelius O'Leary, "The Elimination of Corrupt Practices in British Elections, 1868–1911," (1962); Kathryn Rix, "'The Elimination of Corrupt Practices in British Elections'? Reassessing the Impact of the 1883 Corrupt Practices Act," *The English Historical Review* 123, no. 500 (2008).

60. A summary is available in "New Laws: Elections Regulation Act," *The Argus*, April 15, 1856.

61. Christopher Kam, "The Secret Ballot and the Market for Votes at 19th-Century British Elections," *Comparative Political Studies* 50, no. 5 (2017). We return to questions of vote buying in chapter 5.

62. The People's Charter; with the address to the Radical reformers of Great Britain and Ireland, and a brief sketch of its origin, p. 1.

63. The People's Charter, 22.

64. Barbara Haeberlin, "The Industrialization of Democracy," in *Computing for Science, Engineering and Production—Mathematical Tools for the Second Industrial Revolution*, ed. Karl Kleine (Norderstedt: Books on Demand, 2013), 324.

65. Roy Saltman, *The History and Politics of Voting Technology: In Quest of Integrity and Public Confidence* (Springer, 2006), 111.

66. Jones, "Early Requirements for Mechanical Voting Systems."

67. "A Brief Illustrated History of Voting," http://homepage.cs.uiowa.edu/~jones/voting/pictures/#lever.

68. See James W. Cortada, *Before the Computer: IBM, NCR, Burroughs, and Remington Rand and the Industry They Created, 1865–1956* (Princeton University Press, 2000); James Beniger, *The Control Revolution: Technological and Economic Origins of the Information Society* (Harvard University Press, 2009); James Essinger, *Jacquard's Web: How a Hand-Loom Led to the Birth of the Information Age* (Oxford University Press on Demand, 2007).

69. Saltman, *The History and Politics of Voting Technology: In Quest of Integrity and Public Confidence.*

70. Ibid., 109–10.

71. Robert Krimmer, "The Evolution of E-Voting: Why Voting Technology Is Used and How It Affects Democracy," *Tallinn University of Technology Doctoral Theses Series I: Social Sciences* 19 (2012).

72. Bruce Schneier to Schneier on Security, August 14, 2004, https://www.schneier.com/blog/archives/2004/11/the_problem_wit.html.

73. Adrian Vermeule, "Open-Secret Voting," *Secrecy and Publicity in Votes and Debates* (2015).

74. Saltman, *The History and Politics of Voting Technology: In Quest of Integrity and Public Confidence*, 110.

Chapter Three

A Framework for Institutional Collective Choice

INTRODUCTION

Effectively understanding how blockchain facilitates collective choice requires a theoretical framework to analyze how technologies shift the possible range of institutions. In this chapter we draw on new comparative economics to examine the comparative efficacy of governance solutions in economizing on the costs incurred in making collective choices under uncertainty. We develop a new framework of institutional choice—what we call the Democratic Institutional Possibility Frontier (DIPF)—that maps institutions for collective decision making by *agency costs* and *decision costs* over the governance of bundles of voting rights. The DIPF enables us to examine collective choice as a contract-theoretic problem of governance in the face of transaction costs and uncertainty, and understand where new technologies such as blockchain open up new institutional possibilities of governing voting property rights. We proceed as follows. In the second section we outline some typical democratic procedures of a Westminster system of government as a chain of delegation running between voters, representatives, and public servants. This understanding lays the foundations for understanding the structure of democracy as an institutional trade-off between various social costs. The third section begins from the understanding that votes are bundles of rights—potentially incorporating the right to vote, delegate, and sell—and that non-zero transaction costs means that exercising those rights requires governance. The DIPF arrays different governance structures as they trade-off between the dual costs of agency costs and decision costs of collective choice. The DIPF framework enables us to focus on some of the potential new voting rights that could be exercised in a cryptodemocracy—the right to delegate votes in chapter 4 and the right to trade and exchange those voting rights in chapter 5—as opened up through new technologies.

A PROCEDURAL ACCOUNT OF DEMOCRACY

Modern democratic governance resembles a chain of delegation, from the citizenry (who exercise the right to vote) all the way to the public servants who implement policy decisions.[1] In this section we consider an ideal Westminster system of government. In the first instance citizens delegate decision-making power to their representatives in the legislature. These representatives are chosen from a list (perhaps with a write-in candidate) presented to each eligible voting citizen at the ballot box, and grouped into geographic constituencies, such as an electoral division or a state. Individual citizens also have the right to put themselves on the ballot and run for office (subject to eligibility criteria and usually a fee). The ballot box is merely the first step in delegation. A second step consists of those representatives electing or otherwise forming an executive government to whom they delegate decision-making power for the operation and priorities of the state. Political parties exist as a coordination mechanism to form government and choose the head of government (often in coalition with other political parties). They coordinate members of the legislature into groups, allocate responsibilities, and act as centralized authorities for ideological positioning and political negotiation. As a third step the executive delegates to ministers who assume authority over a domain. A fourth step involves the delegation of operational decision making to bureaucrats who implement the executive's policies and enact and enforce the parliament's legislation. A corresponding chain of accountability goes in the other direction: public servants are accountable to ministers, who are accountable to the head of the government, who is accountable to the elected legislature, who are individually accountable to voters.[2]

We ought to distinguish between two delegations at each step: delegation of governance and delegation of decision making. In *delegations of governance*, voters delegate to an executive government the responsibility for governing the jurisdiction. This is the mundane work of administration. Taxes have to be collected and public goods have to be provided. In this case the purpose of the governance—the mixture of taxes, public goods, and other activities—have already been set, whether constitutionally or legislatively. In this sense, by delegating to government voters are outsourcing, collectively, the delivery of services they have purchased. *Delegations of decision making* allow delegates to adjust the policy settings—the mixture of taxation and services—on behalf of delegators. In a representative Westminster democracy this most prominently involves the negotiation of legislation. However, at the sub-legislative level, ministers and bureaucracies also are vested with decision-making authority that changes the tax-spending mixture. Many statutory authorities can enact subordinate or delegated legislation on their own behalf (often disallowable by the legislature). Many departments and agencies make decisions—such as targeting specific activities for regulation, or favoring certain activities for subsidy over others—that are as much policy choices as they are governance. Such delegated authority is the consequence of the fact that legislative mandates are incomplete contracts: they do not have comprehensive foresight about the range of possible futures that the policy framework may need to contend with.[3] Which policies are allocated into which level of delegation can be either domain specific (such as constitutional questions) or themselves delegated by enabling legislation and governed by norms of legitimate government action.

Adherence to any ideal democratic procedure varies considerably in different policy domains. Contemporary democracies have adaptations that seek to reduce agency and incentive problems that can occur in each delegation, and to enhance or reduce the lines of accountability. Constitutions and other legal instruments direct the consideration of certain domains or policy questions to different levels of government, or prevent certain questions from being subject to direct democratic choice (such as freedoms of speech and religion). Other approaches seek to bypass or sever lines of accountability. For example, freedom of information laws allows individual voters to access information from within the bureaucracy without having to go through the tiers of delegation. Independent statutory agencies such as central banks and some regulatory agencies are delegated power but are formally or informally separated from the lines of accountability to reduce the potential for political interference.[4] Direct participation also bypasses the usual delegations. Referendums are used in certain jurisdictions (such as Switzerland) and in certain circumstances where the delegation of decision-making power is seen as undesirable. Australia has held "non-binding" referendums on four occasions. These have been on conscription (in 1916 and 1917), the national anthem (1977), as well as a voluntary national postal survey on same-sex marriage (2017).

We have presented here perhaps a peculiarly procedural account of democratic structure. Robert Dahl has argued that democracy is a bundle of characteristics and rights (including semi-political rights such as freedom of speech and effective participation) rather than a single voting exercise.[5] A state which maintains the freedom to vote for representatives but eliminates freedoms of speech and suppresses participation erodes its democratic character. While this is unquestionably true, it should not obscure the heavy load that this first step plays in legitimizing the exercise of political power in a democracy. That votes constitute the symbolic transfer of power from democratically empowered citizen to elected, legitimate government. Where further transfers of authority are legitimate—from parliament to executive, from executive to ministers, to bureaucracy—a necessary (although not sufficient) source of that legitimacy is the original transfer of legitimate power.[6] In the following section we develop a framework—situated in the tradition of new comparative economics—to analyze the various ways that bundles of voting rights can be institutionally governed in order to transfer that legitimate power.

THE DEMOCRATIC INSTITUTIONAL POSSIBILITY FRONTIER (DIPF)

Our Democratic Institutional Possibility Frontier (DIPF) framework allows us to analyze the governance of votes—understood as bundles of property rights—where different institutions trade-off between decision costs and agency costs in different ways. The DIPF is a tool to examine the institutional possibilities that blockchain technology opens up in a cryptodemocracy. As we saw above, the chain of delegation in a democratic system is designed to reduce the costs of decision making while retaining the normative value of democratic sovereignty. There are of course many other forms of democratic decision making. For instance, we could contrast the Westminster system with a system of direct democracy. In a system of direct democracy votes might contribute directly to policy choices through voting not on representatives but on specific issues or issue sets. Both the Westminster system and a direct democracy can be considered efforts to create bundles of voting property rights that enable a collective choice to be made under uncertainty and with positive transaction costs. From this Demsetzian perspective it is a constitutional choice to determine the bundle of rights that constitutes a vote.[7] How can we better understand this institutional choice within a consistent analytical framework?

Votes are bundles of property rights to participate in a collective choice. Those rights might include the right to vote on particular issues, under certain conditions, at specified time intervals, and so on. Different combinations of these rights will achieve the objective of the collective choice in different ways because the rights economize on the transaction costs of collective choice under uncertainty differently. Votes as property rights is a useful starting point to understand the nature of choosing institutions for governing collective choice. As with property rights more broadly, votes are not homogenous. Rather, votes include bundles of rights to be used within an economic and social environment. In the same way that the structure of property rights in a market can be judged on their ability to internalize externalities (or the emergence of property rights can be understood as a response to the emergence of new externalities), such a property rights analysis may be useful to understand how we solve democratic problems. Votes as property rights is also a useful analytical frame from which to build a "contract-theoretic" (c.f. "choice-theoretic") understanding of collective choice institutions because it focuses on the individual voter and their constraints when they solve their perceived economic problem. [8]

What combination of rights constitutes the right to vote? In modern democracies the right to vote is a tightly limited bundle of rights that is homogenously granted across the (adult) population. It consists of the right to participate in a collective decision—but that participation is subject to a large number of constitutional, statutory, and regulatory constraints. For example, voters only have the right to choose a representative or presidential leader on a fixed schedule—once every four years for a US presidential election, for instance. That choice, once made on election day, cannot be exercised again until the subsequent election. The range of choices that can be made are also tightly prescribed. Voters can choose their representative from a pre-set list of candidates (although some elections allow for write-in candidates) and those candidates are grouped territorially. A voter in the Victorian federal electoral district of Deakin cannot, for instance, choose as their representative a candidate who is standing in the district of Goldstein, regardless of whether they believe that the Goldstein candidate is more likely to reflect and represent their political views. Furthermore, voters are also often prohibited from participating in secondary markets for votes—that is, votes cannot be bought or sold—and sometimes they are penalized for failing to vote (such as compulsory voting restrictions in Australia).

What constitutes a bundle of voting rights is a product of constitutional design to achieve some democratic purpose. Some of those restrictions will be the result of norms, such as banning the sale of votes. What systems are possible, however, is ultimately constrained by transaction costs. We can therefore examine votes as bundles of property rights from the perspective of institutional economics—how are voting rights governed to economize on the costs in the democratic process? How do different governance arrangements change the voting rights that are possible, and how can those governance arrangements be compared?

We introduce a framework for analyzing the governance of bundles of voting rights through the lens of comparative institutional analysis as a trade-off between different types of costs. The choice over voting rights and the procedure of collective choice are understood as attempts to economize on costs of making a collective choice under uncertainty. Different institutions achieve this in different ways. To develop an understanding of comparative institutional analysis in collective choice, we draw on the Institutional Possibilities Frontier (IPF) as first outlined by Andrei Shleifer and his co-authors. [9] The IPF is an analytic framework to understand comparative economic systems. Shleifer and co-authors arranged the institutions of governance—including markets, the common law, regulation, and public ownership—

according to how they balanced dictatorship costs and disorder costs. Dictatorship costs are the risk of appropriation from state actors, maximized under public ownership, while disorder costs are the risk of appropriation from private agents, maximized under the market order. No institution is costless. Rather, institutions economize on the costs of disorder and dictatorship in comparatively effective ways, and can be arrayed within the IPF space. Following institutional economists such as Ronald Coase, Oliver Williamson, and Elinor Ostrom, human institutions are shaped by the need to economize on transactions costs. The IPF is unique because it enables a dynamic analysis of institutional possibilities from the perspective of trade-offs in costs. While originally the IPF was specifically applied to the economic problem of governing business, it has since been applied to specifically to economic problems including innovation policy, public broadcasting, and environmental law.[10] The IPF has also been extended to incorporate the notion of subjective costs—that is, each person views the shape of the IPF in a different way depending on how he or she expects different institutions to be implemented.[11] The original architects of the IPF argue that the distance from the origin is determined by a number of factors including civic capital and technology.

What costs are traded-off in making collective democratic choices? In the DIPF, systems of democratic decision making exist on a spectrum representing a trade-off between decision costs and agency costs. These are the dual costs incurred by individuals in the process of making a collective choice. Different institutional points—that is, different formations of the bundles of voting property rights that are constitutionally afforded to citizens—solve this problem differently. Figure 3.1 below explores this trade-off along a DIPF with four real-world examples. We will return to these examples shortly, but first it is useful to examine the nature of the axes.

Decision costs are a fundamental cost of making a collective choice. At the most basic level decision costs include the physical activity involved in registering a valid vote—such as keeping voter registration ledgers, attending polling booths, and navigating the voting procedure. Decision costs have two further drivers: (1) the information and cognitive costs of decision making; and (2) the nature of choice in an uncertain and constantly changing environment. Decision costs cover both the cognitive load and the frequency of voting. Empirical evidence suggests that an increase in the number of electoral contests decreases participation.[12] These cognitive costs involve understanding the questions being put to collective choice, awareness of the alternatives, and the consequences of those alternatives. The information to make policy choices is Hayekian: it is distributed, uncertain, and contextual.[13] Locating and putting to use that information, and the mental processing necessary for this understanding, is costly. If the mind is a scarce resource, as Herbert Simon wrote, we would expect individuals to seek to economize on its use.[14] Individuals may also have other values they are trying to maximize

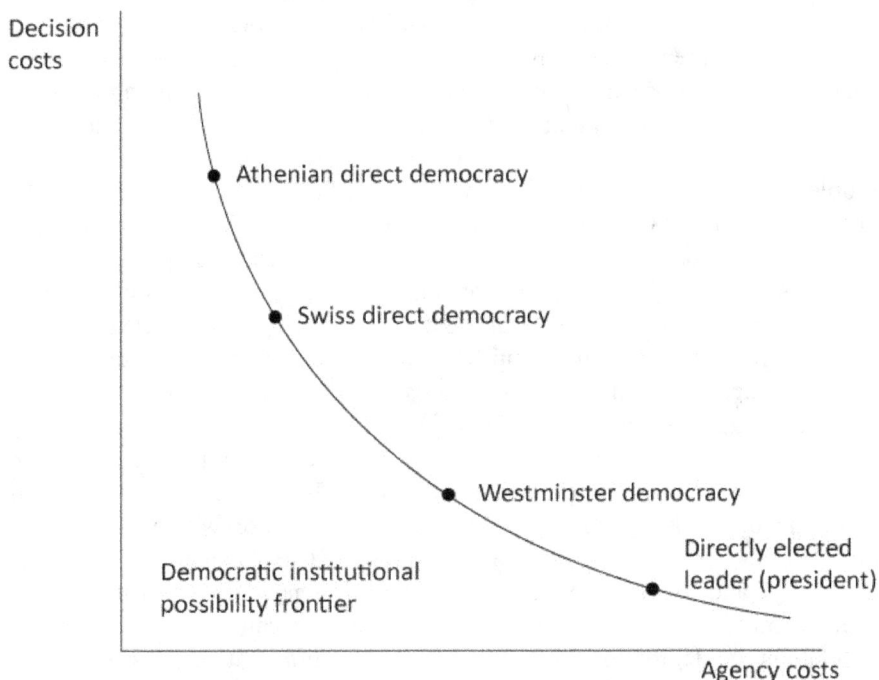

Figure 3.1.   The Democratic Institutional Possibility Frontier (DIPF)

apart from the search for the "best" (however defined) choice among those alternatives. The "rational irrationality" described by Bryan Caplan in his revision of the public choice of voting describes the choice not only to minimize the search for information about public policy while sometimes maintaining an emotion attachment to an irrational opinion.[15]

How can we economize on decision costs? One approach is to decline to participate. At the level of the social aggregate, autocracies economize decision costs by converting collective choices into hierarchical choices. While autocrats may claim to speak on behalf of "the people" or represent them in some way, without some mechanism (outside exit or revolution) by which "voters" can exercise control over the choice of autocrat or the decisions of state we cannot describe it as a system of collective choice. An alternative approach to economizing on decision costs is to delegate decision-making power.

While delegation reduces decision costs it simultaneously increases *agency costs*. The inherent bounded rationality of voters and the uncertainty over the nature of future decisions by a representative means that delegation must always be incomplete in a contractual sense.[16] No delegation contract can adequately foresee all future contingencies. By design, delegation offers delegates space to make decisions on behalf of delegators. Agency costs describe the divergence between the preferences of delegators and the preferences of delegates. Agents (that is, delegates) might interpret the preferences of their principles (delegators) wrongly, or act in ways contrary to those preferences. The former is a problem of bounded rationality, and the latter a problem of opportunism. To be more concrete, the message of populist politics that is opposed to "the elites" is an expression of high agency costs—the belief that delegates (politicians) have failed to transmit the preferences of the voters into action. We can economize on agency costs by: (1) implementing safeguards; and (2) taking on more decision costs (i.e., less delegation).

We can array this relationship between decision costs and agency costs within a space of institutional possibilities. Figure 3.1 arrays four real institutional settings to create a DIPF. Each point along the spectrum is equally "democratic" to the extent that it maintains political equality—that is, 1p1v. But each position economizes on costs differently. The DIPF is convex toward the origin, suggesting some point at the interior where the sum of decision costs and agency costs are minimized. The shape of the curve (its convexity) and its distance from the origin are determined by a mixture of social capital, trust, and prevailing technologies. We can see that the relevant variable is the degree of directness or representation that each system relies on. Here we wish to emphasize that the difference is one of degree rather than kind. There are a plausibly infinite number of intermediate steps along the DIPF, many of which are yet to be discovered. Real-world political systems typically feature a mixture of institutions from direct democracy to representative or presidential systems. The United States combines a representative system (the Congress) with a semi-directly elected presidential system (a vote of the population mediated by the Electoral College). Australia has a Westminster system where constitutional questions (and a small number of non-constitutional questions) are subject to a direct ballot.

To understand the formation of a DIPF it is useful to briefly explore the four institutions we have placed on it. Athenian direct democracy minimizes agency costs but maximizes decision costs. In the Athenian Assembly, all free Athenian male citizens had the right to speak and vote on laws and decrees governing the city. Athenian direct democracy was not absolute or complete. The Athenian system, as we have seen, was a complex system of overlapping authorities. The 500-member council, selected by sortition, could pass decrees on minor matters, and had power to set the Assembly's agenda. Nonetheless, the system placed a heavy load on the votes of the Assembly. History has left us some shadows of this burden. At the democracy's height, there were forty scheduled Assembly meetings per year. Demosthenes complains of his fellow citizens failing to remember agreements in the Assembly despite being "present at every assembly."[17] The system of payments for attendance at the Assembly is testimony to the costs felt by citizens for democratic participation.

The Swiss system of direct democracy reduces the costs of decision making by introducing a system of representation, but this does so by increasing agency costs. It can be seen either as an intermediate step between direct democracy and a representative system or a mixture between the two. The Swiss federal government is organized through a combination of representative parliament and regular referendums. Referendums are mandatory for constitutional questions. These are proposed by Swiss legislatures or executives and are subject to endorsement or rejection by popular vote. In the absence of parliamentary or executive leadership, Swiss citizens can initiate their own votes: popular initiative referendums (at the federal and cantonal level for constitutional questions) are triggered when a proposal receives 100,000 valid signatures collected over eighteen months. This direct democracy resembles that of an ideal direct democracy, where proposals come from the citizenry itself.

A hybrid institution between direct and representative democracy in the Swiss system is the optional referendum. Mandatory referendums allow Swiss citizens to challenge legislation passed by the representative parliament within 100 days of that legislation being published. As these referendums are optional, a petition of 50,000 valid signatures is required to trigger the popular vote. The optional referendum is a mechanism to return decisions made by representatives to the responsibility of the voting population as a whole. One way to think about this is as a safety valve to reduce agency costs. In the normal process, legislation and government decision making proceeds on a delegated basis, economizing on decision costs. However, in circumstances that this delegation imposes high agency costs—such as the delegates acting on their own interests, rather than that of voters—the population can bear some decision costs and reconsider the previously delegated decision.

Further down the DIPF is Westminster government and a directly elected presidential system. These institutional settings are delegations to a parliament and to an executive respectively. The principle of subsidiarity in political science suggests that the closer governments are to the voters the more responsive they will be to their preferences. But given that some public goods have to be (or are understood to have to be) provided at a national, rather than local, level, the institutional choice is how large the constituencies for delegation should be drawn. The smaller the delegative constituency the closer the delegate is to the voters. There is a long tradition in political philosophy seeing the delegate-voter relationship as a two-way relationship. Not only does closeness allow for monitoring of delegates, but theorists from Montesquieu and Alexis de Toqueville onward emphasized that by encouraging a form of civic virtue this binds citizens to their government. Andrew

Rehfeld describes this latter rationale as the "attachment justification" for territorial constituency (that is, arranging and grouping constituencies on a geographic basis).[18]

Delegative subsidiarity is limited by practical and philosophical considerations. At a national level, the smaller the constituency (and closer the delegate to voters) the larger the national legislature. Globally, the number of members of an individual democratic legislative body tops out at around 700. With this practical bound, small countries are able to have delegates representing smaller numbers of voters. Iceland, for example, has six national constituencies allocating sixty-three seats in the Alþingi proportionately. Each seat represents approximately 5,000 Icelandic citizens. India by contrast has 545 seats in its national lower house, the Lok Sabha, meaning each seat represents approximately 2.4 million citizens.

Representative democracies bundle these rights together to determine decision-making authority. Voters are grouped into geographic divisions and then through majority (or plural) vote choose their representative. Those representatives are then bundled together for a majority vote to choose the head of the executive. Direct democracies, by contrast, are disaggregated, allowing for citizens to provide majority or plural votes on policy choices. In Athenian direct democracy the Assembly was open to all male citizens above the age of twenty and the Assembly directed policy-making power through voting. However some hint of the high cost of direct decision making is suggested by the less than full participation at the Assembly: a space for 6,000 people to vote was apparently sufficient while there were around 30,000 potential voters.[19] The implementation of policy was the responsibility of the 500-person Boule. Swiss semi-direct democracy retains features of direct participation for non-constitutional proposals but only if triggered by a petition of a certain number of citizens.[20]

The DIPF that we arrayed above is on the basis of our subjective perceptions of how the four different institutions of collective choice might economize on decision costs and agency costs. Indeed, all costs within the DIPF framework are subjectively perceived by individual voters.[21] Institutional costs are not institutional facts but are perceived differently by individuals according to their matrix of preferences, values, and experiences. Let us take the example of populism. Populism has two overriding concerns: the perceived disconnection between elites and "the people," and where the line between the people and outsiders are to be drawn. Both of these we can see as agency costs. The division between elite representatives and the people is obvious. The more subtle and perhaps more significant is how the aggregation of preferences in the election of delegates (presidents, representatives) is perceived as a loss of control. Populism is in large part a concern with group formation—a concern that control is being lost because outsiders to the group are now sharing, and diluting that control. While we cannot speak to how individuals perceive the costs of institutional choice, we can say that over time new technologies—including the technologies outlined in chapter 1 as well as blockchain technology—open up new institutional possibilities closer to the origin of the DIPF. That is, the institutional points within the DIPF space that society must constitutionally choose are not fixed in time— new possibilities emerge as technologies better help govern new combinations of bundles of voting rights to facilitate a collective choice infrastructure that is closer to the origin. We can therefore use the DIPF framework to understand what new institutional possibilities are opened up—by economizing on decision costs and agency costs—by the invention and application of blockchain to collective choice.

CONCLUSION

In this chapter we developed a contract-theoretic framework over choice of democratic institutions from a comparative property rights governance perspective. The DIPF analyzes votes as bundles of property rights that must be governed under uncertainty between agency costs and decision costs. We can map collective choice institutions along a DIPF where different institutions achieve collective choice goals in comparatively effective ways. Following our historical approach in chapter 1, the development of new technologies opens up the potential for new institutional possibilities closer to the origin. In this context we can analyze how blockchain technology might open up new institutional possibilities in a cryptodemocracy. What we propose in the following chapters, however, is that a cryptodemocracy is unique because it doesn't presuppose a particular procedural or institutional structure. Rather, a cryptodemocracy is a constitutional framework—an underlying infrastructure—within which individual voters contractually determine where in the DIPF space they wish to engage in the political process. We argue that this nature of cryptodemocracy—where individuals can decide how they perceive their agency costs and decision costs and engage selectively—makes it uniquely emergent and polycentric compared to existing collective choice institutions. In a cryptodemocracy voters are given the liberty to contract their property rights in new ways using blockchain technology, putting to use their local knowledge and preferences to discover cost-economizing solutions. What those rights include is determined by individual contracting, but those are constrained by the technologies available in governing, expressing, and monitoring those rights. This contrasts with a centrally planned system of voting where the majority of voting rights that can be exercised are determined constitutionally or through other means. Indeed, voting rights even within a representative democracy are tightly constrained: you can only vote at certain times, for certain candidates, and you cannot exchange or transfer voting rights to others. This opens the question of what new institutional possibilities voters will seek to create when they are given freedom of voting rights governed through blockchain. In the following two chapters we focus on two rights that voters might seek to express: the right to *delegate* votes to others through contracts administered through blockchain smart contracts (chapter 4), and the right to *bargain* and *exchange* those property rights (chapter 5).

NOTES

1. Kaare Strøm et al., *Delegation and Accountability in Parliamentary Democracies* (Oxford University Press, 2003).
2. G. Bingham Powell and G. Bingham Powell Jr, *Elections as Instruments of Democracy: Majoritarian and Proportional Visions* (Yale University Press, 2000).
3. This was described by the Australian High Court in a case in 1909: "Now the legislature would be an ineffective instrument for making laws if it only dealt with the circumstances existing at the date of the measure. The aim of all legislatures is to project their minds as far as possible into the future, and to provide in terms as general as possible for all contingencies likely to arise in the application of the law. But it is not possible to provide specifically for all cases, and, therefore, legislation from the very earliest times, and particularly in more modern times, has taken the form of conditional legislation, leaving it to some specified authority to determine the circumstances in which the law shall be applied, or to what its operation shall be extended, or the particular class of persons or goods to which it shall be applied." (Baxter v Ah Way [1909] 8 CLR 626 at 637–38).
4. Martino Maggetti, "Legitimacy and Accountability of Independent Regulatory Agencies: A Critical Review," *Living Reviews in Democracy* 2, no. 1 (2010); Marc Quintyn, "Independent Agencies: More Than a Cheap Copy of Independent Central Banks?" *Constitutional Political Economy* 20, no. 3–4 (2009).
5. Robert Alan Dahl, *Polyarchy: Participation and Opposition* (Yale University Press, 1973).
6. Allen Buchanan, "Political Legitimacy and Democracy," *Ethics* 112, no. 4 (2002).
7. Harold Demsetz, "Toward a Theory of Property Rights," *The American Economic Review* 57, no. 2 (1967).
8. James M. Buchanan, *Cost and Choice: An Inquiry in Economic Theory* (University of Chicago Press, 1979).
9. See Andrei Shleifer, "Understanding Regulation," *European Financial Management* 11, no. 4 (2005); Simeon Djankov et al., "The New Comparative Economics," *Journal of Comparative Economics* 31, no. 4 (2003).
10. For specific policy questions that the IPF has been applied to, see S. Davidson, "Environmental Protest: An Economics of Regulation Approach," *Australian Environment Review* 29, no. 10 (2014); Sinclair Davidson, "Submission to Parliamentary Joint Committee on Law Enforcement Inquiry into Illicit Tobacco," (2016); Sinclair Davidson and Jason Potts, "A New Institutional Approach to Innovation Policy," *Australian Economic Review Policy Forum: Research and Innovation* 49, no. 2 (2016); Chris Berg, "Safety and Soundness: An Economic History of Prudential Bank Regulation in Australia, 1893–2008" (RMIT University, 2016); Chris Berg and Sinclair Davidson, "Section 18c, Human Rights, and Media Reform: An Institutional Analysis of the 2011–13 Australian Free Speech Debate," *Agenda: A Journal of Policy Analysis and Reform* 23, no. 1 (2016); Berg and Davidson, "Media Regulation: A Critique of Finkelstein and Tiffen," *available at SSRN 2669271* (2015); Sinclair Davidson, "Productivity Enhancing Regulatory Reform," *Australia Adjusting: Optimising National Prosperity* (2013); Sinclair Davidson and Jason Potts, "Social Costs and the Institutions of Innovation Policy," *available at SSRN 2565574* (2015); Trent J. MacDonald, "Theory of Unbundled and Non-Territorial Governance" (RMIT University, 2015); Darcy W.E. Allen and Chris Berg, "Subjec-

tive Political Economy," *New Perspectives on Political Economy* 13, no. 1–2 (2017); Chris Berg and Sinclair Davidson, *Against Public Broadcasting: Why and How We Should Privatise the ABC* (Queensland, Australia: Connor Court Publishing Pty Ltd., 2018); Darcy W.E. Allen, Aaron M. Lane, and Marta Poblet, "The Governance of Blockchain Dispute Resolution" in *The Australasian Law and Economics Conference* (Brisbane, Australia, 2018).

11. Allen and Berg, "Subjective Political Economy."

12. Daniel Stockemer and Patricia Calca, "Presidentialism and Voter Turnout in Legislative Elections," *Parliamentary Affairs* 67, no. 3 (2012); Margit Tavits, "Direct Presidential Elections and Turnout in Parliamentary Contests," *Political Research Quarterly* 62, no. 1 (2009); Mark N. Franklin, "Too Much Democracy? How Elections to the European Parliament Depress Turnout at National Elections in Europe" (paper presented at the Congress of the European Consortium of Political Research, Marburg, Germany, 2003).

13. Hayek, "The Use of Knowledge in Society."

14. Herbert A. Simon, "Rationality as Process and as Product of Thought," *The American Economic Review*, 68, no. 2 (1978); Williamson, *The Economic Institutions of Capitalism*, 46.

15. Bryan Caplan, *The Myth of the Rational Voter: Why Democracies Choose Bad Policies* (Princeton University Press, 2011).

16. Jean Tirole, "Cognition and Incomplete Contracts," *American Economic Review* 99, no. 1 (2009).

17. Dem. 18.273.

18. Rehfeld, *The Concept of Constituency: Political Representation, Democratic Legitimacy, and Institutional Design*, 86.

19. John Thorley, *Athenian Democracy* (London: Routledge, 1996).

20. Hanspeter Kriesi, *Direct Democractic Choice: The Swiss Experience* (Lanham, MD: Lexington Books, 2005).

21. Allen and Berg, "Subjective Political Economy."

Chapter Four

Delegating the Vote

INTRODUCTION

This chapter examines how voters might delegate their voting rights to others within a cryptodemocracy. What are the implications for collective choice when voters freely delegate, decompose, and contract their voting rights? At first a delegative democracy appears similar to representative government, yet it is a step-change in the relationship between voter and delegate, and opens up new emergent forms of democratic ordering. Delegating power to others is an institutional method to reduce decision costs, and is a feature of all democratic and semi-democratic systems. Delegation in a cryptodemocracy, however, is a non-territorial process where voters can choose delegates based on criteria other than geographic location. Delegation through block-chain is the key organizational possibility of cryptodemocracy, propelling a voluntary process where voters and delegates negotiate terms and conditions of delegation—through contractual arrangements. The scope of potential contracts are unlimited—for instance, parties to the contract can specify any terms, abolish contracts according to any agreed criteria at any time, exclude votes on certain policy issues from the delegation, and so forth. The extent to which these delegation contracts are possible will primarily relate to problems of delegation contract incompleteness. Our aim in this chapter is to examine how delegation in a cryptodemocracy might shift the dynamics of collective choice. We contrast existing models of delegation in representative democracies with delegation in a cryptodemocracy. In doing so we emphasize both how votes are grouped into constituencies through voluntary contractual negotiation and how delegation of voting rights becomes decomposable and divisible along multiple dimensions.

We proceed as follows. In the second section we outline the origins, costs, and proposed alternatives to territorial voting, focusing on the concept of constituency. Given that delegative democracy has seen a resurgence in attention in the digital era—and particularly since the development of blockchains and smart contracting—in the third section we introduce the intellectual origins of delegative democracy. In the fourth section we sketch what delegation in a cryptodemocracy might look like. Our presentation is distinct from these earlier works because of the emphasis and integration into a more generalized framework of property rights over votes, the decomposition of delegations along multiple dimensions, and the decentralized enforcement of those votes through smart contracts in a blockchain-based infrastructure. The fifth section concludes.

WHY GROUP VOTES?

The "representative claim" in representative democracy is a contested, dynamic, and elusive one.[1] What does it mean to represent voters, or a constituency? Representative claims are highly sensitive to territoriality and group identity. Against the Burkean trustee model of representation, as a first step, delegation in a cryptodemocracy is firmly on the side of "representations" being contractual delegations made by freely choosing individual voters. Nevertheless, as we shall discuss in later chapters, the contractual discretion of a cryptodemocracy means that voters, if they so choose, may decide to contract with delegates in a way that frees the delegate to follow her conscience. In this way the trustee model can be an emergent order on a delegative cryptodemocratic foundation. Most democracies group voters together, organizing their votes into constituencies for the purposes of determining a representative in a legislature. Yet as Andrew Rehfeld argues, while the constituency (and its typically territorial definition) is one of the most common institutional features of democratic form, it is also one of its least scrutinized.[2] In democratic Athens, offices selected by lot were not chosen from the undifferentiated mass of Athenian citizens. Rather, they were allocated into 139 demes—territorial communities usually centered around a village or harbor. Each deme was allocated a certain number of places in the *boule* or offices, depending on the size of the deme. Most modern democracies group voters into territorial constituencies. These constituencies can be defined according to population numbers (periodically readjusted) or aligned to fixed geographical territories (such as pre-existing states and provinces). Even some single offices filled on a seemingly majoritarian basis can be filtered through constituencies. One of the most prominent examples of this is the US presidency, which is indirectly elected through the Electoral College system. Eligible voters chose delegates on a territorial (state) basis, who in turn elect the president and vice president. By contrast, the French president is directly elected on a majority basis in two run-off elections. Robert Elgie shows a long-term shift from countries with hereditary heads of state, to indirectly elected presidents, to directly elected presidents over the course of the twentieth century.[3] Territoriality is not the only way voters have been grouped: we can observe constituencies of race, social class, and political party in historical and modern democracies. But organizing delegations on a territorial basis is such a widespread feature of ancient and modern democracies that it deserves careful scrutiny if we are to step away from it in a cryptodemocracy.

Representative democracy can be conceptualized as a stepped set of delegations to reduce decision costs. As we noted in chapter 1, the territoriality of the early English parliament (and its pre-parliamentary ancestors) was its key design feature. Parliament was a gathering of neither delegates, nor representatives, but informants (in the non-pejorative sense), who assembled in order to solve the information problem characteristic of large early medieval states.[4] Early parliamentarians delivered information to the monarch as well as back to their local communities. In the centuries after the Magna Carta, the role evolved into an endorsement of the taxation requirements of the monarch. In its earliest forms, parliamentarians were less representatives, or delegates, and more agents—a simple stand-in for a pre-existing community, such as a town or county.[5] As the role and political significance of parliament changed over time—as it became a fundamental part of the constitution, and began to displace the sovereignty of the king—its territorial organization remained fixed, while being subject to little attention.

The principles of vote grouping have been subject to attention on the question of how large constituencies should be and how many agents/representatives each constituency should send to parliament. The creation of the United States was one historical episode in which these questions came into prominence: an event which was accompanied by a remarkable outpouring of political thought. The driver for these debates was the sheer size of the new federal government compared to the states that it bound together. Where small communities could be plausibly represented in state legislatures, it was harder to see how the four million people of the United States could be allocated into representative constituencies for the purposes of forming a legislature. The major cleavage on constituency size was the relationship between factionalism on the one hand and local interests on the other. The first position was that constituencies should represent local interests. While territoriality was not directly considered in these debates, this suggests that voters in an agricultural community are more likely to vote in the interests of agricultural industries, and voters who live around a port are likely to be more focused on the interests of shipping. They would send representatives to the legislature based on those interests. The larger the constituency, the more diluted those communities of interest would become. The local interest argument therefore tends to favor smaller constituencies. The more homogenous the members of the constituency, the more likely their interests will be represented in parliament.

Arrayed against this argument was hostility to factionalism—the opposing belief that local interests would be excessively self-interested and fail to support the public good of the larger whole. Representatives of agricultural or shipping interests might seek to favor those interests against the public interest. Class interests might pit themselves against other classes. Large constituencies diluted interests and therefore the pernicious creation of factions. In Federalist 60, Alexander Hamilton argued that if districts were large enough, interests would be scattered—randomly distributed—thus preventing concentration. Factions would remain, of course, but inter-factional competition would occur at the local level, rather than in the national legislature. The claim was that factions would cancel each other out. When the anti-Federalists challenged the Hamilton argument, one ground on which they did so was that interests were not in fact randomly distributed: that in urban areas particularly large constituency definitions would encourage strategic behavior to concentrate votes. Better, then, to have small constituencies where the interests were unambiguous and the factions would compete in the legislature, rather than the layer below.

From this division between the interest-centric model of constituency and its alternative of large constituencies diluting interests, Rehfeld develops a restructure of electoral constituencies to ensure they "look like the nation they collectively represent."[6] It is worth looking closely at this proposal in order to understand the potential trade-offs in alternative democratic orderings, and to underline the novel implications of our own cryptodemocratic system. Rehfeld proposes (described as a thought experiment) that citizens be randomly allocated to equally sized permanent national constituencies. No constituency or allocation to a constituency would have any relationship to territory. For example, once a voter has reached the age of voter registration, a random number between 1 and 435 (or however many seats in the national legislature were desired) could be drawn, and the new voter allocated to a corresponding constituency. This constituency allocation would be permanent—the constituency they have been allocated to would be the constituency they remain in their whole life. Once they have been allocated, they would be given access to a means of communicating with their representative and other members of the constituency. Each constituency would elect one member to the legislature (although of course multi-member electorates would also be possible under this scheme).

What would permanent random constituencies look like? At the first instance, they would be a near-exact statistical reflection of the national population. Each interest—class, industrial, racial or ethnic group, gender and sexuality—would be equally present in each constituency. If first-generation immigrants represent 27 percent of the population as a whole (assuming they all had voting rights) then 27 percent of each constituency would be first generation immigrants. The population of any constituency would be an approximate stand-in for the national population. The permanence of the constituency allocation is designed to ensure that the voters that authorized a representative at the time of their first election are the same voters that assess the representative at the time of their subsequent election.

Rehfeld is concerned to emphasize that digital communication technologies could substitute for the democratic deliberation that might currently occur on a territorial basis. In current democratic systems, any given voters neighbors are (assumed to be) registered to vote in the same electoral division. Territorial constituencies therefore facilitate—in theory—the creation of communities of deliberation, where the voters can debate and develop policy positions which are then transmitted through to their representatives. One of us has argued that this is one of the functions of free expression—the Hayekian discovery of subjective institutional costs.[7] This possibly overstates the territoriality of deliberation. Internet communication, the decline of local newspapers, and national newsroom consolidation has meant that policy deliberation on national issues tends to be conducted in national fora. Nonetheless, where voters in modern democratic systems have extensive interactions (if not necessarily deep interactions) with many other voters in the same division, voters in randomized constituencies will rarely interact in their daily life with other voters in their division. Here Rehfeld offers a technological solution—a system of secure chat rooms (text, audio, and video, as necessary) for deliberation between members of a single constituency.

The purpose of Rehfeld's randomized constituencies is to reduce interest-centric behavior and eliminate strategic constituency definition—such as gerrymandering. While it is likely to be successful at achieving these goals, the model would have some perverse consequences. As each constituency is demographically exactly the same as every other constituency, we can assume that (as a first approximation) in a two-party system the voters would uniformly elect members of the same party to all seats in the legislature. As the fortunes of that party declined, the next election might see the legislature switch completely to the opposing party. This periodic switching is by design—recall the Hamiltonian argument that policy deliberation should ideally occur within a diverse constituency, rather than in a diverse, interest-centric legislature (as the anti-Federalists favored). While on the surface this looks like it would mean wild policy swings as opposing parties gained and then ceded absolute control of the legislature, Rehfeld suggests that the median voter model suggests that each party would over time converge toward the political median, smoothing policy variation, moderating extremism, and maximizing voter satisfaction.

If we relax the strict assumptions of the median voter model, we expose some weaknesses in the randomized constituency, while at the same time resolving others. One implication of the median voter model is that the demographics representatives will themselves (possibly) reflect the median voter. As Rehfeld notes, for the United States this would probably result in a legislature dominated by white males. It could look strikingly less diverse than it does now. One method of mitigating this could be changing the qualifications for being a representative: for instance, diversity quotas could mandate that a certain percentage of representatives were women or African American. But this solution exposes the down-stream consequences of Rehfeld's Hamiltonian approach. He concludes that white male representatives under the random constituency are going to be more responsive to the median voter, but that there may be a need for having a diverse "range of voices" in the national legislature. Could this reasoning not be applied to diversity on other margins, that is, class, wealth, industry, or even geographic location? Urban representatives, rural representatives, working-class representatives, and aristocratic representatives also bring to the national parliament a diversity of perspectives and accumulated experiences. "Interests" need not be material, and diversity quotas smuggle interest-centric democratic philosophy back into the national legislature even in a random constituency model.

This may be somewhat less a concern if we relax the strict assumptions of the median voter model, which posits single peaked preferences on a single-dimensional model. Assuming that the national legislature considers policy questions that do not neatly map onto a linear, symmetric left-right ideological spectrum, the composition of that legislature and the outcome of its votes are likely to be more "chaotic" than Rehfeld suggests.[8] In the absence of clear preference about what the median voter desires, representatives have to make suppositions about what position will satisfy the maximum number of constituents. This is of course a feature of the status quo, but the random constituency eliminates one of the most useful heuristics available to representatives today—interests. For all the perverse consequences of strategic territorial behavior such as gerrymandering, interest-centric territoriality provides information to the representative about the preferences of their voters. The random constituency model severs that information flow. One possibility is that this would free representatives up to be trustees rather than delegates of their constituencies, potentially enhancing agency problems between voters and their representative. Nonetheless, the random constituency is a compelling thought experiment that exposes clearly some of the embedded assumptions within modern representative democracies. We can now turn to the question of how a form of delegative cryptodemocracy—delegating votes to others to form constituencies—changes the nature of collective choice. A cryptodemocratic process of delegation can be compared to modern representative democracy or randomized constituencies, as well as a new interior point within the DIPF outlined in chapter 3. The model of delegative democracy we detail here is a foundational one that sets up further structures of vote exchange in chapter 5.

THE IDEA OF DELEGATIVE DEMOCRACY

What is delegative democracy? Delegative democracy describes a democratic system in which voters are able to transfer their vote to delegates that act on their behalf. If a voter decides not to delegate their vote, then they can exercise their vote themselves. If they do delegate their vote to another person, then that person votes for them. Delegative voting systems might be used for elections around policy questions or to vote for leaders. In the former, a delegative voting system allows voters to decide whether they wish to exercise their vote as if it was a direct democracy or a representative democracy. For the latter, a delegative voting system allows voters to exercise their vote as if it was a direct presidential system (where voters choose their president in a direct vote) or a Westminster system (where voters elect representatives who then choose prime ministers). The basic outlines of this system are sometimes described as voluntary proxy voting (underlining its relationship to proxy voting systems in corporate democracy) or the evocative "liquid" democracy (which emphasizes the transitive characteristics of delegation, as voter preferences flow into collective choice).[9] What a delegative democracy means in practice is that individual voters can engage in the political process in a selective way, effectively revealing their preferences for points within the DIPF space outlined in chapter 3. That is, in a delegative democracy individuals can draw on their local knowledge to economize on the decision costs and agency costs of different paths of action within some collective choice.

Delegative democracy is not a new idea. Its basic feature—the transitive proxy of voting from one person to another—was first described by the mathematician and novelist Charles Dodgson (better known as Lewis Carroll, author of *Alice's Adventures in Wonderland*) in his 1884 book *Principles of Parliamentary Representation*. Dodgson's primary focus was the development of a scheme of proportional representation, where "the number of unrepresented Electors should be as small as possible."[10] Delegative voting comes up when Dodgson considers the problems of two or more candidates from the same party in a multi-member electorate diluting the vote for their party, and "wasting" surplus votes. He considers, and rejects, preferential voting schemes (where voters rank their preferences for candidates, and votes flow down the rank ordering) and a system where the vote total is continuously announced during the period of voting, so voters could direct their votes to alternative candidates once their first preference had received enough votes to be elected. The alternative, for Dodgson, is to have the candidates themselves redirect votes according to their own preferences. In doing so, he sketches a property rights model of voting:

> Clearly somebody must have authority to dispose of [surplus votes]. . . . There remains *the Candidate himself, for whom the votes have been given.* This seems to solve the whole difficult. The Elector must understand that, in giving his vote to *A*, he gives it to him as his absolute property, to use for himself, or to transfer to other Candidates, or to leave unused. If he cannot trust the man, for whom he votes, so far as to believe that he will use the vote for the best, how comes it that he can trust him so far as to wish to return him as Member?[11]

Dodgson's focus was proportional representation and his *Principles* was seen at the time as one of the more sophisticated explorations of such a system that was being widely discussed.[12] The delegative model he develops—almost as an afterthought—was not seriously considered for another eighty years.

In a paper published in *Public Choice* in 1969, James C. Miller III (later Budget Director in the Reagan administration) described clearly the delegative model: "instead of electing representatives periodically for a tenure of two years or more, why not allow citizens to vote directly or delegate proxy to someone else for as long as they like."[13] One crucial clarification Miller makes is that under such a system, the nature of "representation" would change. Where representatives in the legislature currently have a single, equivalent vote regardless of the population they are representing, delegates acting by proxy in a legislature would have their vote weighted by that population. In Miller's view, "the advancing technology of electronic computers" reduced both the decision costs and agency costs of direct decision making and delegation respectively, allowing for this new form of organization. A "recording console" for each voter, secured by a "special metal key, a coded combination, or even a thumbprint" would be available to register decisions. This can be interpreted as new technologies opening up new institutional possibilities in the DIPF space.

Unsurprisingly, the development of digital technology throughout the 1990s and 2000s has led to a surge in interest about delegative democracy. This book is no exception. However, to date, the bulk of the work about this form of government has consisted of restatements of the basic principles. The novelist Robert Heinlein and political scientist Gordon Tullock both briefly raised the possibility of a delegative voting system.[14] The computer scientist Bryan Ford has been one prominent advocate of delegative democracy, publishing a paper in 2002.[15] For Ford, delegative democracy is a democratic system based on individual self-determination. Voters can choose their role (passive delegators or active participants), there are low barriers to participation (delegations are negotiated rather than structured around large-scale political campaigns), there are high degrees of accountability, and delegates can potentially specialize (we will return to this question of entrepreneurial specialization of delegates later). Dan Alger's exploration of proxy voting in 2006 (also published in *Public Choice*) posited that a preferential voting system for the choice of proxies—combined with a supermajority rule to change government—would buttress the stability of the system.[16] This relates to broader questions around the trade-offs in institutional innovations—discovering new points in the DIPF space closer to the origin—and the stability of the system, however defined. Over time voters in a cryptodemocracy may change their preferences for stability. It is also possible that delegation in a cryptodemocracy is more robust because it involves individuals engaging in the political process along a spectrum in reference to their own preferences, rather than squeezing those preferences within a centrally planned institutional procedure. For Alger, a delegative system "seems to offer an improvement for everyone except for the party elites, the special interests, and those voters with preferences quite close to theirs."[17]

A complementary analysis offered by James Green-Armytage in 2014 argues that delegative systems would likely reduce the dual information problems in democracy—the lack of information voters may have when voting in a direct democracy, and the lack of information representatives may have about their voters' preferences in a representative democracy—as well as encouraging political participation.[18] Indeed, as we will elaborate in chapter 5 and chapter 8—the preferences of voters over collective choice questions are not necessarily known or given. Rather, the act of political deliberation and discourse forms these opinions over time as they gather and interpret information, and a cryptodemocracy might be a favorable institutional environment for this dynamic process. Another genre of analysis on delegative democracy has focused on the relationship between this system and existing digital networks, where delegative democracy is related to social networks or inspired by Google's PageRank formula.[19]

For the purposes of this chapter, we do not offer any significant modifications of delegative democracy as it has emerged through this literature. Indeed, delegation in a cryptodemocracy is similar to the delegative democracy literature in that individuals may selectively engage and participate in collective choice. However, delegation in a cryptodemocracy differs compared to previous attempts in two main ways. First, delegation in a cryptodemocracy potentially rests on more nuanced and bespoke contracts that are administered through smart contracts. Indeed, our conception of votes as bundles of property rights within a collective choice enables voters within a cryptode-

mocracy to decompose those votes along new dimensions. Second, delegation in a cryptodemocracy is unique because, through the use of smart
contracts, the enforcement of delegations can occur in a decentralized way.
Voters can develop their own private governance mechanisms to enforce the
conditions of a delegation. We explore the implications of these unique features in the following section.

A DELEGATIVE CRYPTODEMOCRACY

What would delegation in a cryptodemocracy mean in practice? The delegative or proxy relationship is best understood as a contractual transfer of
property rights. In a cryptodemocracy those relationships are governed using
decentralized blockchain technology, including the application of smart
contracts. For simplicity's sake, let us assume there is collective choice about
a minimally simple choice—who should lead the government—which needs
to be made through a vote in a jurisdiction with twenty registered voters.
Figure 4.1 contrasts a Westminster representative system (on the left) against
a delegative system (on the right).

In a Westminster representative system, voters elect representatives to the
parliament who in turn elect the leader of the government. This is shown as
two roughly equally sized electoral divisions (Electorate a has nine voters,
while Electorate b has eleven voters), electing two members of parliament (r^a
and r^b). While it is not shown in the figure, it is important to note that both
the representatives and the leader are themselves members of electoral divisions, and (in the Westminster case) the leader is also the member of the
legislature. The numbers represent the weighting of each vote. Each voter in
the electorate has a vote weighting of one. Each representative likewise has a
vote weighting of one in the legislature, regardless of how many voters have
elected them.

The right side of figure 4.1 shows a simple delegative system. Voters are
not formally grouped into voting blocs. Formally, this conceptualizes the
political system as a single electoral division, and the head of government at
the first instance is directly elected. However, voters have a choice: they can
either exercise their vote themselves (or abstain), or contract with a delegate.
Delegates (shown in the figure as d^{a-e}) exercise the vote on their behalf. A
voter-delegate contract constitutes a transfer of property rights. As a consequence, each delegate has as much voting rights as they have acquired
through voluntary delegation. A delegate who contracts with seven voters
has seven votes in the final election for head of government. On the right
side, we show a voter who has chosen to vote him- or herself. A single vote is
unlikely to significantly influence the result but the voter is able to exercise it
(as if it were) a referendum or a direct leadership election. As the delegates

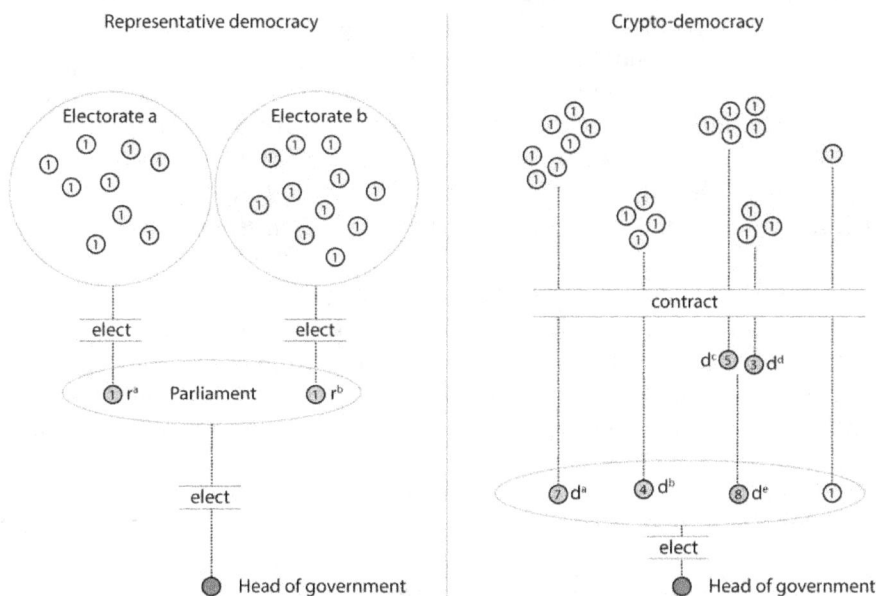

Figure 4.1. Simplified Models of Delegation in a Representative and Cryptodemocracy

have exchanged the right to exercise votes through contract, they may also re-delegate their vote as well (assuming the original delegation contract does not prohibit doing so). This is shown in the diagram as d^c and d^d delegating to d^e. In this way the cryptodemocratic delegative process is an emergent chain of delegation. Each contractual step draws on the local knowledge of the voter and the delegate. This leads to a unique process of coalition and constituency building over time that is built entirely from the voluntary interactions of the citizenry.

While the diagram makes clear one benefit of delegation—grouping more votes together exerts more influence over the final decision—we conceive two main costs to delegation. The first are the agency costs of delegating votes to others under uncertainty with the potential for opportunism. However, in a cryptodemocracy the agency costs related to opportunism would significantly decline as a result of the use of self-executing smart contracts.[20] The second is the loss of expressive value that a voter may experience. However, the latter is comparative: voters may in fact experience more expressive value in a delegative democracy compared to a representative democracy because they are free to delegate to whomever they wish.

Representatives are typically residents of or registered in the electoral divisions that they represent. They are members of their subgroup. In the simplest form of a delegative relationship, a delegate could be a member of a small group of politically aligned individuals who accepts the responsibility for acting on the group's behalf. In that form, delegates are members of the population of voters for whom they act. However, that membership is not a necessary feature of delegative democracy. Delegates may offer to act on behalf of individuals whose politics they do not share, as a commercial relationship (we discuss vote buying in chapter 5). Nor is it necessary for delegates to even have the right to exercise a vote themselves. Delegates may come from outside the political jurisdiction. In a national delegative democracy, it is feasible that delegation services could be provided by multinational firms domiciled overseas or even artificial intelligences, neither of which might hold constitutional property rights to vote on their own. Of course a society may make the constitutional choice to only enable delegates who are part of the franchise—but this must be understood as a reduction in voter liberty.

What is the institutional significance of delegation in a cryptodemocracy? At the first instance, delegative democracy is distinct from other democratic systems because it is contractual. Rather than centrally specifying the circumstances in which voters are allowed to exercise their votes constitutionally, voters themselves are able to write contracts with delegates that specify their own conditions for exercising the delegated vote. In this way voters choose the institutional context in which they express their voting rights. We have conceptualized this as a contractual transfer of property rights. The democratic order—that is, the shape and characteristics of the political system—is the result of voluntary negotiations between voters and their agents. In chapter 3 we presented the DIPF, depicting the relationship between direct democracy and representative democracy as a trade-off of decision and agency costs. In the DIPF decision costs and agency costs apply on a jurisdiction-wide basis. Two of us (Allen and Berg) have offered a critique of the comparative institutional literature in that it is insufficiently sensitive to subjective preferences. Institutional costs are not objective. Each actor in a political-economic system has different perceptions of those costs that are mediated both intersubjectively and according to personal material and ideological preferences. Different individuals feel agency costs and decision costs differently. In a delegative cryptodemocracy we decentralize decision making over the cost-minimizing approach to political action the utilization of political voting rights.

Delegative democracy allows voters to "customize" their political engagement according to their subjectively felt agency and decision costs. Alternative democratic forms—representative and direct democracy—impose the same structure on all voters regardless of those preferences. However preferences about political engagement are unevenly distributed. Disengaged or uninterested voters are likely to accept agency losses for reductions in decision costs. In voluntary voting systems those who are disengaged or disinterested are likely to be non-voters. In a delegative system they would be capable of establishing long-term delegative relationships that minimize their effort but still contribute their vote to collective choices. (Constitutional-level rules could require delegative relationships to be re-confirmed after a certain period of time.) Highly engaged voters are more willing to bear decision costs—or subjectively perceive lower decision costs—and are potentially more sensitive to agency costs.

There are alternative models that seek to resolve the problem of diverse preferences over political engagement, but they tend to do so either by emphasizing processes that occur outside the formal structures of voting, or undermine the 1p1v democratic ethic. For example, "monitory democracy" emphasizes the role of third parties (such as the press, citizen media, nonprofit third-sector organizations, and public watchdogs) to discover and publicize information about collective choices.[21] The political scientist John Keane has described this is as form of "post-electoral" democracy (although in a monitory democracy the institutions of voting and elections are maintained).[22] Political power in a monitory democracy is unevenly distributed by design, as individuals self-select into roles of influence. Advocates of monitory democracy respond that currently existing democratic systems already have uneven distributions of power, for instance through corporate political donations and "dark money."[23] A group of libertarian scholars who focus on the externalities caused by low-information voters have proposed technocratic solutions such as embedding expert panels into the political system or more fundamental changes such an epistocratic system that would require voters to demonstrate knowledge about political issues before they could vote.[24]

While this is not the place for extended critiques of these proposals, these alternatives provide some guide to how the challenges facing democracy have been conceptualized. Monitory democracy is useful as a positive description of the evolved democratic order but as a normative ideal risks entrenching interest groups and open up further opportunities for rent seeking.[25] Entrenching independent experts likewise induces potential capture. Epistocracy either undermines the 1p1v system (and then cannot be said to be democratic) or establishes a system whereby the knowledge threshold is also susceptible to capture. Delegative democracy by contrast targets the *variability* of preferences about engagement.

Just as policy knowledge is variable between voters, it is variable within an individual voter as well. Voters are not equally engaged or informed on all policy or political domains. In voluntary voting systems, this is clearly evident in the differences in rates of participation between national elections, legislative elections, and state and local elections. Swiss voters typically select which referendums they participate in: while the turnout for an individual referendum is rarely above 40 percent of eligible voters, it has been estimated that more than 90 percent of eligible voters had participated in at least one ballot within a five-year period. These so-called selective voters— neither always participating nor always abstaining—make up the bulk of the Swiss electorate.[26]

One unique feature of delegative democracy is that it allows votes to be conditionally decomposed. Contracts between voters and delegates can be formed that limit delegations to certain policy domains. For example, a voter might delegate his or her vote on economic and foreign policy but retain his or her voting power on questions of social policy. This not only enables individuals to engage selectively based on how intense their preferences are, but also for those voters who don't fit easily on the left-right spectrum of politics. Votes could be delegated on the basis of the knowledge of a delegate—some descriptions of liquid democracy emphasize the role of domain expertise—or to a trusted generalist, who might vote herself or re-delegate specific votes to experts. Delegative relationships could also plausibly have retention clauses in them that allow voters to retain voting control on an ad hoc basis. The most effective structures for these delegative contracts would have to be discovered, allowing voters the desired level of control over their vote without impeding the delegates' ability to fulfill the delegative contract. All of this becomes institutionally possible and enforceable through blockchain smart contracts—where it could be publicly verifiable about who owns what voting rights at any given time. Furthermore, introducing a compensation and bargaining process into this relationship, as we present in the next chapter, would speed the discovery of such contractual arrangements, and expand the potential space of mutually beneficial delegations.

An obvious but non-trivial characteristic of the delegative democracy described here is that, as voters and delegates are free to write the terms of the contract themselves, delegative relationships could be terminated (as James C. Miller III wrote) "on a day-to-day or even an hour-to-hour basis."[27] Under a simple representative system, voters can only withdraw their consent for a given representative at an election (typically every three to five years). The withdrawal of delegative power looks superficially like a recall election under a representative system, provided for in some electoral systems (including some Swiss cantons, British Columbia, and a number of American states). Recall elections have been criticized for encouraging "permanent campaigns," enhancing the powers of special interest to target individual office-holders outside the normal election cycle, and undermining the delicate balance between the delegative and trustee model of representation.[28] While some constitutions allow for recall only in the cases of incompetence and misconduct, many recalls can be made for "political" reasons: as opponents of office-holders who did not originally vote for the incumbent relitigate that collective choice.[29] The withdrawal of delegative power is, however, quite distinct from recall elections. Only direct parties to the delegative contract are able to dissolve the contract. That is, where recall campaigns can be launched by opponents of a representative, only those who had originally delegated their vote to a particular delegate can dissolve that delegation. It is also possible voters would waive any recall powers for a period longer than a traditional election or voting cycle, leading to a system which is more amenable to long-term political goals.

One significant objection might be raised at this juncture: that of political instability. The term "liquid democracy" suggests a democracy in constant flow. Voters may withdraw their consent to delegates at any time. Recall elections have been criticized for their unpredictability, and much political reform (such as fixed election cycles in Westminster systems) has been pursued in order to give governments the security of tenure to make decisions in the long-term interest. However in the simple model of a vote on who is to be head of government, this is not necessarily any more unstable than the existing system: heads of governments could still be elected on fixed schedules. Nor are legislative decision-making processes likely to be more unstable than representative systems.

To explain why, let us imagine a delegative democracy system that closely parallels the Westminster system. Voters chose either directly or through delegates the head of government, who in turn forms a government (from the population at large, rather than from a national parliament). That government manages the administration of policy and potentially other executive functions like foreign policy. In a representative democracy, changes to legislation have to be endorsed by the representative level below the government—that is, parliament. In the delegative system by contrast decisions on legislation (as with any other collective choice) would be made by a combination of direct votes and delegated votes. There would be no "parliament" *per se*. Any decision to reverse a collective choice—such as repeal existing legislation, or replace the head of government—would be made not by a parliament, but by the entire population and their delegates acting under instruction. Leadership changes in a Westminster system tend to swing on a small number of marginal votes in the governing parliamentary party.[30] James Madison was likewise concerned that a legislature that was too small would be susceptible to control by "the cabals of a few."[31] At a first approximation, delegative systems are likely to be only as unpredictable as public opinion. We are not comfortable however making formal predictions about the stability of a delegative system as much will rest on the provisions of the delegative contracts which are established. What kind of contracts prevail is a matter for entrepreneurial discovery. Delegative contracts could be written that prevent delegates from reconsidering leadership positions within a certain time frame, for example. How stable the system will be will be a function of the population's preferences for stability. We should also note, however, that messiness is not necessarily inefficient. Just as Elinor and Vincent Ostrom pushed back on the idea that institutional arrangements that looked messy and chaotic were inefficient, a delegative democracy might be effective for coordinating the diverse local knowledge of individuals into a collective choice. Polycentrism, where centers emerge from the bottom-up through individuals, draws on the local knowledge of voters as a mechanism to form constituencies.

One consequence of a delegative system is that it dispenses with the formal institutions of parliament. Parliament is not only a place for voting on legislation and leadership, it is an institution of deliberation. Through committee systems representatives scrutinize legislation, typically drawing on outside expertise and stakeholders. On the floor of the parliament representatives debate legislation, interrogate the government, and make statements on issues of national importance. These formal institutions are not a necessary feature of a delegative democracy. However, they can be constructed in one of two ways. One mechanism by which they exist sees a formal legislature built into the system at a constitutional level with delegates empowered to vote on national collective choices. Alternatively, a national deliberation body could *emerge* from the preferences of the voters and their delegates as an efficient institution of policymaking. In chapter 5 and chapter 8 we consider the emergent properties of cryptodemocracy.

Nonetheless, it is certainly possible that no recognizable "parliament" emerges. How would that affect the working of the democratic system? In his model of random constituencies Rehfeld is concerned about replicating the democratic deliberation that—at least in a naïve theory of popular democracy—occurs between neighbors and within small communities. His solution is the establishment of digital democratic forums among constituent members for deliberation. At a more general level, however, he emphasized the internet as the primary domain for political consideration. Rehfeld's book was written in 2005—that is, the year before Facebook became accessible to the general public, and before the release of Twitter the same year. In the interim decade, digital forums such as social media have become central domains for political deliberation, coordination, and campaigning. While there has been some interest in using these tools to enhance local democracy, for the most part the non-territorial nature of digital communications has focused their effects on national-level governments.[32] Digital citizens do not tend to cluster online around territorial electorates, and do not deliberate as electorate communities.

Digital citizens do, however, cluster around communities of interest—ideological, class, industrial, or environmental. It is within those communities of interest that we expect to see delegative coordination. How will voters and delegates cluster and form constituencies? The relationship between a voter and a delegate is a two-sided matching problem. Both delegate and voter have to identify possible counterparties in a potentially population-wide search field. And, as we elaborate in the following chapter, we will see how introducing the potential for financial exchange might enable between-community delegation and exchange. Clustered communities of interest are pre-existing communities on which to establish delegative relationships. Technology workers cluster around digital and real-world communities and could coordinate to choose a delegate between them. Likewise construction workers cluster and could choose a delegate among that community. Such clustering provides beneficial effects for democratic participation and deliberation. Voters who wish their delegated votes to have influence over collective choices have an incentive to form those communities of interest and coordinate over shared goals: the more proxy voting power a delegate holds the more likely they are to exercise control over the national collective choice. The ability for any community to politically coordinate as a group should also encourage political deliberation and engagement. In a representative democracy the choice of representative is mediated through the structures of party control. This privileges those who exercise power through formal party structures, which can come at high cost. By contrast, delegative democracy allows voters to exercise political power through pre-existing communities of interest.

CONCLUSION

In this chapter we have examined how in a cryptodemocracy voters might delegate their voting rights, and how that might change the nature of democratic representation and the formation of constituencies. In a cryptodemocracy voters can decide to either exercise their vote directly, or to delegate those rights to others. We have not examined who individuals might delegate their vote to, or why someone would wish to be a delegate. Over time delegation contracts could become highly complex and the freedom of delegates to act could be highly constrained—that is, depending on the conditions of their contractual arrangements. While a delegative democracy represents a step-change in the way voters may exercise their voting rights, the delegative democracy we have described is still highly constrained. For instance, voters and delegates would have to be matched and aligned in terms of policies. However, opening up delegative democracy to incorporate payments—that is, the buying and selling of bundles of voting rights—creates an entirely new space of potential exchanges. On one hand, voters could pay delegates to act on their behalf. Indeed, in a modern representative government, politicians are paid for their services with a salary. (A wide range of other motivations to enter politics are of course common—including public service, ideological passion, opportunities for corruption, and love of power—but the same is true of any industry. Being a political representative is, first and foremost, a job.) Being a delegate is not cost-free and needs to be compensated for in some fashion. On the other hand delegates could approach voters and pay them for their voting rights (effectively providing them compensation for the transfer of property rights). In the following chapter we expand the potential bundle of voting rights that voters might hold to incorporate the potential for exchange and compensation in both directions, thereby introducing the cryptodemocratic parallel to voting markets.

NOTES

1. Michael Saward, *The Representative Claim* (Oxford University Press, 2010).
2. Rehfeld, *The Concept of Constituency: Political Representation, Democratic Legitimacy, and Institutional Design*.
3. Robert Elgie, "The President of Ireland in Comparative Perspective," *Irish Political Studies* 27, no. 4 (2012).
4. Maddicott, *The Origins of the English Parliament, 924–1327*.
5. Rehfeld, *The Concept of Constituency: Political Representation, Democratic Legitimacy, and Institutional Design*, 71.
6. Ibid., 210.
7. See Chris Berg, "An Institutional Theory of Free Speech," in *RMIT Blockchain Innovation Hub Working Paper Series* (2017). We return to these questions of knowledge discovery and the different epistemic characteristics of alternative institutional arrangements in chapter 5 and chapter 8.
8. See the famous "chaos theorems": Richard D. McKelvey, "General Conditions for Global Intransitivities in Formal Voting Models," *Econometrica: Journal of the Econometric Society* (1979).
9. James Green-Armytage, "Direct Voting and Proxy Voting," *Constitutional Political Economy* 26, no. 2 (2015); "Direct Democracy by Delegable Proxy," DOI= http://fc.antioch.edu/~james_greenarmytage/vm/proxy.htm (2005).
10. Charles Lutwidge Dodgson, *The Principles of Parliamentary Representation* (Harrison and Sons, 1884), 1.
11. Ibid., 34.
12. A valuable discussion of Dodgson's work in the history of voting occurs in Iain S. McLean, Alistair McMillan, and Burt L. Monroe, *A Mathematical Approach to Proportional Representation: Duncan Black on Lewis Carroll* (Springer Science and Business Media, 2012).
13. James C. Miller, "A Program for Direct and Proxy Voting in the Legislative Process," *Public Choice* 7, no. 1 (1969): 108.
14. Gordon Tullock, *Toward a Mathematics of Politics* (University of Michigan Press, 1967), 144–57. Robert Heinlein, *The Moon Is a Harsh Mistress* (Tom Doherty Associates, Inc., New York, 1966).
15. Bryan Ford, "Delegative Democracy," *Manuscript.* (2002).
16. Dan Alger, "Voting by Proxy," *Public Choice* 126, no. 1–2 (2006).
17. Ibid., 24.
18. Green-Armytage, "Direct Voting and Proxy Voting." For other academic analyses of delegative democracy, see Zoé Christoff and Davide Grossi, "Liquid Democracy: An Analysis in Binary Aggregation and Diffusion," *arXiv preprint arXiv:1612.08048* (2016); Gal Cohensius et al., "Proxy Voting for Better Outcomes" (paper presented at the Proceedings of the 16th Conference on Autonomous Agents and MultiAgent Systems, 2017).
19. Paolo Boldi et al., "Voting in Social Networks" (paper presented at the Proceedings of the 18th ACM Conference on Information and Knowledge Management, 2009); Baldi et al., "Viscous Democracy for Social Networks," *Communications of the ACM* 54, no. 6 (2011);

Steve Hardt and Lia C. R. Lopes, "Google Votes: A Liquid Democracy Experiment on a Corporate Social Network," in *Technical Disclosure Commons* (2015); Yefim I. Leifman, "Secret and Verifiable Delegated Voting for Wide Representation," *IACR Cryptology ePrint Archive* 2014 (2014).

20. Chris Berg, Sinclair Davidson, and Jason Potts, "Blockchains Industrialise Trust," *SSRN https://www.ssrn.com/abstract=3074070* (2017).

21. John Keane, *The Life and Death of Democracy* (Simon and Schuster, 2009).

22. John Keane, "The Origins of Monitory Democracy," *The Conversation*, September 24, 2012.

23. On dark money, see Jane Mayer, *Dark Money: The Hidden History of the Billionaires Behind the Rise of the Radical Right* (Anchor Books, 2016).

Also, see the Sydney Democracy Network Dark Money Project, http://sydneydemocracy-network.org/portfolio_page/dark-money/.

24. For the former, see Caplan, *The Myth of the Rational Voter: Why Democracies Choose Bad Policies*. For the latter, see Jason Brennan, *Against Democracy* (Princeton University Press, 2016). We turn to some of these proposals in chapter 5.

25. See also Christopher Snowdon, "Sock Puppets: How the Government Lobbies Itself and Why" (London, United Kingdom: Institute of Economic Affairs, 2012); Chris Berg, "The Biggest Vested Interest of All: How Government Lobbies to Restrict Individual Rights and Freedom" (Melbourne: Institute of Public Affairs, 2013).

26. Pascal Sciarini et al., "The Underexplored Species: Selective Participation in Direct Democratic Votes," *Swiss Political Science Review* 22, no. 1 (2016).

27. Miller, "A Program for Direct and Proxy Voting in the Legislative Process."

28. Zachary J. Siegel, "Recall Me Maybe: The Corrosive Effect of Recall Elections on State Legislative Politics," *University of Colorado Law Review* 86 (2015).

29. Karen Shanton to The Thicket at State Legislatures, September 12, 2013, http://ncsl.typepad.com/the_thicket/2013/09/most-recall-elections-are-politically-motivated.html.

30. Paul Kelly, *Triumph and Demise: The Broken Promise of a Labor Generation* (Parkville, Victoria: Melbourne University Publishing, 2014); Wayne Errington and Peter Van Onselen, *Battleground: Why the Liberal Party Shirtfronted Tony Abbott* (Parkville, Victoria: Melbourne University Publishing, 2015); Niki Savva, *The Road to Ruin: How Tony Abbott and Peta Credlin Destroyed Their Own Government* (Melbourne, Victoria: Scribe Publications 2016).

31. James Madison, "Federalist No. 10," *November* 22 (1787).

32. For social media and local democracy, see Nick Ellison and Michael Hardey, "Social Media and Local Government: Citizenship, Consumption and Democracy," *Local Government Studies* 40, no. 1 (2014); Enrique Bonsón et al., "Local E-Government 2.0: Social Media and Corporate Transparency in Municipalities," *Government Information Quarterly* 29, no. 2 (2012).

Chapter Five

Bargaining and Exchange in a Cryptodemocracy

INTRODUCTION

This chapter extends the rights of voters in a cryptodemocracy from simple delegation to include buying and selling votes. This is a logical yet likely controversial extension. This is not an exercise in advocacy or evangelization. Instead, we aim to examine the arguments for and against voting markets, explore how a cryptodemocratic market process might work, and compare it to other attempts to integrate price signals into voting. One of the primary institutional features of a cryptodemocracy is the incentives for the creation, discovery, and coordination of the dispersed, contextual, and imperfect information about political preferences. We suggest there will be more discourse and coordination between voters to seek out mutually beneficial bargains and exchanges. In this way exchanging voting rights with others is civilizing—encouraging people to seek mutually beneficial exchanges outside of their existing preferences. Through this process, democratic orderings may become more spontaneous, built from the bottom-up through individual contracts. This might be institutionally desirable because of its dynamic process of coordinating local knowledge through polycentric constituencies. In this chapter we proceed as follows. In the second section we describe some of the challenges of collective choice and the institutional innovations that attempt to overcome them. This understanding motivates our examination of voting markets. The third section explores the arguments for and against voting markets. In the fourth section we examine some of the transaction costs in voting markets that are economized on in a cryptodemocracy, with a particular focus on the costs of enforcing contracts. The first section turns attention to the institutional characteristics of a cryptodemocracy, particularly how price generation differs from another recent approach to integrating preference intensity into democracy, quadratic voting (QV). The final section concludes.

WHY VOTING MARKETS?

The democratic process by nature occurs under uncertainty, between dispersed people with subjective preferences, and in an environment of positive transaction costs. One of the challenges this presents is the tyranny of the majority. The tyranny of the majority is that, from a utilitarian perspective, a majority rule can lead to undesirable results when a majority with weak or indifferent preferences overpowers a minority with intense preferences.[1] Minorities may be oppressed through expropriation of property or restrictions of basic liberties such as the right to vote. This threat is inherent within a system of 1p1v and with any decision rule less than unanimity.[2] Any majority decision rule must be set in the context of a trade-off between a system vulnerable to a tyranny of the majority and a system prone to gridlock. There have been several institutional innovations that seek to overcome this challenge, including supermajority rules and delegating power to independent statutory authorities.

Supermajority decision rules are set at an arbitrary level between simple majority rule and unanimity.[3] These rules emerged as a second-best alternative to unanimity rather than as an extension from simple majority rule.[4] Supermajority rules emerged in Ancient Rome and became more widely used throughout the twelfth century through papal elections.[5] Today both direct and indirect impositions of supermajorities are common. Mixed constitutions imposing bicameralism seek to integrate the preferences of multiple social groups. Because the House of Commons and the House of Lords have non-identical constituencies, this theoretically provides greater veto power for minorities as compared to a simple majority rule. While it is unclear the extent to which a supermajority protects minority interests—for instance it may simply favor minorities who can form coalitions—it is clear that moving from a simple majority to a supermajority is to some extent an attempt to constrain the tyranny of the majority, albeit all the while favoring the status quo.

Delegating power to experts, such as through the creation of independent statutory authorities, also attempts to overcome the information aggregation problems of collective choice. Independent authorities are often tasked with applying their expertise to objectively weigh the benefits and costs of policy. Independent decision makers try to overcome democratic decision-making problems—for instance, where some "uneducated" majority will make poor decisions—through centralized expert calculation. This approach distributes decision-making power from democratically elected representatives to un-elected bureaucrats. Public choice theory, however, would lead us to examine whether those independent experts are benevolent.[6] Even if they were, given the subjective costs of institutional choices, there are clear epistemological challenges of undertaking any cost-benefit analysis in the design of policy.[7] Experts do not hold the knowledge necessary to make omnipotent—or even necessarily comparatively efficient or effective—policy choices.

One alternative argument based on the perceived incompetence of voters is limiting democratic participation. Recent proposals to move power toward those who are knowledgeable—such as Jason Brennan's arguments for an epistocracy where voter intelligence is tested before they can vote—are troubling.[8] The motivation to overcome some of the challenges of democracy is reasonable—indeed, this book is an attempt to overcome similar concerns—but the practical issues are clear. An epistocracy is an attempt to construct a centrally engineered barrier to political action. It assumes a better solution to democratic problems can be arrived at through implementation of stricter rules. But how realistic is it that an expert can better integrate the preferences of minorities than the minorities themselves? How can a society objectively determine who the knowledgeable people are?

Attempts to move power away from the governed seek to overcome the messiness or imperfections of democratic deliberation. Democracy is often thought of as a problem of optimum preference aggregation to discover an objective truth. That is, some objectively verifiable solution to collective decisions is assumed to exist. The claim, then, is that restricting who can participate will better reveal this solution. But collective choice must always occur under uncertainty, with positive transaction costs, distributed information, and within a changing environment. Any institutional structure of democracy—including the introduction of voting markets in a cryptodemocracy—must be made in this context. Given that democracy is a means rather than an end, Friedrich Hayek argues that the limits of democracy must be determined by the purpose that the democratic process serves.[9] The most compelling of these purposes for Hayek is democracy as a process of "forming opinion," and that the value of democracy "is in its dynamic, rather than its static, aspects." A cryptodemocratic system recognizes that democracy is inherently messy. Individuals use local contextual knowledge to determine where decision-making power should reside. Individual voters, through contracts, determine who is best placed to make decisions and to hold power. The question, then, is whether voting markets in a cryptodemocracy better serve this purpose as an institutional mechanism to facilitate the democratic process of coordinating and creating knowledge to aid in collective choice.

Attempts to incorporate market processes into collective choice processes are not new. The desirable properties of markets stem from the Hayekian view of the economic problem as one of coordinating and putting to use dispersed information.[10] Market-generated prices act as signals of the opportunity costs of alternate choices that incorporate local contextual knowledge over distributed people. From here markets facilitate an organic process of voluntary cooperation. Do the epistemic characteristics of markets also apply to collective choice?[11] Indeed, the delegative process outlined in the previous chapter incorporates voters' preferences, including the choice to selectively engage in the political process by acting directly on the political process or delegating to others. Moving from simple delegation to enabling exchange for compensation (with funds flowing in either direction) is both an expansion of democratic liberty, and one that integrates more knowledge and preferences into a collective choice. Financial compensation could occur in both directions: delegates may pay voters, or voters might pay delegates. While the margins at which individuals determine this contractual relationship will be the result of bargaining and the way that they perceive agency and decision costs when engaging in democracy, it is entirely possible that an individual would pay delegates to act on his or her behalf. Extending the bundle of rights that each voter holds opens up the space of mutually beneficial delegations within the political sphere. Indeed, an understanding of Coasian bargaining might apply to collective choice. With well-defined voting rights and sufficiently low transaction costs, will people bargain away externalities and tend votes to those who most value them?[12]

Voters in a cryptodemocracy could not only delegate their votes, but buy or sell them. This enables voters to better express their subjective local contextual knowledge. Although controversial, voting markets have the potential to incentivize the forming of opinion and the integration of knowledge into the collective decision. The buying and selling of votes allows political interactions to become a positive sum game.[13] If two voters disagree over a collective choice, allowing them to exchange votes with compensation may: (1) by definition, in the absence of coercion, be mutually beneficial for the voters involved; and (2) integrate more intensity of preferences and act as a constraint on the tyranny of the majority. Ultimately the exchange of votes enables individual voters to express their intensity of preference because they can better take into account the opportunity costs of their choice rather than through other forms of rationing.[14] These potential benefits, however, are curious when we see vote buying almost universally outlawed. Why should individuals be restricted from buying and selling votes? Why doesn't the bundle of rights associated with voting include the right to alienability and exchange?

The democratic process itself can be conceived as an exchange between political representatives and the franchise. James Buchanan's normative framework for analyzing political choice incorporates this premise of "politics as exchange." This contrasts with the conception of politics as a process of truth seeking or as a zero-sum game of distribution.[15] Indeed, from an economic perspective, voting itself can be understood as a form of market exchange for collective goods:

> In a democracy, the government always acts so as to maximize the number of votes it will receive. In effect, it is an entrepreneur selling policies for votes instead of products for money. Furthermore, it must compete for votes with other parties, just as two or more oligopolists compete for sales in a market. [16]

The type and degree of vote trading takes many forms: informal or formal, centralized or decentralized, regulated or unregulated, or at various levels of collective choice. [17] *Logrolling*, for instance, is the process of political representatives trading votes on different issues. One political representative may vote one way on an issue in return for action on another issue. This is understood as mutually beneficial for those representatives, enabling minorities to have greater veto power of legislative change. *Campaign finance* is another example of voting markets. Although restricted in many ways, the ability for the franchise to contribute monetary support to political campaigns enables them to express their intensity of preference on various issues, shifting the actions of representatives. This is considered an exercise in freedom of speech. *Campaign promises* occur where political representatives during an election make a conditional promise for the provision of goods or services—or some other benefits such as tax cuts—on the condition of being voted into office. These are a form of non-binding contract purchased through public funds. Indeed, the existence of campaign promises as vote markets persists despite the obvious reality that campaign finance promises are paid for collectively, perhaps making them even more objectionable than direct core voting markets.

All of the above examples are quasi vote markets with a similar underlying principle: individuals and representatives can trade-off their preferences on issues with others for mutual gain. Some of these practices are also justified or seen as acceptable because they enable people to more closely participate and express their preferences and persuade others. This accepts heterogeneous intensity of preferences and the potential for gains from revealing these preferences. This is a similar argument to those over the efficiency of markets in allocating resources: the process of vote exchange and bargaining may reveal information and tend scarce resources toward their most valued use. If we accept that the exchange of commodities and property rights in markets leads to both efficiency gains through better coordination and gains for those voluntarily entering the exchange, then it may also be true that the virtues of the market process will help overcome the tyranny of the majority. [18] The value of a voting right can only be discovered through the coordination of distributed voter knowledge, through time, under uncertainty, between individuals.

The delegative cryptodemocracy outlined in the previous chapter is a type of voting market without financial compensation. Delegation is not considered direct or core vote buying because there is no money exchange—but the principle is the same. What happens when we extend the bundle of rights voters hold to include buying and selling votes? Indeed, delegative cryptodemocracy is familiar in the context of modern representative democracy: there is a franchise, a collective choice, political representatives, and so on. The most basic application of economic theory suggests that including monetary transfers will increase the number of mutually beneficial exchanges of votes. A bargaining and compensation process means voters must take into account the opportunity cost of their vote. Furthermore, because individuals can selectively decompose the various components or rights within that vote, these opportunity costs are more complex than in a simple 1p1v system. This may therefore help to ameliorate one of the central challenges facing majoritarian governance by incorporating intensity of preferences. Indeed:

> By introducing the possibility of bargaining and vote-trading in the process, the intensity of preferences is reflected in the decision-making process. With bargaining and side-payments the "one man, one vote" rule would provide the initial entitlement for each vote-trader. The exchange mechanism would then reveal the relative strength of the individual preferences. [19]

Despite the potential of voting markets as a mechanism to facilitate collective choice, this suggestion does not come without controversy.

THE OBJECTIONS TO A MARKET IN VOTES

Voting markets are controversial. Will economic inequality map onto political inequality? What is the impact of negative externalities imposed on others? What if people with strong or extreme preferences do not act in the "public interest"? While these are legitimate questions, the institutions of democracy must also be understood as imperfect. Democratic structures trade-off the costs of decision and agency costs to achieve the deemed objectives of democracy. Indeed, to the extent that a democracy is a process of learning and forming opinion, there are also a range of arguments *for* the introduction of voting markets. As we will see, many of these arguments stem from an epistemic perspective of integrating better knowledge into the democratic process. [20] Restricting voting markets also opens up a range of questions about our current democratic institutions. For instance, given that many familiar collective action processes resemble voting markets, such as campaign promises, are these forms of voting markets unacceptable too? [21] Here we examine some of the moral, ethical, and economic challenges and opportunities of voting markets.

There are three main arguments against vote buying: equality, efficiency, and inalienability.[22] The first and most initially intuitive objection focuses on *equality*—that the poor will be more willing to sell their vote than the rich.[23] The likely low price of each vote—given its small chance to be decisive in a large election—means that poor individuals will be more willing to sell their votes than wealthier voters. This might comparatively push more voting power toward the wealthy, with the fear of how economic inequalities may map onto the distribution of votes.[24] This equality objection to voting markets ignores the notion that generally we consider opening markets to poorer citizens to be wealth enhancing—namely because they have the most to gain from acquiring greater rights over another asset, and that they may be able to sell votes to gain revenue to spend on other elections, goods, or services.[25] Further, a voluntary vote exchange implies mutual benefit.[26] Nevertheless, this leaves the question: if we were able to constrain the equality problem through some restrictions (e.g., a progressive tax on acquiring votes) would a market for votes remain objectionable? This leads us to the efficiency and inalienability arguments.

Efficiency arguments against vote buying primarily focus on how voting markets may lead to more rent seeking. Specifically, while there may be mutual benefits to the individuals involved in a vote exchange, the effect of that may impose externalities on others.[27] This argument may be a legitimate reason to restrict the sale of votes.[28] Vote buyers could also finance their purchases using public funds through promises.[29] But there are several objections to these inefficiency claims. Collective action by its very nature imposes externalities on others.[30] The nature of collective choice with any decision rule less than unanimity is being bound by that choice (assuming of course some pre-constitutional consent in a constitutional contractarian sense). Any analysis of democratic institutions must be made in the context that institutional choice is imperfect and those decisions are always comparative. Furthermore, it is possible that there is less rent seeking in a system of vote buying than where vote buying is banned.[31] Efficiency arguments focus on how elected officials are elected into office, ignoring that they could extract benefit for themselves whether or not they were voted in through vote buying. Efficiency arguments are also paternalistic. If we are worried that individuals will vote and act in their own private interest, why should they be able to vote? If banning vote markets is justified on how someone might vote, then should the process of democratic discourse itself be restricted?

Other objections to vote buying call on the nature of democracy itself and that votes should be *inalienable* and *anti-commodifiable*. This suggests that votes belong to the community to participate in a collective decision-making experience and should be used for the common good.[32] Pamela Karlan summarizes the argument, noting that vote selling "involves selling an asset that is not entirely theirs to sell" and "because voting is a public function, not solely a private right, the worth of an individual's vote to the community as a whole may exceed the worth of the vote to that individual."[33] For example, Michael Sandel argues that voting markets views "[the mistaken] purpose of democracy is to aggregate people's interests and preferences and treat them into policy" then "there is no good reason to prohibit buying and selling of votes."[34] A variation on these arguments is the paternalistic argument that vote buying protects voters from themselves; voters need to be protected from being compelled into selling their votes.[35]

What can we take away from these equality, efficiency, and inalienability objections to vote buying, and thus to bargaining and compensation in a cryptodemocracy? Arguments against voting markets on efficiency and equality grounds suggest that the democratic process should be more restricted than it currently is. It is inconsistent if not paradoxical to ban core "retail" vote buying yet enable "wholesale" trading.[36] That is, it is paradoxical to make it illegal to offer individual voters money in return for votes, but it is common practice to offer voters regulatory privileges and benefits on the condition of being elected.[37] Richard Epstein argues that "a simple restriction on selling votes should not be disparaged even if it does not offer a complete answer" to the other challenges of political abuse and more indirect forms of vote buying.[38] Yet is unclear at what margins the problems outlined above outweigh the potential gains from enabling voting markets.

Putting these objections aside we can now examine the potential of voting markets in a cryptodemocracy as an institutional mechanism to facilitate knowledge coordination. While on one hand this may appear a radical embrace of voter rights, including alienability and exchange, on the other hand there are only small functional differences between a cryptodemocracy and the processes of logrolling and campaign promises.[39] A cryptodemocracy facilitated through blockchain removes some of the frictions and restrictions that these market-like mechanisms face. Restricting voter rights is a pre-constitutional choice. As such, in the following section we begin by examining why we are exploring the potential for a cryptodemocracy today, before outlining how blockchain provides new collective choice infrastructure.

ENFORCING VOTING CONTRACTS

The exact form that any democratic institution might take will be constrained by the transaction costs of the underlying problem and the ability to set up governance structures that ameliorate those costs. A central barrier to voting markets is the transaction costs of facilitating such exchanges, including the agency and decision costs outlined previously. How can individuals who sell their vote determine if that vote was cast in a particular way? How would the matching market between voters—to enable mutually beneficial trade—be structured? When voting rights cannot be properly enforced or observed, there will be a higher potential to defect, making parties cautious in exchanging votes.[40]

The secret ballot itself was an attempt to increase the transaction costs of voting markets. It increased the agency costs of creating trusted and verified markets for votes and increased the costs of discovering potential counterparties, which was effectively an increase in search costs.[41] From this perspective it is unsurprising that the introduction of the secret ballot decreased voter numbers—the incentive payments to vote became harder to govern and fewer mutually beneficial exchanges were possible.[42] Many of the theoretical questions surrounding vote buying return back to the question of enforceability of contracts—that is, agency costs. Dennis Mueller outlined two problems with bargaining and voting markets in a political context:

> First, because [trading agreements] do not remove the incentives each voter has to conceal his true preferences—which is the basic problem with which we began; second, because no one can be expected to keep these agreements once the number of voters is very large.[43]

The first problem is one of concealing preferences. We do not address this challenge here: it is a problem with markets generally. Therefore we focus on the latter challenge—enforcement—as a problem of economizing on transaction costs of exchange. The second challenge is primarily one of enforcement transaction costs, compounded when votes are not cast concurrently:

> When voting decisions are made sequentially, the temptation to violate voting agreements is large. If two voters agree to swap votes on a pair of issues, as soon as the first issue is decided one of the voters will have fulfilled his part of the bargain. The second voter then has a greatly reduced incentive to live up to his part of the agreement and vote against his own wishes.[44]

The agency costs within an exchange of votes are high when an individual cannot easily observe or verify how a vote was cast. When the transaction costs of an exchange are higher than the benefit of the parties, those exchanges will not take place—and votes will not be bought and sold. Blockchain technology—including the potential for smart contracts between voters—economizes on these costs and opens up new institutional possibilities for voting markets. Blockchain provides the political infrastructure for cryptodemocratic delegation and compensation over their political rights. Allocating property rights over voting on a blockchain and enabling individuals to trade those votes dramatically opens up the space of exchange. Voters can more securely delegate their votes to others, and the public can have cryptographic proof that vote has been delegated. This effectively disintermediates the vote buying process as compared to existing wholesale logrolling to more retail vote buying between individuals.

Without the invention of blockchain it is unclear whether the exchange of votes with conditions attached is realistically enforceable. Blockchain technology enables individuals to decompose parts of their votes to others—including compensation—and they can later verify how those votes were eventually cast. While the internet may have reduced the costs of search for potential counterparties—a form of decision cost—the exchange of those votes through contracts still had high agency costs. How could individuals exchange votes over the internet and ensure that the votes were cast in a particular way, or that the delegate didn't break the agreement? This challenge becomes even more exacerbated when individuals wish to decompose their votes, and only sell or delegate some rights over some issues.

Through the deployment of smart contracts—automatically executing contracts written into code that execute on the information fed in from a third party—individuals may decompose their voting rights in different ways while maintaining trust that those agreements will be fulfilled. Opportunistic behavior by a delegate—for instance, not voting in the way intended—might be ameliorated through conditions coded into a smart contract, where a breach could result in the automatic transfer of voting rights back to the original holder. The process of vote buying and selling can be coded into smart contracts that rely on third party information oracles. Voters can effectively retain ultimate property rights over their vote even once it has been delegated to others, with trust that the code will execute if the agreement is broken. This enables much more complex structures of voting markets to emerge.

The exchange of voting rights and compensation would likely occur in both directions. Individual voters could decide to cast their vote themselves (i.e., not delegate). This would tend a cryptodemocracy to be similar to direct democracy. When voters delegate their vote to someone else, however, they might pay their delegate, or the delegate might pay them. It might be rational for a low-information voter to transfer his or her voting rights to a delegate and compensate him or her for acting on his or her behalf, in a similar way to politicians being paid a wage. Blockchain technology acts as the infrastructure upon which individuals can make these individual choices of their engagement within the democratic process. Blockchain technology enables more complex constituency and coalition building by lowering the transaction costs of collective action over political rights. A cryptodemocracy enables individuals to better economize on the way they perceive the agency costs and decision costs over their voting rights.

The notion of delegation and compensation connects closely with the work of Ronald Coase. Blockchain might facilitate a Coasian bargaining process—that is, the process of bargaining may tend property rights to their most valued use—by lowering agency costs of enforceability.[45] At the level of the transaction it is true that the exchange of voting rights is mutually beneficial. However, would we expect an ongoing process of mutually beneficial exchanges to move votes to those who value the voting property rights most? Will votes move from those who have low preference intensity to those with high preference intensity? We cannot answer this question at any level of analysis above a transaction. It is not possible to aggregate individual preferences to the societal level because of their subjective nature. If the Coase Theorem was to operate at the society level this would suggest some objectively verifiable and true solution to political problems—that is, where all externalities are internalized.[46] We can never say at the aggregate level whether a particular number of trades have achieved some Pareto-efficient outcome. Each exchange does internalize some externalities, but also imposes some external costs. We must also note that while the initial allocation of voting rights in a cryptodemocracy is evenly spread across the population, the relative power of individuals to acquire other votes suffers from the potential wealth effects described above. From a methodologically individualist perspective, each trade is mutually beneficial to those engaged in it, and that over time enabling cryptodemocratic bargaining and exchange might tend rights toward those who value them the most. We would expect this to be the case the lower the transaction costs or frictions in the democratic process.

Before turning to a comparison of cryptodemocratic bargaining and centralized pricing, it is useful to explore another argument that has been held against voting markets—that voting market bans are a solution to a collective action problem—and observe why a cryptodemocracy might help.[47] Because each vote in an election has a theoretically trivial price due to its low expected impact on an election election—despite the fact a large bloc of votes might be valuable—each voter might rationally sell his or her vote at a low price. A ban on vote selling, in this view, is itself a collective agreement to not sell votes. A cryptodemocracy may help ameliorate this same collective action problem not through a centralized ban, but through self-governance. The process of delegation outlined in the previous chapter—whether or not that delegation has associated compensation—allows multiple votes to be held by single individuals and sold in blocs. This enables a self-governance solution to the collective action problem because votes are not sold purely in individual terms, they may be entrepreneurially grouped together and sold as blocs, increasing their marginal value. Furthermore, individuals are able to attach conditions to their voting rights when they sell them, disaggregating votes into multiple parts. This theoretically raises the expected cost of the votes and helps to overcome the collective action problem.

There are numerous ways that blockchain technology could be used to facilitate collective decision making. What we have discussed above is the potential for a cryptodemocratic process of bargaining and compensation between individuals. To further draw out the institutional and dynamic properties of such a system, in the following section we compare a cryptodemocracy with another recently proposed system of quadratic voting (QV). Together, cryptodemocratic delegation and compensation (an emergent contracting process) and a system of QV (a centralized system governed by a quadratic pricing rule and subsequent redistribution system) helps us understand the epistemic and polycentric nature of a cryptodemocracy.

HOW PRICES ARE GENERATED

We can compare a *cryptodemocracy* with *quadratic voting* (QV) to draw out their institutional characteristics. This comparative institutional analysis emphasizes assumptions over the nature of voter preferences and the generation of prices for votes. A cryptodemocracy does not take preference intensities and voting intentions as given, but rather focuses on the institutional incentives and characteristics for that knowledge to be discovered, over time, under uncertainty. Contracting in a cryptodemocracy is a decentralized process of learning and discovery. Prices are determined through individual discourse and contractual negotiation. In contrast, in QV prices are enforced through a quadratic pricing rule. A cryptodemocracy also theoretically incentivizes actors within the political system—specifically delegates—to discover and produce information about voter preferences. Eventually, as we elucidate in chapter 8, these delegates may provide goods or services in return for votes, acting as new emergent polycentric state-like structures within the cryptodemocratic framework. All of this is premised on the notion of voter liberty and voluntary contractual exchange.

QV is a system of collective choice where voters may purchase additional voting rights for a price that is a square of the number of votes purchased.[48] The budget constraint that individuals face may be based either on their own wealth—perhaps with money paid into a centralized fund and distributed back to the population on a per capita basis—or on some constraint equally imposed across all votes, such a "voice credits." The former enables individuals to express their intensity of preference using other scarce resources—thereby taking into account the opportunity cost of voting relative to their wealth—while the latter enables voters to decide their intensity across multiple issues, removing wealth effects. We focus on the former situation where individuals can spend their own money to buy more votes through a pricing rule. One central goal of QV is to integrate intensity of preferences into collective choices, and ameliorate the tyranny of the majority. Because of the quadratic nature of the purchasing potential, it becomes prohibitively expensive for a small group of wealthy individuals to affect the outcome. Compared to standard 1p1v majority rule, QV moves toward a market for votes. However, those market-like properties are implemented through an effective regulation of how those votes may be purchased. A QV may indeed be an improvement on other arrangements such as supermajorities and representational democracy that

> . . . either give insufficient power to minorities, allowing tyranny of the majority, or they give excessive power to minorities, which leads to gridlock, as well as unfair political outcomes. No existing system calibrates the power afforded to minorities to the strength of their interests in a given policy decision. [49]

Why is the pricing rule quadratic? As a pricing rule increases the voting cost curve becomes highly convex. It quickly becomes extremely expensive for an individual to buy even a single additional marginal vote. As the pricing rule approaches infinite the collective choice begins to approximate the current 1p1v system because most individuals would not purchase additional votes. This fails to integrate intensity of preferences. On the other hand, with a linear pricing rule—where the marginal price of an additional vote is the same—powerful minorities are given excessive power, leading to "dictatorship of the most intense voter." [50] This leads to concerns over the wealth effects of economic equality mapping onto political equality. QV seeks an optimum trade-off between these challenges with an effort to integrate voter preferences.

As is the case with all imperfect democratic institutions, QV has a number of drawbacks. At the outset it is important to note that one of the central challenges of QV is that the transaction costs of implementing such a system have been too high to make it realistic. How would individuals be given a digital identity that is verifiable and secure? As we have established in this book, blockchain technology has the potential to facilitate this process. [51] Further, the robustness of the efficiency of QV has been questioned, particularly in the context of voter collusion or when voter numbers are too low. [52] However, our focus here is not on the efficiency or optimality of QV. Rather, we wish to draw out the institutional differences between QV and cryptodemocracy:

- QV is based on a single pricing rule that approximates Pareto optimality. In a cryptodemocracy monetary compensation—and thus integration of incentive intensity—emerges from voluntary contractual bargains between voters.
- In a cryptodemocracy voters maintain equal political representation through 1p1v. In contrast, QV uncaps the number of votes, because individuals can continue to buy votes within their budget constraint.

- In a cryptodemocracy all vote trades must be matched and contracted with counterparties. This means individuals have the capacity to maintain their voting rights and cast their vote. In QV the purchasing of votes by one person dilutes the stake of others.
- The preceding two points also lead to different types of information costs. In a cryptodemocracy the main information costs relate to discovering counterparties and determining their point within the DIPF space, while in a QV individuals calculate how many votes to purchase given their existing preferences.
- In QV the purchasing of votes maintains a singular voting unit (votes are not decomposed), while in a cryptodemocracy individuals can conditionally decompose their vote depending on the conditions under which they wish to (this assumes that these decompositions can be contracted and enforced through smart contracts.).
- The process of compensation for additional political power in a QV system is pooled and centrally redistributed (potentially on a per capita basis). In a cryptodemocracy any compensation occurs directly through discourse and individual contracting—stemming from the concept of votes as property rights.
- A cryptodemocracy has a process of delegation where voting rights can move between multiple parties, while in QV the system is essentially a one-step centralized process. In a cryptodemocracy voting rights might move between a dynamic chain of owners, with various conditions and values attached.
- In QV the acquisition of additional voting power always comes with a positive cost, set through the quadratic pricing rule. In a cryptodemocracy the compensating differential can go in both directions (where voters could pay for a delegate to represent them), opening up new potential polycentric structures within the democracy.

There are several upshots from this comparison of QV and a cryptodemocracy. A cryptodemocratic solution to the knowledge problem of collective choice does not attempt to make a democracy clean or take away its messiness. A cryptodemocracy is not based on an Arrowian perspective of the aggregation of political preferences into a collective social welfare solution. This aggregation perspective is often the approach of other attempts to create a more digital democracy, such as those where particular questions are posted through a blockchain-based voting platform, or moves to introduce independent statutory authorities and experts to make decisions. Rather, a cryptodemocracy is the collective choice infrastructure on which individuals contract over voting property rights. We take the perspective of Hayek and Buchanan that "the virtue of democracy is now predominantly assessed according to its ability to serve as a rule-guided procedure for the formation, discovery and utilization of opinions and conjectural problem-solutions."[53]

The structure of a cryptodemocracy is created over time from the bottom-up interaction of individuals—it is emergent. A cryptodemocracy doesn't suggest that the role of democracy is to come to some clear or objective truth. Further, we don't assume an optimal democratic governance structure. Collective choice is a process of coordinating imperfect, fragmented, and distributed knowledge between people as well as generating those subjective preferences through discourse. There are no imposed pricing rules in a cryptodemocracy—compensation payments come from bargaining over the subjective costs faced by individual voters. Indeed, while a cryptodemocracy may appear as an attempt to radically shift the shape of democracy, it is not an attempt to rationalize or construct a better structure. Rather, we empower people to discover new structures through a process of contracting.

Preferences in a cryptodemocracy are not taken as given—they form and evolve through interactions with others. Many attempts to integrate intensity of preference within collective choice effectively take the preferences and opinions of voters as given—then assume the problem is to incentivize voters to reveal those preferences and their intensities. However, as Julian Muller argues: ". . . the problem-solving capability of a political architecture depends not only on its capability to exploit the available knowledge but also on its capability to create new knowledge, to expand its stock."[54] So too in a cryptodemocracy. A cryptodemocracy is messy, and along some dimensions individuals will face additional choices, such as in what manner and to whom to delegate. By maintaining 1p1pv and enabling delegation and bargaining, however, any transfer of voting rights must have engaged with another member of society (or machine) to acquire or delegate those rights.

The cryptodemocratic process is likely to stimulate rhetoric and discourse. A cryptodemocracy is a discovery and learning process of coordinating and forming the preferences of individuals within society. Like the market process as outlined by Hayek, it is institutionally effective because of its epistemic properties in the face of uncertainty within collective choice. A cryptodemocracy is not justified or desirable for its cleanliness or in terms of preference aggregation. Rather it is the infrastructure that enables individuals to engage in a dynamic and constantly shifting set of questions and knowledge.

The shape and form that a cryptodemocracy could ultimately take is an entrepreneurial question, but its analysis should begin from the perspective of voter exchange. Individuals who hold voting rights are democratically empowered to make choices and form contracts over their political rights. For analytical purposes, a cryptodemocracy must begin with the premise of voter liberty—that voters hold the widest possible range of rights—before later restricting those rights. These restrictions are a constitutional choice.

Voters may rightly have concerns over the freedom of political voting rights. They may change the protocol of voting rights. For instance, if the franchise is concerned about wealth effects and a mapping of economic inequality onto political equality then some form of supermajority or consensus mechanism could be built in. This would raise the barrier for individuals with extreme preferences to control the election. Alternatively, individuals comprising the collective choice could limit the scope of the public sphere—that is, through constitutional restrictions—or by increasing the decision rule closer to unanimity, directly limiting government power. Indeed, while covering the potential of these changes are beyond the scope of this book, decreasing the power of the state or the barrier to use the coercive powers of the state may be necessary for cryptodemocracy to be implemented.

The decision of whether to place further restrictions on the bundle of property rights within a vote—to delegate, to receive compensation, and so on—should be understood as a restriction of voting rights. Restrictions should be seen in the context of the presumption of voter liberty: a reason to "allow citizens to use their vote as they see fit and that the burden of justification rests with those who would abridge that liberty."[55] As Friedrich Hayek argued, the question of economics and political ordering is not whether planning occurs, but who does the planning. In a cryptodemocracy voters effectively choose at what margin they wish to make plans themselves, or delegate those planning rights to others.

CONCLUSION

In this chapter we examined extending the bundle of voting property rights to buying and selling of votes. Vote buying and selling, we have argued, enables a dynamic process of bargaining and exchange between voters. We have proposed that in a cryptodemocracy with vote exchange there may be better coordination of local contextual knowledge of voter preferences—including the formation of those preferences. We have not argued for a cryptodemocracy on the basis of optimality or efficiency, but rather suggested its potentially desirable properties from an epistemic perspective. For the same reason we make no claims that cryptodemocracy will tend collective choice toward a "public interest." Rather, a cryptodemocracy rests on the assumption that knowledge is dispersed, contextual and often unformed, and that a cryptodemocracy of delegation and bargaining may incentivize the coordination and formation of that information. This also means that we cannot say how voting markets in a cryptodemocracy would operate. Rather than a centralized process of vote purchasing, such as in the example of QV, or at the level of political representatives through vote trading, logrolling, and lobbying, a cryptodemocracy pushes the power of compensation and bargaining down to the level of individuals. It gives the power to individual voters to engage within the political process at selective levels—deciding to trade-off decision costs and agency costs—and to best determine how they wish to subjectively execute their political rights.

Predicting the potential of exchange in a cryptodemocracy is fraught with problems. How many voters would delegate their vote, let alone bargain for compensation? On one hand there is evidence of vote trading within general elections having little effect, although one of the reasons is the difficulty of enforcement due to the secret ballot.[56] Furthermore, strong social norms against vote selling—the taboos around money and politics—might mean implementing a cryptodemocracy has little impact. What would be the impact on expressive voting? Given the potential decomposition of voting rights we would expect greater numbers of expressive voting contracts. Interestingly, voters could be expressive with some issues yet not with others. There are also questions over the price of individual votes and collective bundles of votes. Perhaps votes would be prohibitively expensive to buy precisely because individuals believe in some social duty to cast their own vote. We have little information about demand curves for votes given the currently restricted ability of individuals to reveal the price of their vote. Further, as bundles of rights as disaggregated—such as through the delegation of decomposable conditions—the potential predictability of pricing structures rapidly declines, and comes up against the bounded rationality of the human mind.

While a cryptodemocracy would reignite the understanding of democracy as an institutionally constrained process of knowledge generation and cooperation between voters, it is likely to come up against some opposition. To ground our analysis into perhaps more potentially implementable scenarios, in the following chapters we explore some private governance examples of cryptodemocratic processes—including shareholder voting (chapter 6) and labor unions (chapter 7) —as smaller case studies in the process of learning and discovery in a cryptodemocracy. These represent more specific applications of cryptodemocratic principles—and, as we will see in the following chapter, some of those principles of voter rights already exist within corporate governance.

NOTES

1. Henry G. Manne, "Some Theoretical Aspects of Share Voting. An Essay in Honor of Adolf A. Berle," *Columbia Law Review* 64, no. 8 (1964): 1428.

For a description of the two central challenges of majoritarian voting, see Hardy Lee Wieting Jr., "Philosophical Problems in Majority Rule and the Logrolling Solution," *Ethics* 76, no. 2 (1966). One of the problems of democratic governance that we do not examine here is the Condorcet problem of intransitivities when aggregating preferences. That is, while the individual preferences may be transitive, the preferences of the electorate as a whole may not be.

Majoritarian voting systems face Arrow's Impossibility Theorem. Arrow suggests that no voting system perfectly aggregates individual preferences to satisfy Pareto efficiency. See Kenneth J. Arrow, "A Difficulty in the Concept of Social Welfare," *Journal of Political Economy* 58, no. 4 (1950).

2. The "tyranny of the majority" has a long history. See Alexis de Tocqueville, *Democracy in America* (2003 [1835]); John Stuart Mill, *On Liberty* (London: J. W. Parker and Son, 1859).

3. These are an attempt to devise a "workable approximation of unanimity." See Thrasher and Gaus, "James Buchanan and Gordon Tullock, the Calculus of Consent," 10.

4. This is unsurprising from the perspective that unanimity, not a simple majority, is the conceptual yardstick or criterion for judging decision rules. On the optimality of unanimity with veto power, see James M. Buchanan and Gordon Tullock, *The Calculus of Consent* (Ann Arbor: University of Michigan Press, 1962).

5. See Melissa Schwartzberg, *Counting the Many: The Origins and Limits of Supermajority Rule*, vol. 10 (Cambridge, MA: Cambridge University Press, 2013).

6. For the demand and supply of regulation, see George J. Stigler, "The Theory of Economic Regulation," *The Bell Journal of Economics and Management Science* (1971); Sam Peltzman, "Toward a More General Theory of Regulation," in *National Bureau of Economic Research Working Paper 133* (National Bureau of Economic Research, Cambridge, MA, 1976).

7. See Roger Koppl, *Expert Failure* (Cambridge: Cambridge University Press, 2018); David M. Levy and Sandra J. Peart, *Escape from Democracy: The Role of Experts and the Public in Economic Policy* (New York: Cambridge University Press, 2016). On the subjective costs of institutional choice, also see Allen and Berg, "Subjective Political Economy."

8. See Brennan, *Against Democracy*.

9. Friedrich A. Hayek, *The Constitution of Liberty: The Definitive Edition* (United Kingdom: Routledge, 2013), 95.

10. For an analysis of the marvel of the market mechanism in generating prices that communicate information, see Hayek, "The Use of Knowledge in Society."

11. See Peter J. Boettke, Vlad Tarko, and Paul Aligica, "Why Hayek Matters: The Epistemic Dimension of Comparative Institutional Analysis," in *Revisiting Hayek's Political Economy* (Emerald Group Publishing Limited, 2016).

12. On the process of bargaining and the allocation of property rights under different transaction cost conditions, see Ronald H. Coase, "The Problem of Social Cost," *Journal of Law and Economics* 3 (1960).

Also see Francesco Parisi, "Political Coase Theorem," *Public Choice* 115, no. 1–2 (2003): 1. Parisi applies the Coase Theorem to politics claiming that: "if all voters are allowed to enter into Coasian bargaining over the policy outcome to be adopted by the majority coalition (i.e., if political bargains are possible and are enforceable), uniqueness and stability are obtained."

13. Walter Block, "Alienability: Rejoinder to Kuflik," *Humanomics* 23, no. 3 (2007).

14. For an early treatment of intensity of preference in relation to Arrow's Impossibility Theorem, see James S. Coleman, "The Possibility of a Social Welfare Function," *The American Economic Review* 56, no. 5 (1966).

15. See Geoffrey Brennan, "Politics-as-Exchange and the Calculus of Consent," *Public Choice* 152, no. 3–4 (2012).

16. Downs, "An Economic Theory of Political Action in a Democracy," 137.

17. Vote buying can mean different things in different contexts including instrumental compliance, normative compliance, or coercive compliance in exchange for money, goods, or services. See Frederic Charles Schaffer, "What Is Vote Buying? Empirical Evidence," *Vote Buying: Who, What, When and How* (2002).

18. See Buchanan and Tullock, *The Calculus of Consent*; Christopher Freiman, "Vote Markets," *Australasian Journal of Philosophy* 92, no. 4 (2014); Richard L. Hasen, "Vote Buying," *California Law Review* 88, no. 5 (2000); James Tobin, "On Limiting the Domain of Inequality," *The Journal of Law and Economics* 13, no. 2 (1970).

19. Francesco Parisi, "The Market for Votes: Coasian Bargaining in an Arrovian Setting," *George Mason Law Review* 6 (1997): 748.

20. Jason Brennan, *The Ethics of Voting* (Princeton University Press, 2012); Freiman, "Vote Markets"; and John Thrasher, "The Ethics of Legislative Vote Trading," *Political Studies* 64, no. 3 (2016). For the potential efficiency gains of enabling voting markets being unsettled and the complexity of measurement, see Buchanan and Tullock, *The Calculus of Consent*.

21. Hasen, "Vote Buying."

22. For a review of the literature on vote buying, including the contradictions between a ban on core vote buying and non-core vote buying, see ibid.

23. For an early outline of these equality concerns see Manne, "Some Theoretical Aspects of Share Voting. An Essay in Honor of Adolf A. Berle."

24. For a treatment of the egalitarian concerns of vote buying, see Michael S. Kochin and Levis A. Kochin, "When Is Buying Votes Wrong?" *Public Choice* 97, no. 4 (1998): 648.

25. Saul Levmore, "Voting with Intensity," *Stanford Law Review* 53 (2000): 115.

26. Block, "Alienability: Rejoinder to Kuflik," 128.

27. This is known as the "paradox of vote trading." See William H. Riker and Steven J. Brams, "The Paradox of Vote Trading," *American Political Science Review* 67, no. 4 (1973).

28. For more on this externality problem, see Richard A. Epstein, "Why Restrain Alienation?" *Columbia Law Review* 85, no. 5 (1985).

29. Ibid., 988.

30. See Freiman, "Vote Markets."

31. For claims on rent seeking behavior in a free market for votes, see Gary M. Anderson and Robert D. Tollison, "Democracy in the Marketplace," *V in Pre* (1990).

32. On inalienability in the context of voting, see Margaret Jane Radin, "Market-Inalienability," *Harvard Law Review* 100, no. 8 (1987). For a discussion on inalienability in voting rights also see Levmore, "Voting with Intensity," 119.

33. Pamela S. Karlan, "Not by Money but by Virtue Won? Vote Trafficking and the Voting Rights System," *Virginia Law Review* (1994): 1457.

34. Michael J. Sandel, "What Money Can't Buy: The Moral Limits of Markets," *Tanner Lectures on Human Values* 21 (2000): 118.

35. See Kochin and Kochin, "When Is Buying Votes Wrong?"

36. For the distinction between "wholesale" and "retail," see Karlan, "Not by Money but by Virtue Won? Vote Trafficking and the Voting Rights System." As ibid., 1467 argues, vote buying restrictions "are best justified as protecting the integrity of the political process rather than the autonomy of individual voters." For an argument on how this would go against what politics means, see Cass R. Sunstein, "Incommensurability and Valuation in Law," *Michigan Law Review* 92, no. 4 (1994): 849. Sunstein argues, "If votes were freely tradable, we would have a different conception of what voting is for—about the values that it embodies—and this changed conception would have corrosive effects on politics." See also Karlan, "Not by Money but by Virtue Won? Vote Trafficking and the Voting Rights System," 1457: "Tactics that are outlawed when they target individual voters are condoned, or even constitutionally protected, when they are aimed at the electorate at large. In effect, candidates can implicitly buy what individual voters are forbidden directly to sell."

37. Kochin and Kochin, "When Is Buying Votes Wrong?"

38. Epstein, "Why Restrain Alienation?" 988.

39. For a discussion of how other democratic processes involve an *incomplete commodification* of votes, see Pamela S. Karlan, "Politics by Other Means," *Virginia Law Review* 85 (1999).

40. See Thrasher, "The Ethics of Legislative Vote Trading," 4: "If it is impossible or hard to check whether or not a trading partner voted the way that they promised to vote, the urge to defect will be high and parties will be wary of engaging in trades."

41. For a brief history, see Malcolm Crook and Tom Crook, "The Advent of the Secret Ballot in Britain and France, 1789–1914: From Public Assembly to Private Compartment," *History* 92, no. 308 (2007).

42. On how secrecy in voting perhaps limited a core motivation for voting payments, see Jac C. Heckelman, "The Effect of the Secret Ballot on Voter Turnout Rates," *Public Choice* 82, no. 1–2 (1995).

88 *Chapter 5*

43. See Dennis C. Mueller, "The Possibility of a Social Welfare Function: Comment," *The American Economic Review* 57, no. 5 (1967): 1306. Mueller was responding to the model in James S. Coleman, "The Possibility of a Social Welfare Function," *The American Economic Review*, 56 (1966).

44. Mueller, "The Possibility of a Social Welfare Function: Comment," 1306.

45. See, for instance, Daron Acemoglu, "Why Not a Political Coase Theorem? Social Conflict, Commitment, and Politics," *Journal of Comparative Economics* 31, no. 4 (2003): 622: ". . . any enforcement problem potentially limits the applicability of the Coase theorem. In the context of the PCT [Political Coase Theorem], widespread enforcement problems arise because most contracts are enforced by the state. Contracts that the state, or social groups controlling the state, would like to write with others, e.g., the citizens, will be non-enforceable by definition because groups controlling the state cannot commit to not using their power to renege on their promises or to not changing the terms of the contract."

46. For a discussion of the Coase Theorem and subjective opportunity costs, see James M. Buchanan, "Rights, Efficiency, and Exchange: The Irrelevance of Transaction Costs," *Berlin: Duncker and Humblot* (1984).

47. For an outline of this argument, see Levmore, "Voting with Intensity."

48. See Steven P. Lalley and E. Glen Weyl, "Quadratic Voting: How Mechanism Design Can Radicalize Democracy" (paper presented at the AEA Papers and Proceedings, 2018); Richard A. Posner, 2016, http://ericposner.com/quadratic-voting; Eric A. Posner and E. Glen Weyl, "Voting Squared: Quadratic Voting in Democratic Politics," *Vanderbilt Law Review* 68 (2015).

49. Posner and Weyl, "Voting Squared: Quadratic Voting in Democratic Politics," 446.

50. Lalley and Weyl, "Quadratic Voting: How Mechanism Design Can Radicalize Democracy," 2.

51. See Darcy W.E. Allen et al., "Cryptodemocracy and Its Institutional Possibilities," *The Review of Austrian Economics* (2018); Allen, Berg, and Markey-Towler, "Blockchain and Supply Chains: V-Form Organisations, Value Redistributions, De-Commoditisation and Quality Proxies."

52. Glen E. Weyl, "The Robustness of Quadratic Voting," *Public Choice* 172, no. 1–2 (2017).

53. Michael Wohlgemuth, "Democracy and Opinion Falsification: Towards a New Austrian Political Economy," *Constitutional Political Economy* 13, no. 3 (2002): 228.

54. Julian F. Müller, "Epistemic Democracy: Beyond Knowledge Exploitation," *Philosophical Studies* (2018): 1271.

55. Freiman, "Vote Markets," 763.

56. See ibid.

Chapter Six

Cryptodemocratic Corporate Governance

INTRODUCTION

For all the seeming radicalism of the cryptodemocratic form discussed so far in this book, much of this system already exists. The joint-stock company is one of the most popular institutional choices for structuring collective decision making in a commercial context. Andrei Shleifer and Robert Vishny explain that "corporate governance deals with the ways in which the suppliers of finance to corporations assure themselves of getting a return on their investment."[1] It has been maintained—correctly in our view—that shareholder voting is "fundamental to the corporate governance process."[2] This chapter examines how shareholders are already contracting, delegating, and exchanging voting power within this context to achieve consensus around commercial outcomes. This builds on the previous chapter by providing concrete examples of the types of coordination, discourse, and exchange that occurs in the corporate world—and provides further insight into the kinds of arrangements that may emerge in a political cryptodemocratic environment.

The taxonomy of voting bargaining offered in this chapter will show how shareholders seek to economize the transaction costs involved in corporate voting. The equality and inalienability arguments against vote buying in the political context, discussed in the previous chapter, are not strong when translated to the corporate context. As Richard Hansen has observed "few expect shareholders to consider anything but narrow economic self-interest in corporate elections, whether or not votes are for sale."[3] This makes the purpose of shareholder voting clear: arriving at collective decisions to maximize the return on capital investment. Nevertheless, this chapter will canvass a number of other issues with voting markets and will review how

corporate voting markets could be strengthened through traceable share registries that promise to "fix the plumbing" of the corporate governance framework.[4]

We proceed as follows. In the second section we describe the history of
the corporation and the key corporate principles underlying shareholder voting rights in the corporate institutional environment. The third section explores a number of examples of shareholders delegating and exchanging
voting rights. In the fourth section we examine some of key problems or
"pathologies" of shareholder voting that could be further economized in a
corporate cryptodemocracy. The fifth section concludes the chapter.

THE PROPRIETARY NATURE OF
SHAREHOLDER VOTING RIGHTS

Historically, the corporation "emerged in England during the Middle Ages as
a means for conferring on a group of people the capacity to hold and deal
with property and interest to advance their collective aims."[5] English jurist
Sir William Blackstone explained that corporations are "artificial persons"
designed to "preserve entire and for ever those rights and immunities, which,
if they were granted only to those individuals of which the body corporate is
composed, would upon their death be utterly lost and extinct."[6] In other
words, the key benefit of the corporate form is "perpetual succession"—the
principle that collective ownership of assets and the contractual obligations
of an organization will remain intact even if any or all of the participants
change over time. This allows commercial entities to form under uncertainty
about the group's future composition.

There are two other important related legal concepts flowing from the
principle of perpetual succession. First, the fiction that a corporation is a
separate legal person. This means that the law treats the corporation as legally distinct from its managers or participants, rather than as merely an agent or
an alias for individuals.[7] Second, members or shareholders of most corporate
entities are afforded limited liability in contrast to members of a partnership,
for example, where partners are jointly and severally liable for the debts of
the business. This status encourages investment by enabling individuals to
limit their risk exposure when they contribute capital resources to an enterprise but are not otherwise involved in the management of the business.

In the nineteenth century, legislation in various forms around the world
allowed for the incorporation of joint-stock companies. In doing so, companies were endowed with the benefits of perpetual succession, separate legal
identity, and limited liability—legal privileges that were previously limited
to ecclesiastical bodies, municipalities, and a small number of merchant ven-
tures incorporated through Royal Charter or Acts of legislature. Today, joint-

stock companies (where shares are issued to members and can be bought, sold, or transferred without the permission of the other members) can be easily registered under authorizing legislation and are now the "most common and economically significant form of the corporation."[8]

Joint-stock companies are creatures of statute, so there is no single type of company. Variations exist in each jurisdiction around themes of control (e.g., proprietary, closely held, or public), liability (e.g., no liability, limited liability, or unlimited liability), and liquidity (e.g., listed on a stock exchange or unlisted). This chapter will confine itself to shareholder voting within for-profit listed public companies, as this is the best example to observe the dynamics of bargaining, delegation, and exchange that are of interest to our cryptodemocratic analysis.

Notwithstanding the significant regulatory differences between jurisdictions, there are a number of key features of a listed public company. In particular, public companies are legally permitted to raise capital from members of the public through a public offering. Each public offer results in the creation of additional shares in the company. As a result, public companies tend to have a large number of shares on issue across numerous investors. This means that ownership is less concentrated—and therefore less likely to have a single majority shareholder—as compared to closely held or proprietary companies. By listing the company on a stock exchange, individuals are able to obtain shares in the company outside of public offerings. In this case, individuals can buy or sell shares, through a stockbroker and mediated by a stock exchange, but the number of shares on issue does not change.

To hold shares is to hold a proprietary interest. It is an interest capable of being bought, sold, or transferred. Shares in a company are an intangible form of property, referred to in legal nomenclature as a "chose-in-action."[9] This means that when an individual purchases shares in a company, he or she does not actually receive any direct legal or equitable interest in the company's assets. This flows from the principle of separate legal identity, discussed above, where the company itself is the legal owner of the company's property. Instead, a shareholder obtains a bundle of rights on becoming a member of the company. What rights are contained within this bundle? The answer to this depends on the specific rights that are conferred by the company's constitution or mandated under corporate legislation. However, for ordinary shares this bundle of rights will include the ability to vote on members' resolutions at general meetings of the company. That is, shareholders are provided with decision-making power within the company—expressed through voting. In corporate law, "shareholder primacy" requires management to focus on maximizing the return to shareholders and to provide decision-making power through voting to shareholders in preference to the company's other stakeholders.[10] Some corporate governance scholars have described the shareholder franchise as a "myth" in that the voting power to control management is limited.[11] Nevertheless, shareholders, therefore, have a stronger interest in the company than others that may have other contractual relationships, such as customers or creditors. Just as in chapter 5, we argue that in a corporate context voting rights are a key part of the bundle of property rights that go along with share ownership.

The proprietary nature of corporate voting rights is also supported by looking at the alignment between voting rights and other rights in the shareholder's bundle such as the residual claim on a company's assets.[12] As the University of Chicago's Frank Easterbrook and Daniel Fischel observe, "someone must have the residual power to act (or delegate) when contracts [i.e., the company's constitution and corporate legal rules] are not complete."[13] Who should this decision-making power be allocated to? Easterbrook and Fischel make the persuasive case that the reason shareholders are granted voting rights is because "shareholders are the residual claimants to the firm's income."[14] Although a share certificate does not represent a "piece" of a company in a technical legal sense, shareholders will share in the company's surplus assets in the event that the company is wound up. This means that shareholders are the ultimate beneficiaries—and bear the ultimate risk—of the company's performance in contrast to other groups like employees or creditors whose interests are generally fixed ahead of time. Accordingly, when the company is solvent, decision-making power is vested in the shareholders because they have the strongest incentives to make good decisions in the best interests of the company. On the contrary, when the company is insolvent, it is the company's creditors that are empowered to make decisions about the future of the company's operations because there will be no residual assets for shareholders and the best interests of the company will generally align with the best interests of the creditors. As such, although our key focus in this chapter is on shareholder voting, creditors are also relevant to a wider view of corporate democracy.[15]

How are these voting rights exercised? Corporate decision making is fundamentally polycentric. Formal decision-making power is separated between shareholders and directors of the company. The usual separation of powers is that the board of directors generally control the day-to-day enterprise and capital decisions of the company, while the shareholders ultimately elect those board members and decide the constitutional rules governing the company. This settlement economizes on decision costs—it would take a prohibitive amount of time for every shareholder of a listed company to have genuine input into operational decisions of the business. However, it has long been recognized that the polycentric nature of corporate decision making leads to agency problems.[16] Traditionally, corporate law tempers agency costs by imposing fiduciary duties on directors requiring directors to act with care and diligence and to exercise their powers in good faith and for proper purposes in the best interests of the company.[17]

Indeed, in deciding to operate or invest in any commercial business or other type of organization, individuals face choices about how best to structure their involvement. The company as an institutional business structure sits somewhere in the middle of a broad range of other institutional possibilities from close individual ownership through sole proprietorships at one end of the spectrum (characterized by relatively higher decision costs), to collective ownership through government-owned or nationalized businesses at the other end (characterized by relatively higher agency costs). One of the strengths of the corporate entity is the ability for shareholders to collectively agree on the extent of the powers that are vested in the directors and which powers are reserved for the shareholders in general meeting.

Shareholders may not have day-to-day management control of the company, but their decision-making power is still big business. Obtaining a directorship of a major listed company hinges on winning the support of shareholders. Similarly, the board of directors are generally required to obtain shareholder approvals for mergers or major acquisitions. Changing a company's internal rules usually requires a supermajority vote of shareholders. Activist shareholders concerned about ethical and environmental issues may seek to influence management decisions by proposing advisory motions at company meetings. Executive and director remuneration is usually determined by a sub-committee of the board, but this is subject to shareholders' "say on pay." At the end of the corporation's business, shareholders or creditors may vote to wind up the company and have a liquidator distribute the company's assets. Each of these decisions has major commercial consequences for the company's management and investors. In this environment it is not surprising that many investors engage professionals to provide advice on corporate voting options. Equally, it is not surprising that those shareholders seeking to get an outcome are willing to compensate other shareholders in exchange for support. In the next section of the chapter we will review a range of ways that shareholders seek to economize on decision costs by exercising their voting rights of delegation, bargaining, and exchange.

CORPORATE VOTING MARKETS

There is a long history of drawing on political theory as a lens for analyzing corporate voting.[18] Here we seek to do something of the opposite, examining a number of practical examples of corporate voting arrangements to gain insight into some of the ways that people may bargain and exchange votes in a cryptodemocracy. There are a number of examples of corporate voting markets. Specifically we will examine proxy advisors, proxy voting (including proxy solicitation), collective action through activist shareholder organizations, and conclude with reviewing the methods of corporate vote buying.

Proxy Advisors

One indirect market for corporate voting is paid research and advice. Institutional investors (such as banks, insurance companies, mutual funds, and pension or superannuation funds) may own shares in hundreds of companies at any one time. Each of these companies may have several shareholder resolutions requiring shareholders to either vote in favor, against, or abstain altogether. So how do these investors decide how to exercise their voting rights in each case? The preferences of shareholders are not necessarily known or given. Historically, institutional investors might have once followed the "Wall Street rule"—that is, decide to vote in favor of management's recommendation on the shareholder resolutions or sell your shares in the company.[19] The logic behind the Wall Street rule is the expense involved in researching the merits of various proposals. However, over recent decades, proxy advisory services have "transformed proxy voting" by driving down the decision costs of voting.[20] For the institutional investor, the introduction of proxy advisors presents a classic "make or buy" decision. Instead of employing a team of researchers to monitor companies and investigate the merits of each resolution, an institutional investor can outsource the work to a proxy advisory firm to make recommendations on how to vote and benefit from economies of scale. As George Dent explains in his defence of proxy advisors:

> It makes economic sense to pay a third party a small fee (which is also charged to many other investors holding the same stock) to research whether each proxy resolution serves [the goal of maximizing portfolio value] rather than to incur the expense of doing that research in-house.[21]

There are a number of benefits to proxy advisors aside from rationalizing monetary cost. Proxy advisory firms may be able to offer more specialized expertise. For example, proxy advisory firms may train researchers to specialize in analyzing particular types of shareholder resolutions. Proxy advisors or the firm may develop or invest in specialized analytical technology to assist clients and are able to draw on a greater pool of data as inputs for analysis. Using proxy advisors may mitigate the actual or reputational risk to the institutional investor, noting that voting decisions are not only important in their own right but also because an institutional investor will have its own fiduciary obligations to its clients.

There is a body of empirical evidence showing that proxy recommendations are highly influential.[22] There is nothing surprising about these results as paid advice is often followed. Proxy advisors are no different in this regard to the institutional investor's external legal counsel or marketing agencies. But there is also evidence that suggests institutional investors do not blindly follow the recommendations of their proxy advisors. Instead, the advice is "one of many inputs in deciding how to vote."[23] In this way the payment of advice can be seen as a type of discourse—shareholders gathering information to discover their voting preferences.

The increased use of proxy advisory services has been met with calls to restrict the use of this practice or otherwise impose greater regulation on the industry.[24] One criticism is that the market for proxy advice is highly concentrated. For instance, in the United States, Institutional Shareholder Services (ISS) and Glass Lewis (GL) are two of the most prominent proxy advisory firms. A 2013 report from the Mercatus Center estimated that ISS and GL have a combined market share of 96 percent.[25] Although a concentrated market might be theoretically problematic for the usual reasons (monopolistic prices, possibilities for collusion, etc.), in the absence of any evidence of this in practice, economists would do well to recall Ronald Coase's salient warning about not jumping to monopoly explanations at the first sight of business practices that cannot be readily understood.[26] Other criticisms include that the proxy advisory firms have too much influence, are prone to making errors of judgment, may drive agendas that are irrelevant to the business interests of the company, and have conflicts of interests.[27] Nevertheless, the high demand for proxy advisors surely evidences institutional investors derive value from their services—and growing complexity in capital markets decisions is likely to see this demand continue into the future.

Proxy Voting

Proxy voting moves beyond obtaining professional advice to delegating votes, but without any direct payment. A shareholder may authorize a third party to exercise votes on their behalf. This practice drives down the decision costs of voting because it allows investors to exercise their decision-making power in the company without having to be physically present at a general meeting that could be located in a different city or country. The ability to vote by proxy is an important part of exercising the property rights associated with share ownership in a truly global capital market where investors own stocks in a number of countries. Further, the majority of investors will have diversified portfolios (i.e., holding shares in a variety of different public companies) and it will not always be possible for investors to physically attend every general meeting. Of course, there is a practical necessity with delegation of voting power in the corporate setting; institutional investors are themselves large corporate entities and will require a human delegate to execute the proxies.

The legal ability of shareholders to proxy votes has evolved over time, as the Court of Appeal for the District of Columbia held over a century ago.

> The common-law rule in respect of voting by proxy had its origin in reasons
> peculiarly applicable to the earlier forms of corporations, namely, municipal
> and charitable corporations. Membership in these was coupled with no pecuni-
> ary interest. The voting privilege was in the nature of a personal trust, commit-
> ted to the discretion of the member as an individual, and hence not susceptible
> of exercise through delegation. Suffrage, and the right of representation in the
> elections and other affairs of the modern trading or business corporation, stand
> upon essentially different foundations. The stock represents property only—
> money as an investment—and is transferable as freely as other property. Upon
> the transfer of a share the transferee becomes a member in the place of the
> transferrer. In this corporation the transfer by one member to another of prop-
> erty and the policy covering it, would pass the transferrer's right to vote—one
> vote for each risk—to the transferee, to be exercised by the latter in addition to
> any prior right he may have enjoyed. There is sound reason in favor of, and
> none opposed to, permitting an owner of property of this character, as in case
> of other property, to act by agent in all matters affecting his interests when
> inconvenient to act in person. [28]

To be sure, the exercise of proxy voting rights will be constrained by the
constitutional rules of the company and other corporate regulation—such as
mandating the form, method, and timing for exercising proxies. For instance,
shareholders may be able to exercise a proxy vote through a delegate in
person, by mail, by telephone, or over the internet. Shareholders will be
provided with this information ahead of the general meeting. But it is clear
that the law now recognizes proxy voting as an inherent part of the proprietary nature of shareholder voting rights. [29] Proxy votes can be delegated or
initiated in two directions:

- The investor could contract or engage a professional proxy firm.
- The voting right could be solicited externally.

First, the investor could contract with a professional proxy advisory firm,
discussed above, to exercise the vote on behalf of the investor. Many proxy
advisory firms offer this service in addition to conducting paid research and
providing advice. Some shareholder associations, discussed further below,
also act as proxies for their members. The investor can provide instructions
about how votes are cast or the investor could provide the proxy with discretion to exercise their own judgment. In theory, in either case the investor
retains ultimate control of the voting power until the vote is exercised. Although this practice economizes the decision costs of voting, there is an
obvious agency cost in that votes may not be exercised in accordance with
instructions, or the exercise of discretion may not be made in the best interests of the investor. However, proxy firms often develop guidelines—informed by the individual investor's requirements and preferences—and exercising votes in accordance with these policies mitigates agency risks. This

could be a semi-automated process, known as a "standing proxy" or "standing voting instruction," where investors delegate a proxy advisor or shareholder association to undertake research and execute votes according to the agreed guidelines but retain the power to revoke or redirect the proxy. This could theoretically be coded in an automatically executing smart contract. In practice, proxy firms deliver services through technological platforms, removing some friction involved in the proxy voting process. As Jill Fisch summarizes:

> ISS offers a service to its subscribers called ProxyExchange that permits them to outsource the mechanics of the voting process including executing ballots and maintaining voting records. Glass Lewis provides its clients with Viewpoint, a web-based voting platform. Broadridge offers ProxyEdge, an Internet-based system that allows institutional investors to manage, track, reconcile and report their proxy voting through electronic delivery of ballots and satisfy SEC requirements regarding vote reporting and record keeping.[30]

In chapter 4 we mentioned that delegative democracy allows voters to "customize" their political engagement according to their subjectively felt agency and decision costs. Similarly, by choosing to engage proxy firms or associations and delegate corporate voting shareholders economize costs of voting, providing an ability for shareholders to individually tailor the combination of decision and agency costs with their service provider.

Second, proxy votes could be solicited from shareholders. The key difference compared to shareholders engaging proxy firms is that this is on the initiative of a third party that has an interest in supporting or opposing an upcoming resolution. This is known as a "proxy contest" (also called a "proxy battle" or "proxy fight") between the company's management and "shareholder activists." In some contests, there may be more than one activist. The actors may choose to engage a professional proxy solicitor to "identify, locate and communicate with shareholders to secure votes on certain issues."[31] This practice tends to be more commonly observed in the United States than elsewhere and is regulated by the US Securities and Exchange Commission.[32] Common contests are for the elections of directors (such as the high-profile contest in 2017 within Proctor and Gamble, where activist hedge fund Trian Fund Management made a pitch for nominees to the board) or corporate takeovers (such as the 2001 management-sponsored Hewlett Packard merger with Compaq, vigorously opposed by key shareholders and ending up in litigation).[33] There is a stream of research evaluating the question of whether proxy contests produce value for shareholders in the long run.[34] This may seem like a fair empirical question, given that the considerable fees paid to proxy solicitation firms (for example, the 2017 proxy contest between Trian and Proctor and Gamble was estimated to cost a combined US$100 million).[35] Cost-benefit analyses of these disagreements, however, miss the point. The value in proxy contests is twofold; there is information and knowledge generated by the delegation and solicitation process, and the contest acts as a discovery process about which outcome is the most valued by the participants. Because shareholders are not compelled to exercise voting rights, management or activists need to work to persuade potential supporters about the merits of resolutions and turn out the vote. Strategically, management will need to provide a response to the issues raised by the activists. Indeed, the mere prospect of a proxy contest may motivate management to proactively engage with shareholders and activist groups. Proxy contests are also likely to generate significant media interest and analysis— generating further knowledge about the decision facing shareholders. David Yermack points out that even if activists fail in their efforts, "these protest votes may often intimidate management into changing the composition of the board, dismantling takeover defenses, revising executive compensation packages, and implementing other changes."[36] Combined, the ability to delegate votes to either activists or management through competing proxy solicitors has the effect of increasing shareholder turnout, generates information about voting preferences, and ultimately drives down shareholders' decision costs.

Shareholder Organizations

Another way that shareholders can put pressure on the company's management is through participating in shareholder organizations. Yermack describes this as being "among the most controversial forms of shareholder voting for they seem to offer only vague benefits to targeted companies while potentially imposing large costs in terms of adverse publicity and distraction of management."[37] One reason that it is controversial is because the issues that shareholder organizations pursue are politically charged and may undermine the long-term profitability of the company. Another reason for sparking controversy is that shareholder organizations may be seeking to interfere with management's powers over the day-to-day running of the business— contrary to the usual separation of powers.[38] Nevertheless, organizations are providing their members with a service where shareholders care about ethical or other social issues that may not otherwise covered by proxy advisory firms.

As one example, the Interfaith Center on Corporate Responsibility (ICCR) is among the most prominent shareholder organizations in the United States. Founded in 1971, its most recent Annual Report claims that the organization leads a "coalition of over 300 global institutional investors . . . [representing] more than $400 billion in managed assets."[39] ICCR reports that the current issues it is pursuing are in the categories of human rights and human trafficking, climate change, food justice, water, health, corporate lobbying and political expenditure, and financial lending practices.[40] In a similar way to proxy advisory firms, discussed above, the ICCR conducts research and issues guidance to investors on shareholder resolutions.[41] Other organizations, like the Australian Centre for Corporate Responsibility, operate by purchasing small shareholdings (sometimes as little as AU$500) in listed public companies that gives the organization the ability to file shareholder resolutions directly—providing their membership with cover.[42]

Regardless of the membership model, shareholder organizations use "the shareholder resolution tool as a means of seeking social change through changing business behaviour."[43] This power is used as a stick to leverage into other engagement strategies such as direct discussions with company management and lobbying through the media and the political process. These efforts can lead to company management committing to action outside of the general meeting of the company's shareholders. The value to shareholder democracy of this exchange is that it provides an opportunity for discourse between the company and shareholder organizations—with the potential for long-term collaborative relationships to be established.[44] However, at the same time, there is a worry that the shareholder resolution process is being used to achieve social and political policy changes. The risk to shareholder democracy in this case is that company management give undue weight to the views of a small number of noisy shareholders whose resolutions are almost never successful when put to a vote.[45]

Corporate Vote Buying

Agreements to buy votes provide shareholders with bolstered voting power without requiring that they purchase additional shares or launch takeover bids. Whether vote buying should be permitted under corporate law is an old question.[46] Simply put, vote buying is where a shareholder sells their voting rights to a third party without transferring the underlying stock. As such, corporate vote buying is an extension of delegating votes by proxy, but with the shareholder receiving some form of compensation in exchange for their voting rights. In the case of proxy advice and proxy voting, discussed above, compensation flows from the shareholder or the company to the proxy advisory firm. Corporate vote buying allows compensation to flow from third parties to shareholders.

Traditionally, corporate vote buying was prohibited. However, it appears that courts in the United States and the United Kingdom have moved toward a position of legality, so long as that the agreement to purchase voting rights is not fraudulent or does not constitute oppression of minority shareholders.[47] Other commentators offer a narrower interpretation of the case law, claiming that "courts [in the United States] will allow vote buying only when such a deal aligns the financial interests of the shareholders with those of the corporation."[48] This may exclude some forms of "vote lending," discussed below.

In any case, the development of the law is in keeping with other common law developments on proxy voting, discussed above. It is also consistent with the inherent proprietary properties of corporate voting rights.

How can corporate vote buying be structured? There are several options depending on the commercial needs of the parties and the particular regulations in a jurisdiction.

These options include:

- Voting agreements—where shareholders agree to pool votes and vote unanimously;
- Voting trusts—where voting rights are assigned to a third party trustee for a specified period of time;
- Irrevocable proxies—where shareholders agree to assign voting rights to a third party on the condition that it cannot be revoked for the term of the agreement, generally coupled with an interest such a derivative option; and
- Vote lending (also referred to as "empty voting" or "new vote buying")—where shareholders agree to provide shares to a third party in exchange for a fee and the return of equivalent shares at the end of the loan period. [49]

Although some of these arrangements are relatively commonplace, it is not to say that there are no ethical or practical issues with corporate voting markets. This is a contested space. Some have called for a ban on vote lending that separates voting rights from the underlying economic interests. [50] Others seem to prefer that practice to be unrestricted. [51] Another, more specific, ethical issue with vote buying is "greenmail," a practice where the company's management or a majority of shareholders repurchase shares or lend voting power at a premium price from a "transient, threatening investor" that is seeking to "raid" or "loot" the company. [52] This questionable practice was popular in the 1980s, and notably depicted in the Oliver Stone film *Wall Street*. Greenmail is problematic because the individual shareholder is seeking a short-term profit opportunity by imposing costs on the other shareholders—rather than seeking to have genuine input into corporate decision making.

There are a number of other "pathologies" of corporate voting that undermine the ability of shareholders to exercise their voting rights to bargain, delegate, and exchange. [53] The next section of the chapter will focus on these issues. This will put us in a position to reflect on the ways that blockchain could strengthen corporate governance arrangements in the future.

PATHOLOGIES OF CORPORATE VOTING

Maintaining voter registration ledgers (i.e., electoral rolls) is a key decision cost of voting within the political context (as we have previously outlined in chapter 3). This is also true of corporate voting. How is a shareholder's proprietary interest in a company recorded? It is complicated, and this complexity causes several problems.

Corporate law requires companies to keep and maintain a share register. In theory, the share register contains a record of the identity of members and how many shares each member holds at any one point in time. In most jurisdictions, the share register is the primary evidence of ownership—ranking above other records like share certificates or a stock exchange's share clearing house transaction data. In this way the share register is akin to an electoral role as it also records the number of votes (1 share 1 vote for ordinary shares). But maintaining an accurate share register in real time has always been problematic in practice. In a recent law review article, George Geis makes the important observation that current stock exchange settlement systems do not actually trace individual shares when they are bought and sold; instead the clearance system lumps traded shares together as "unidentified fungible bulk."[54]

Geis paints a picture of the historical backdrop to the present-day settlement systems.

> In the early and mid-1900s, when corporate law lingered in a formative state, investors lived in a paper world. Numbered stock certificates were stashed in private file cabinets, or perhaps broker storerooms, and passed from seller to buyer like the deed to a house or title to a car. But a share of stock can trade hands much more frequently than a used automobile, and by the 1960s the system was snowed under. There was simply too much trading volume. During the height of this paperwork crisis, traders closed the stock markets every Wednesday just so the brokers could inspect the unruly piles of certificates for authenticity, organize them for distribution, and route them to their new owners. Many brokers could not keep up and closed their doors.[55]

The solution to this inefficient trading system was to "immobilize" share certificates and use a clearing house as an aggregator and centralized custodian. Intermediaries exist between the shareholder and the clearing house. Brokerage firms and other financial services institutions maintain accounts with the clearing house and the majority of shares are held in the "street name" (i.e., the name of the brokerage firm). This solved the paperwork problem and mitigated the risk that share certificates were lost or otherwise not delivered. There are also efficiencies when trades occur between a brokerage firm's clients, as the firm can update its own internal records without any changes occurring at the clearing house level. However, this means that the company's share registry will record the "street name" rather than that of the beneficial shareholders with the consequence that "it is often impossible to specify who owns any given share of stock."[56] As a result, many companies engage the services of analysts to identify and track underlying share ownership—particularly important for shareholder engagement in proxy contests. Present-day settlement systems may have created more efficient markets for trading securities. However, as Marcel Kahan and Edward Rock observe in a ground-breaking article, there are a number of observable "pathologies" of corporate voting resulting from confusion over ownership, system complexity, and delays.[57]

The first category of pathologies is a consequence of the confusion over ownership. The previous section of the chapter raised the matter of agreements to lend out shares and associated voting rights. Kahan and Rock pose the example of a "securities lending surprise" where an institutional investor that has sponsored a shareholder resolution cannot actually vote after discovering that its shares had been lent out.[58] Shareholders will often not know that the broker has even lent out the shares—a consequence of untraceable bulk shares. This presents another difficulty—"over voting." The problem of over voting occurs where "securities lending can result in brokers soliciting votes, and receiving instructions, for more shares than are entitled to vote."[59]

A second category of pathologies are a result of the complexity of the system. The mechanics of corporate voting is time consuming given the back and forth that is required between various intermediaries and the ultimate shareholders. Documented problems include printed materials not arriving in time to exercise votes (although this is less apparent now as many companies or proxy firms are using web-based platforms) and votes not being correctly counted.[60]

De Filipi and Wright cite the example of the 2008 proxy contest at Yahoo! to evidence counting errors.

> After a tense vote, Yahoo announced that two of its directors received approval from approximately 80 percent of stockholders, raising the eyebrows of an institutional investor holding about 16 percent of Yahoo's stock. This investor asked Broadridge, the third party administering the vote, to double-check the totals, which uncovered an error that misattributed millions of shareholder votes.[61]

While the errors in the Yahoo! case did not change the result of the ballot, massive errors highlight the need to be able to verify and have confidence in the result. According to Kahan and Rock, the "most troubling pathology of complexity is the system's inability to provide vote verification and an end-to-end audit trail."[62]

A third category of pathologies flows from the delays involved in the clearing house system for settlement when shares are traded through an exchange. In present-day settlement systems there can be delays of several days for the transfer of the economic ownership of shares. To make corporate voting work there is a fixed "record date" to be entitled to vote on upcoming resolutions. What happens when shares are sold after the record date but before the company issues its proxy statement? There is an "internal discrepancy" at play here where an incoming shareholder holds the economic interest but does not yet hold the corresponding voting rights and the outgoing shareholder possesses voting rights without any economic exposure to the consequences of the voting outcome.[63] Henry Hut and Bernard Black have written extensively on the problems of the "decoupling" of economic and voting interests.[64]

This review raises serious concerns about the validity of corporate voting outcomes. This is significant because the problems have the potential to undermine confidence in corporate governance more broadly. For instance, if the process of electing company directors is questionable, how can shareholders have faith in the decisions that they make? Major improvements are needed to the current settlement systems given the central role of voting as a tool for collective decision making within companies.

However, it is important to note that the problems identified in this section of the chapter do not stem from the act of shareholder voting itself or even with bargaining or exchanging voting power. Instead, the pathologies of corporate voting stem from an outdated voting architecture or "plumbing system."[65] The solution to these problems is not removing shareholder voting but developing modern architectural solutions. The good news, according to Vice Chancellor of Delaware's Court of Chancery, is that there is a "plunger to clean up the plumbing" promising to "provide better accuracy, greater transparency, and superior efficiency for settling securities trades and voting in corporate elections."[66] This will be achieved by creating traceable share ownership through a blockchain-enabled system.[67] It is at this point, we return to the core focus of this book—the application and implications of using blockchain as governance infrastructure.

Blockchain enables new types of record keeping. As we have identified earlier in this chapter, the core record for corporate voting is the shareholder register that records the identity and voting power of shareholders. Blockchain provides the ability to tokenize and record share ownership that can be traced whenever interests are transferred. Geis explains that "the defining feature of traceable shares is that every unit of stock will have a clear chain of title identifying all current and prior owners. Stock will no longer need to be physically isolated and held in unidentifiable fungible bulk."[68]

How could creating such a blockchain share registry change corporate voting? Traceable shares using blockchain promises to strengthen corporate voting and increase trust in voting outcomes. For instance, a traceable mechanism would clarify and readily identify the party that is in possession of voting rights, avoiding a security lending surprise and removing the potential for over voting and other errors associated with vote tabulation. Trades—and other associated information—could occur in real time rather than lengthy settlement processes. It would also provide shareholders with an immutable, transparent, and verifiable record of how votes were cast that can be audited by shareholders or other independent third parties. Combined, these characteristics radically lower the decision costs of voting relative to agency costs.

How could blockchain change the corporate voting landscape? Disintermediation is a promised feature of many blockchain applications—and corporate voting is no exception. Blockchain could streamline settlement processes by removing some of the layers of banks, brokers, and other financial intermediaries. It could also mean that a decentralized voting system displaces traditional paper-based or e-proxy service providers.[69] Although, as Geis notes, there are good reasons why complete disintermediation may not fully occur in the context of corporate voting.[70] This is because it is likely that investors may continue to engage professional services for proxy advice and appoint delegates to undertake voting. Likewise, management and activists are likely to continue to solicit support for board positions and proposed resolutions. As Yermack explains, the extent of decentralization depends in part on whether the voting system uses a permissioned blockchain or a public blockchain.[71] This is because permissioned blockchains will require a third party intermediary (or a consortium) to run and maintain the platform. Nevertheless, a traceable share registry opens up new vistas for bargaining and exchanging voting rights in a decentralized way—as shareholders may be able to trade and delegate voting rights directly in a peer-to-peer fashion rather than relying on financial intermediaries and large proxy advisors.

It has been predicted that blockchain may stamp out the practice of empty voting. Geis speculates that "by linking votes to share ownership for a longer period of time, there would be fewer situations where loose votes are available for sale or manipulation" but notes that the same practical effect could be achieved through hedging.[72] Fiammetta Piazza observes that "[empty] voting strategies mostly rely on secrecy . . . a transparent system like shared ledger would effectively render empty voting impossible."[73] Transparency could reduce other forms of rent seeking and other opportunistic behavior.[74] However, a scenario that might emerge is that shareholders make use of paid delegation contracts instead of empty voting to achieve the same outcome.

A traceable share system would give shareholders more control over how voting rights are managed and exercised. For instance, in chapters 4 and 5 we mentioned that decentralizing voting might decompose voting rights in various ways. This could be applied in the corporate setting by expanding the current practices of proxy advisor and proxy solicitor firms. Instead of delegating corporate voting to a single firm, shareholders could delegate to multiple firms or individual advisors, or choose to exercise votes themselves—

depending on the issues before them. Currently, shareholders can already receive advice from multiple proxy advisors (and indeed many do). But shareholders are unable to delegate the exercise of their voting rights to multiple firms on an issue-by-issue basis. Using a traceable system, it will be possible for shareholders to select one delegate to vote on directors, another delegate for "say on pay" matters, another for mergers and acquisitions, and so on. Such a voting system prevents double voting as it will be able to accurately trace whether votes have been previously exercised.

The possibility of a corporate cryptodemocracy is close on the horizon as stock exchanges around the world are moving to blockchain-enabled share registries. It has been reported that stock exchanges including the ASX, Deutsche Bourse, India's Securities Exchange Board, NASDAQ, New York Stock Exchange, and the Tokyo Stock Exchange have begun investing in proprietary blockchain infrastructure to upgrade their current electronic settlement systems for trading shares.[75] To be sure, the motivating factors behind adopting this technology are quicker settlement times and enhanced record keeping. But it is significant because it will provide the new "plumbing" for corporate voting—and the ability to delegate, exchange, and trade.

Wright and De Fillipi are not optimistic about completely decentralizing corporate voting.

> . . . direct voting through distributed consensus may be difficult to achieve because it requires that people remain consistently engaged and attentive to the organisation's activities. For many, gathering all the information necessary to make a well-informed decision will be too time consuming and complex, dissuading participation.[76]

This recognizes the real decision costs involved in participating in the company decisions. It is expected that shareholders will continue to rely on professional advice to economize on these costs, particularly institutional investors that have fiduciary duties to their ultimate clients. However, our conception of cryptodemocracy is one where the company's shareholders can customize their own level of engagement according to their sensitivity to decision and agency costs. Shareholders would be able to establish a variety of delegative relationships that minimize their effort but still contribute their vote to collective choices. The implication, as Yermack has observed, is that shareholder voting will be "much more reliable and less costly."[77] This deepens the scope for engagement and may see shareholders have an even greater role in the corporate decision-making context. While increasing the amount of shareholder voting threatens the historical settlement of powers between directors and shareholders, it certainly fits within the global trend of legislative reforms restraining directors and executives by handing more power to shareholders.

CONCLUSION

In this chapter we have examined the proprietary nature of corporate share-holder voting rights and considered how these voting rights might be strengthened looking toward the prospect of blockchain-enabled share regis-tries. In the corporate context, shareholders have a key function in electing the directors that will take responsibility for the day-to-day operations of the company, approving mergers and acquisitions, voting on advisory policy resolutions, and deciding on the constitutional rules governing the company. Shareholder voting rights are aligned with their financial stake in the compa-ny. While shareholders can exercise their votes directly, there are several ways that shareholders delegate and exchange voting power to economize on decision costs. This chapter discussed different voting markets: seeking paid advice by proxy advisory firms, engaging in proxy voting arrangements (contracts with either a proxy firm or delegation to a proxy solicitor), mem-bership of shareholder organizations, and corporate vote buying. Of course, all these options are in addition to the real prospect that a shareholder or another third party seeking greater voting power within the company could simply increase their stake in the company by buying additional shares. This builds on the previous chapter by providing real examples of delegation and exchange contracts—and examples of compensation flowing from voter to delegate and from delegate to voter. A share registry records the voting rights of shareholders—but this information is often incomplete due to the volume and complexity of share trading settlement exchanges. Solutions to an out-dated paper-based system "immobilized" share certificates but lead to shares being recorded in the "street name" rather than the ultimate beneficial owner. This chapter reviewed several "pathologies" of voting caused by this settle-ment system. The interesting aspect of each of the pathologies is that they represent the relatively high decision costs of voting—issues with identifying who is entitled to cast a vote, complexity about the method of casting votes, and the lack of transparency and integrity about how votes are tallied. Addi-tionally, many of the problems that we have reviewed undermine the ability of shareholders to economize on the information and cognitive decision costs of voting through engaging in voting markets. But there are also unavoidable agency costs present in this environment as several intermediaries are re-quired to make a complex system function. Blockchain provides a new tool for governing voting property rights and could be built on top of blockchain-based stock exchange systems that are being proposed around the world. The possibility for corporate cryptodemocratic governance will surely strengthen proprietary voting interests and provides greater scope for shareholder deci-sion making. Having now examined voting rights associated with capital, the next chapter will look at collective decision making in the employment con-text.

NOTES

1. Andrei Shleifer and Robert W. Vishny, "A Survey of Corporate Governance," *The Journal of Finance* 52, no. 2 (1997).
2. Peter Iliev et al., "Shareholder Voting and Corporate Governance around the World," *The Review of Financial Studies* 28, no. 8 (2015).
3. Hasen, "Vote Buying," 1354.
4. J. Travis Laster, "The Block Chain Plunger: Using Technology to Clean up Proxy Plumbing and Take Back the Vote," *Address to Council of Institutional Investors, Chicago, 29 September 2016* (2016).
5. Pamela Hanrahan and Geof Stapledon, *Commercial Applications of Company Law*, 17th edition (South Melbourne: Oxford University Press, 2016), 11.
6. William Blackstone, *Commentaries on the Laws of England in Four Books* (Indianapolis: Liberty Fund, 1973 [2011]), 293.
7. For example, see the classic English case of *Salomon v Salomon & Co Ltd* [1896] UKHL 1.
8. Hanrahan and Stapledon, *Commercial Applications of Company Law*, 5.
9. Essentially, a "chose-in-action" is a right to sue to enforce rights, in contrast to a "chose-in-possession" interest that allows the interest holder to enforce rights by taking physical possession of an asset.
10. David Millon, "Radical Shareholder Primacy," *University of St. Thomas Law Journal* 10 (2013).
11. Lucian A. Bebchuk, "The Myth of the Shareholder Franchise," *Virginia Law Review* 93, no. 3 (2007).
12. Frank H. Easterbrook and Daniel R. Fischel, "Voting in Corporate Law," *The Journal of Law and Economics* 26, no. 2 (1983).
13. Ibid., 403.
14. Ibid.
15. For example, see Kevin A. Kordana and Eric A. Posner, "A Positive Theory of Chapter 11," *New York University Law Review* 74 (1999).
16. For example, see Adolf A. Berle and Gardiner C. Means, "The Modern Corporation and Private Property" (Harcourt, Brace, Jovanovich; Commerce Clearing House, 1968 [1933]).
17. The specific general law and statutory duties vary across jurisdictions.
18. For example, see Manne, "Some Theoretical Aspects of Share Voting. An Essay in Honor of Adolf A. Berle"; Franklin C. Latcham and Frank D. Emerson, "Proxy Contest Expenses and Shareholder Democracy," *Western Reserve Law Review* 4 (1952).
19. George W. Dent Jr., "A Defense of Proxy Advisors," *Michigan State Law Review* (2014).
20. Ibid.
21. Ibid.
22. For recent discussions, see Andrey Malenko and Nadya Malenko, "The Economics of Selling Information to Voters," *Journal of Finance* (forthcoming); Joerg-Markus Hitz and Nico Lehmann, "Empirical Evidence on the Role of Proxy Advisors in European Capital Markets," *European Accounting Review* 27, no. 4 (2018).
23. Dent Jr., "A Defense of Proxy Advisors," 1302.
24. For example, at the time of writing, H.R.4015—Corporate Governance Reform and Transparency Act of 2017 passed the United States House of Representatives and was before the Senate. If passed by Congress and signed into law, the bill would license and regulate proxy advisory firms operating in the United States.
25. James K. Glassman and J. W. Verret, "How to Fix Our Broken Proxy Advisory System," in *Mercatus Research* (2013).
26. Ronald H. Coase, "Industrial Organization: A Proposal for Research," in *Economic Research: Retrospect and Prospect, Volume 3, Policy Issues and Research Opportunities in Industrial Organization* (NBER, 1972).
27. For a review of these arguments, see generally Dent Jr., "A Defense of Proxy Advisors."
28. *Walker v. Johnson* 17 App. D.C. 144 (1900).

29. For a comprehensive history of the evolution of corporate proxy voting, see Leonard H. Axe, "Corporate Proxies," *Michigan Law Review* 41, no. 1 (1942).

30. Jill E. Fisch, "Standing Voting Instructions: Empowering the Excluded Retail Investor," *Minnesota Law Review* 102 (2017). (footnotes omitted).

31. US Government Accountability Office, "Proxy Advisory Firms' Role in Voting and Corporate Governance Practices," in *Highlights of GAO-17-47, a report to the Chairman, Subcommittee on Economic Policy, Committee on Banking, Housing, and Urban Affairs, U.S. Senate* (2016).

32. See *Securities Exchange Act of 1934*; Regulation 14A—Solicitation of Proxies.

33. For a summary of the resulting HP litigation, see Luh Luh Lan and Loizos Heracleous, "Negotiating the Minefields of Corporate Vote-Buying," *Corporate Governance: An International Review* 15, no. 5 (2007).

34. Recent examples include: Lucian A. Bebchuk, Alon Brav, and Wei Jiang, "The Long-Term Effects of Hedge Fund Activism," *Columbia Law Review* 115 (2015). *Contra*: Leo E. Strine Jr., "Can We Do Better by Ordinary Investors: A Pragmatic Reation to the Dueling Ideological Mythologists of Corporate Law," *Columbia Law Review* 114 (2014). However, it is an old question; for example, see Latcham and Emerson, "Proxy Contest Expenses and Shareholder Democracy."

35. Siddharth Cavale, "P&G Appoints Peltz to Board Despite Losing Proxy Battle," *Reuters*, December 16, 2017.

36. David Yermack, "Shareholder Voting and Corporate Governance," *Annual Review of Financial Economics* 2, no. 1 (2010): 108.

37. Ibid.

38. For a recent Australian case on this point, see Australian Centre for Corporate Responsibility v Commonwealth Bank of Australia [2015] FCA 785.

39. Interfaith Center on Corporate Responsibility, "A Faithful Voice for Justice: Annual Report 2016–2017," (2017).

40. Ibid.

41. Ibid.

42. Australian Centre for Corporate Responsibility, https://accr.org.au/.

43. Jeanne M. Logsdon and Harry J. Van Buren, "Beyond the Proxy Vote: Dialogues between Shareholder Activists and Corporations," *Journal of Business Ethics* 87, no. 1 (2009): 354.

44. Ibid.

45. Yermack, "Shareholder Voting and Corporate Governance."

46. See, for example, Robert Charles Clark, "Vote Buying and Corporate Law," *Case Western Reserve Law Review* 29 (1979).

47. Hasen, "Vote Buying"; Lan and Heracleous, "Negotiating the Minefields of Corporate Vote-Buying."

48. Paul H. Edelman and Robert B. Thompson, "Corporate Voting," *Vanderbilt Law Review* 62 (2009): 165.

49. See Henry T. C. Hu and Bernard Black, "The New Vote Buying: Empty Voting and Hidden (Morphable) Ownership," *Southern California Law Review* 79 (2006); Lan and Heracleous, "Negotiating the Minefields of Corporate Vote-Buying."

50. Edelman and Thompson, "Corporate Voting."

51. Manne, "Some Theoretical Aspects of Share Voting. An Essay in Honor of Adolf A. Berle."

52. David Manry and David Stangeland, "Greenmail: A Brief History," *Stanford Journal of Law, Business and Finance* 6 (2000): 224.

53. Marcel Kahan and Edward Rock, "The Hanging Chads of Corporate Voting," *Georgetown Law Journal* 96 (2007).

54. George S. Geis, "Traceable Shares and Corporate Law," *Northwestern University Law Review* 113, no. 2 (2018).

55. Ibid., 232; Martin J. Aronstein, "The Decline and Fall of the Stock Certificate in America," *Journal of Comparative Corporate Law and Securities Regulation* 1, no. 3 (1978).

56. Geis, "Traceable Shares and Corporate Law," 231.

57. Kahan and Rock, "The Hanging Chads of Corporate Voting."

58. Ibid.

59. Ibid., 1258.

60. Ibid.

61. Wright and De Filippi, *Blockchain and the Law: The Rule of Code*, Kindle Locations 2625–28.

62. Kahan and Rock, "The Hanging Chads of Corporate Voting," 1253.

63. Ibid.

64. Hu and Black, "The New Vote Buying: Empty Voting and Hidden (Morphable) Ownership," 811; Hu and Black, "Empty Voting and Hidden (Morphable) Ownership: Taxonomy, Implications, and Reforms," *The Business Lawyer* (2006); Hu and Black, "Hedge Funds, Insiders, and the Decoupling of Economic and Voting Ownership: Empty Voting and Hidden (Morphable) Ownership," *Journal of Corporate Finance* 13, no. 2–3 (2007); Hu and Black, "Equity and Debt Decoupling and Empty Voting II: Importance and Extensions," *University of Pennsylvania Law Review* 156 (2007): 625.

65. Laster, "The Block Chain Plunger: Using Technology to Clean up Proxy Plumbing and Take Back the Vote."

66. Ibid.

67. Geis, "Traceable Shares and Corporate Law."
See also Wright and De Filippi, *Blockchain and the Law: The Rule of Code*; Fiammetta S. Piazza, "Bitcoin and the Blockchain as Possible Corporate Governance Tools: Strengths and Weaknesses," *Bocconi Legal Papers* 9 (2017); David Yermack, "Corporate Governance and Blockchains," *Review of Finance* 21, no. 1 (2017).

68. Geis, "Traceable Shares and Corporate Law," 267; Larissa Lee, "New Kids on the Blockchain: How Bitcoin's Technology Could Reinvent the Stock Market," *Hastings Business Law Journal* 12 (2016).

69. Wright and De Filippi, *Blockchain and the Law: The Rule of Code*.

70. Geis, "Traceable Shares and Corporate Law."

71. Yermack, "Corporate Governance and Blockchains."

72. Geis, "Traceable Shares and Corporate Law," 227.

73. Piazza, "Bitcoin and the Blockchain as Possible Corporate Governance Tools: Strengths and Weaknesses," 293; Yermack, "Corporate Governance and Blockchains."

74. Wright and De Filippi, *Blockchain and the Law: The Rule of Code*.

75. Eric Ervin, "Blockchain Technology Set to Revolutionize Global Stock Trading," *Forbes*, August 16, 2018.

76. Wright and De Filippi, *Blockchain and the Law: The Rule of Code*.

77. Yermack, "Corporate Governance and Blockchains."

Chapter Seven

Cryptodemocratic Labor Unions

INTRODUCTION

Labor unions—also known as trade unions—are a particular type of organization formed for collective decision making. The union movement's powerful influence in workplace bargaining, industrial relations, and the broader political environment is a common feature of many liberal democracies. The functions and form of labor unions therefore demand particular attention for understanding the opportunities and challenges of the cryptodemocratic framework we have outlined. At the basic level, unions are organizations consisting of workers in a particular trade or industry. The central function of the union has remained unchanged since the beginning of the industrial revolution. A labor union is a "continuous association of wage-earners for the purpose of maintaining or improving the conditions of their working lives."[1] Through collective action labor unions seek higher wages and better working conditions than their members would otherwise be able to achieve in negotiating directly with their employer. Blockchain technology expands and reshapes this process in a new institutional possibility we call cryptodemocratic labor unions.

We proceed as follows. First, in the second section we begin the chapter from the perspective of an individual worker who makes decisions about his or her own labor in the face of decision costs and agency costs. We consider the trade-offs applied to the employment contract in the context of governance. Second, in the third section we turn to the central role of coercion in enforcing collective decision making within labor unions and the issues that this may cause for union governance. In particular we draw on a recent Australian case study of six unions. Then, in the fourth section we examine the ways that blockchain technology could provide solutions to the systemic problems facing the modern labor movement. Finally, in the fifth section we conclude by detailing the characteristics of new polycentric collective action in cryptodemocratic labor unions.

LABOR AS AN INDIVIDUAL PROPERTY RIGHT

To understand unions within a cryptodemocratic framework we must understand labor as a form of property rights, with various institutional governance options. In the natural rights tradition, it has long been argued that everyone has property in their own person. Flowing from this basic proposition is the notion that a worker's labor is unquestionably the property of the worker.[2] Of course, most people engage in work out of necessity; people need to work in order to provide for themselves and their families. More than that though, there is dignity in work—providing people with a sense of purpose and fulfilment. Through income-generating work people have the means to acquire land and capital assets and build their wealth over time. This means that the protection of other private property interests will only be truly meaningful and universal if labor is also recognized and protected as an individual property right.[3]

What is the implication of labor as an individual property right? In an advanced economy, work is rarely an individual pursuit. Each type of good and service being bought and sold is the product of the coordination and cooperation of knowledge and resources by thousands of people, mostly unknown to each other.[4] This system is based on thousands of contracts. Each of these agreements needs to be made and then enforced. Labor is therefore a question of economic organization—a comparative institutional problem. Parties must weigh factors such as the frequency, uncertainty, and asset specificity required for each labor transaction.[5] Yet the overwhelming majority of people exchange their labor under an employment contract: wage earners working for small or large businesses, the not-for-profit sector, or the public sector. So, in these settings, individuals need to come to an agreement with their employers about their pay and conditions. Again, this is a governance matter. While the responsibility falls on an individual to bargain with his or her employer, there is no single method governing this process.

What are the institutional options available for governing labor rights? One possibility is a contract negotiated directly between an individual and an employer. People could also combine into a collective agreement negotiated by a labor union on behalf of employees in a particular workplace. Alternatively, there could be an economy-wide award set by a centralized wage fixing body. How can we combine these understandings into a coherent framework for the governing of labor property rights? We propose that these alternative employment decision-making systems exist on a spectrum representing a trade-off between decision costs and agency costs, illustrated in figure 7.1 below.

Not all possibilities exist for all people, and there are potentially substantive costs of shifting between governance forms. There is a level of path dependency in the governance of labor property rights. Different forms of employment governance may be the norm in different industries. Further, entrenched governance arrangements may well exist for incoming employees. This may be because legislation and other government action may constrain the available choices and increase the relative costs of particular institutional options. In this view governments can distort the various costs of alternatives. For instance, laws could favor enterprise-level bargaining by making this process relatively easier, in turn making the process for negotiating individual agreements relatively more difficult. Although arrangements may be presented to a new worker with little bargaining power, ultimately the individual worker retains control about whether or not to sign up.

Another factor is that the institutional options are not mutually exclusive. For example, a collective workplace agreement may be combined with a

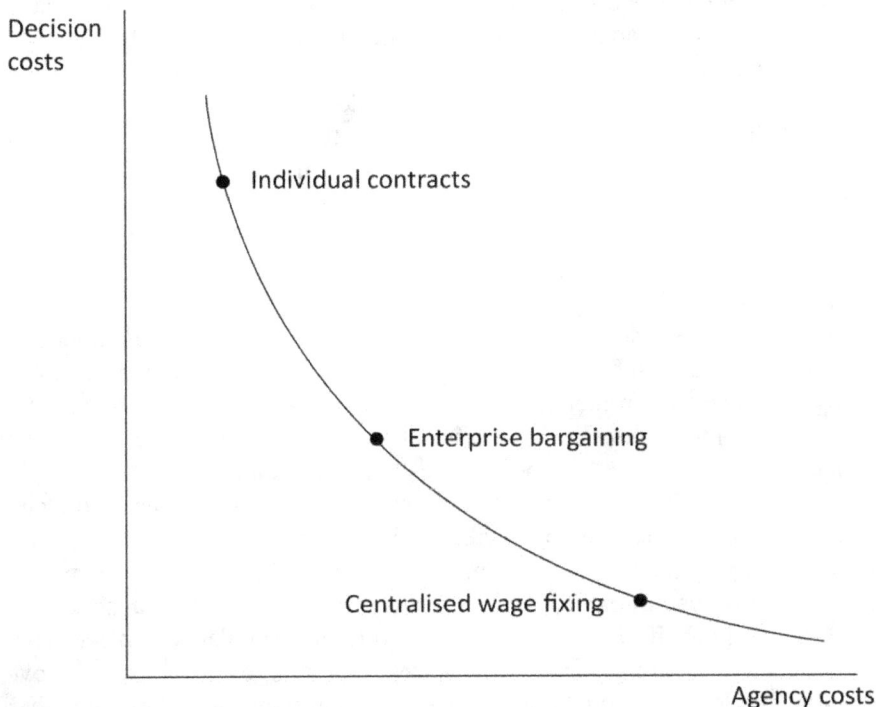

Decision costs

• Individual contracts

• Enterprise bargaining

Centralised wage fixing •

Agency costs

Figure 7.1. An Employment DIPF

separate individual agreement about matters that apply only to an individual worker. Similarly, economy-wide centralized wage-fixing bodies may mandate minimum wages and entitlements for workers in a specific occupation but a collective workplace agreement could still be negotiated above those minimums or in substitution of the award. These combinations are subject to the relevant legislative constraints. Although there is complexity involved in the institutional choices governing employment contracts, the cohesion of the Democratic Institutional Possibilities Frontier (DIPF) is that institutions emerge to economize on decision costs and agency costs in different ways.

What are decision costs in the context of a labor contract? A starting point in the labor market is individual bargaining. Decision costs are those involved in deciding on the terms and conditions of an employment contract. As we saw previously, decision costs include those involved in searching, selecting, bargaining, and enforcing employment contracts.[6] This process is time consuming and costly (in a similar way to democratic voting, discussed in previous chapters). Uncertainty exists on both sides of the employment contract—a key decision cost. So, given decision costs, employers need to develop their own internal processes for recruitment. They must then negotiate the terms and conditions with candidates. Employers will not know the strength of other offers available to a prospective employee, and will have limited information about his or her ability to perform the job. There is duplication involved, as employers need to repeat this process for every new recruit. Employees, on the other hand, face decision costs in that they will seek out the best available employment opportunity, bounded by a limited amount of information about the internal pay structure and actual working conditions at any organization, and what other opportunities exist with other potential employers. The risk that employees are unfairly discriminated against, or are taken advantage of, factor into the decision costs of an agreement.

How have labor decision costs changed through time? The internet has driven down search and bargaining costs in labor markets.[7] Blockchain technology promises to further reduce information costs in making human resources decisions, such as the verification of an employee's credentials.[8] While other applications will be explored at a later point in this chapter, it is probable that decision costs will remain substantial for individual contracts. Collective bargaining attempts to reduce the decision costs associated with forming employment contracts—particularly bargaining and enforcement costs. In this institutional possibility, labor unions negotiate a collective agreement on behalf of employees—tailored for a particular workplace. This is particularly advantageous in workplaces with a large number of employees. Pay scales, working hours, and other conditions of the employment contract are fixed. This reduces the cost of an employer having to individually negotiate every employment contract. It reduces decision costs of the

employees because they do not need to make decisions directly, as employees are represented by the union and the agreement applies to all employees
equally. Enforcement costs of the decision are decreased as collective agreements will typically contain dispute resolution clauses, and unions will often
act on behalf of aggrieved employees. However, as outlined in chapter 3,
reducing decision costs brings agency costs. A labor union requires union
officials. There is the risk that labor union officials might interpret the preferences of employees wrongly or act in their own interest and against the best
interests of employees.

Centralized wage-fixing exists toward the limit of the applied DIPF. In
this institutional form, a central authority issues legally binding awards about
the pay and conditions.[9] Decision costs are further reduced as the award
would apply to all employment contracts—not just those in a particular firm.
Separate awards are made for different industries and occupations. But there
is a heavier reliance on agents compared to collective bargaining at a workplace level—and this reliance comes with agency costs. Labor unions and
employer associations make representations to the central authority. Members of the authority are appointed by the government. The core agency cost
here is one of information; despite any special expertise of the members of
the wage-fixing body, they will never be able to take into account the dynamic preferences of millions of employees and employers.[10] In applying the
stylized model of the DIPF, both collective bargaining and centralized wage-
fixing possibilities reduce decision costs—as compared to direct contracts—
but increase agency costs. Both institutional forms require labor unions to
represent employees. So how then are collective decisions made in this environment? The next section of the chapter will explore this trade-off between
agency and decision costs in more detail.

MONOPOLY, VOICE, AND COERCION IN LABOR UNIONS

In a classic paper, Harvard economists Richard B. Freeman and James L.
Medoff noted that there are two faces of unionism: monopoly and voice.[11] In
the monopoly view, unions create monopolies over the supply of labor which
reduces or removes market competition. This monopoly power allows unions
to seek higher wages, above the competitive market rates that would otherwise prevail if individual workers negotiated with employers directly. In the
voice view, unions provide workers with a collective voice at the workplace
level and in the broader political environment. In this case, collective voice is
used to agitate for better working conditions. Borrowing from Albert Hirschman's *Exit, Voice, and Loyalty,* Freeman and Medoff explain that "voice"
includes "voting, bargaining, discussing and the like."[12] In a similar way, the
American labor activist A.J. Muste characterized this dualism—decades ear-

lier—as a combination of "two extremely divergent types of social structure, that of an army and that of a democratic town meeting. . . ."[13] Ultimately, the two faces of unions are faces of the same coin. There is a debate over whether or not unions are a detrimental force within society and the veracity of the empirical evidence supporting either view. That is, the main concern held by proponents of the monopoly view is that collective action leads to decreased productivity and overall economic output. This empirical claim is not material to the issues being explored in this chapter. Instead, our focus is on how unions reduce decision costs—and increase agency costs—compared to individual bargaining. The dichotomy is helpful for clarifying the role of unions.

Freeman and Medoff's arguments about voice can be applied to our framework. Specifically, they propose two reasons for collective bargaining being more of an "effective voice" in the workplace as compared to individual bargaining.[14] One reason is "that workers who are not prepared to exit will be unlikely to reveal their true preferences to their bosses, for fear of some sort of punishment."[15] This could be extended to prospective employees being unwilling to walk away from a "take it or leave it" contract. This will be particularly the case in larger organizations. As Mancur Olson observed, "unions are naturally supposed to have the greatest function to perform in the large factory, where there can be no personal relationships between employer and employee."[16] To the extent that such preferences are not incorporated into the negotiation process, they will be reflected in higher decision costs. In the Arrowian perspective, the union provides a platform for the aggregation of preferences to be communicated to the employer at arm's length. In truth, however, it is not possible to aggregate individual preferences because these are subjective. Further, it will take time to discover these preferences, and preferences can be transient. Nevertheless, unions provide a platform for ongoing communication. Employee solidarity and the potential threat of strike action or other legal enforcement through the courts—the monopoly face of unionism—add strength to the voice. This is true also of establishing defined grievance procedures under collective bargaining, where union officials may represent employees. In this scenario, voice is a strengthened alternative available to unhappy employees instead of exit—that is, quitting their positions and seeking work elsewhere. Decision costs are reduced on the employer's part by retaining staff and reducing turnover.

The second reason that a collective voice will be more effective than individual negotiation, according to Freeman and Medoff, is that many aspects of working conditions are necessarily shared.[17] The consequence of this is that any positive or negative changes in working conditions will affect all of the employees within a workplace. For example,

Safety conditions, lighting, heating, the speed of a production line, the firm's policies on layoffs, work-sharing, cyclical-wage adjustment, and promotion, its formal grievance procedure and pension plan-all obviously affect the entire workforce in the same way. [18]

Freeman and Medoff note that an individual has limited incentives to invest the time and cost of negotiating these conditions when the benefits and costs will be shared with others. [19] Again, there are decision costs here to the extent that a worker's preferences are not incorporated in the negotiation process. Interestingly, one of the key advantages for workers in the digital workplace is a higher degree of flexibility for workers and a higher degree of autonomy over their place of work and the physical working conditions. [20] This predicts that the decision costs in the digital working environment will be lower than traditional forms of employment. Nevertheless, Freeman and Medoff argue that collective voice is required to overcome the "externality" and "public good" effects of the collective nature of work. Without a collective voice, it is argued, it is unlikely there will be any individual action.

However, introducing collective action creates its own "free-rider" problem: individuals can obtain the benefits of union action without necessarily needing to participate themselves. Mancur Olson in *The Logic of Collective Action* starts from the proposition that "the essence of an organization that it provides an inseparable, generalized benefit."[21] Specifically commenting on labor unions, Olson explained that

> Unions are for "collective bargaining," not individual bargaining. It follows that most of the achievements of a union, even if they were more impressive than the staunchest unionist claims, could offer the rational worker no incentive to join; his individual efforts would not have a noticeable effect on the outcome, and whether he supported the union or not he would still get the benefits of its achievements. [22]

Olson notes that, historically, the solution to the free-rider problem in labor unions has been coercion—requiring individuals to become members of labor unions. [23] Indeed the history of the union movement is a story from coercion of one type to another. In the union movement's infancy in the industrial revolution, there was the threat of government coercion to prevent collective bargaining. The present challenge is the threat of law providing unions with a privileged position by limiting the economic freedom of individuals. On this point, writing in 1960, Friedrich Hayek observed that

> Public policy concerning labor unions has, in little more than a century, moved from one extreme to another. From a state in which little the unions could do was legal if they were not prohibited altogether, we have now reached a state where they become uniquely privileged institutions to which the general rules of law do not apply. [24]

Coercion can take a variety of different forms and extremes. Examples include enforced picket lines, compulsory membership through closed shops, compulsory agency fees, secondary boycotts, rights of entry for union officials, mandatory representation or recognition, and so on. All of these actions suppress the individual property right in labor. However, Hayek predicted that a system based on coercion could not sustain itself in the long run for two reasons.[25] The first reason was due to the inflationary pressures caused by above-productivity wage increases coupled with expansionary monetary policy to maintain full employment. Unless coercion was addressed, the problem would get so great there would be calls "either for the fixing of wages by government or for the complete abolition of unions."[26] Indeed, the inflation problem came to pass in the late 1970s and early 1980s—motivating actions from governments at either end of this spectrum. For instance, Margaret Thatcher's government in the United Kingdom passed laws curtailing the power of labor union officials—requiring ballots of members to approve strike action.[27] In Australia, Bob Hawke—himself a former president of the peak union body the Australian Council of Trade Unions—entered into the Prices and Income Accord, a series of agreements with the union movement to fix wages.[28]

According to Hayek, the second reason that a system of coercion couldn't sustain itself was that eliminating a functioning market mechanism for wage setting necessitates a central government authority.[29] According to Hayek, this would require unions having to make a choice between "becoming the willing instrument of government policy and being incorporated into the machinery of government, on the one hand, and being totally abolished, on the other."[30] On this point there is evidence of the cosy relationship between unions and employer organizations—aided by central governments—making "sweetheart deals" that benefit union officials over workers. For instance, Gerard Henderson documents how historically "Industrial relations in Australia [took] place in club-like atmosphere."[31] Such is the consequence of weak market mechanisms.

What does this all mean for decision making within trade unions? One consequence is that union decision making has become less polycentric over time. Rather than individual unions focused on industrial outcomes and providing workers with a voice to govern their own arrangements in individual workplaces, the focus of the union movement has instead become focused on achieving high-level and centralized political outcomes that impact an entire industry or even the whole economy. Strong lines of demarcation results in no competition between unions for workers in some occupations and professions: members are prevented from exiting and voting with their feet. Union officials are sheltered, allowing them to be more concerned with their own power and positions rather than representing the interests of workers. In other words, coercive protection by the state ends up, in the long run, becoming a cause of the problems with trade union governance.

One key omission from the analysis so far is the impact of technological change. Economic development has driven employment in advanced economies away from heavy manufacturing—where the power to organize and union dominance is strongest—and toward the professional services sector. Because new businesses are able to emerge without the baggage of entrenched and coercive union agreements, these external factors cannot be understated.

With these factors in mind, the rates of union membership have declined across the Western world over the last three decades. Of course, there are exceptions in some industries and in some regions—but at an aggregate level a clear general downward trend can be observed. For instance:

- In Australia, the proportion of trade union members as a percentage of the total workforce has fallen from 49 percent in 1982 to 14.5 percent in 2016.[32]
- In Canada, rates of membership have moderately declined from 38 percent of the workforce in 1981 to around 30 percent in 2017—boosted by high coverage rates of approximately 75 percent in the public sector.[33]
- In Great Britain, trade union density reached a height of 55 percent in 1979 before falling sharply to 41 percent by 1989, followed by a steady decline to 22.9 percent in 2017.[34]
- In the United States, union membership was 20.1 percent in 1983 and has fallen steadily to just 12 percent in 2017.[35]

These trends have led to something of an existential crisis for the labor union movement. And there has been no shortage of introspection from the movement and fellow travelers.[36] One dominant strategy to arrest the membership decline was to merge. The literature distinguishes between *amalgamation* (the merger of two or more unions to form a new union) and *absorption* (the merger of one union into another).[37] For our purposes they provide the same effect; there are economies of scale in that larger unions can devote more resources to representation and provide members with a more powerful voice inside the workplace and in the broader political environment. This aids reducing the decision costs of forming employment agreements.

However, there are trade-offs. Some of the criticisms of the merger strategy include that "Industry-based amalgamations . . . implicitly assume that members' needs within the major industry divisions are largely undifferentiated."[38] It is not clear that this will always be the case, and raises the prospect that union officials will not have the knowledge of members' preferences to represent them effectively. On this point, "super-unions" have been criticized as being "too far removed from their members to be able to respond to their members' needs."[39] These concerns reflect increasing agency costs in this institutional possibility. As unions grow, there becomes a greater disconnect between individual members and union officials. This problem becomes most manifest in abuses of positions within labor unions—another factor that has surely contributed to the downward trajectory of trade union membership.

Agency problems arise from the traditional union model, where members delegate negotiating power to union officials. As we have seen, the union model works by threatening to restrict the supply of labor (the monopoly face) in order to achieve higher rates of pay and better working conditions (the voice face). There is a clear analogy here with representative democracy. Labor unions work by employees electing or appointing union officials as their representatives. Union officials then exercise power to negotiate with employers. A key difference is that legislative rules for finalizing collective agreements may or may not dictate that all employees need to vote on the agreement. This democratic model is far from perfect. For instance, employees may be members of the union under coercion or employees may be covered by a union agreement but have no voting power within the union, while there are difficulties in monitoring whether officials have properly understood and then faithfully represented employees' preferences on particular issues of concern. While this is far from an exhaustive list, it is through these imperfections in the representation model that provides the space for corruption in this process.

Governance problems and union leaders abusing powers are not new phenomena. However, Australia provides a compelling case study following a recent Royal Commission that examined governance and corruption in six Australian trade unions.[40] A Royal Commission is the highest form of public inquiry in Australia, and a Commissioner has quasi-judicial powers including compelling witnesses to appear to give evidence under oath and requiring parties to produce documents. The Royal Commission into Trade Union Governance and Corruption was established in March 2014. The Commissioner, retired High Court Justice Dyson Heydon, handed down an interim report on December 15, 2014 and a final report on December 28, 2015.[41] The Commission sat for approximately twenty-one months. There were 189 hearing days, and 505 individual witnesses were examined. The final report spans six volumes, providing a plethora of real-world examples about the worst of agency costs associated with labor unions.

The Royal Commission revealed systemic misconduct. This included numerous instances of spending union funds for private purposes—such as purchasing luxury cars, funding private travel, constructing personal holiday houses, and even payment for sex services. It also made allegations of criminal conduct such as bribery. The Royal Commission also investigated the widespread use of "slush funds," which are essentially off-the-book bank accounts with union members' money, with the Commissioner's interim report explaining

> Funds of this kind pose significant governance issues. The officials who operate those funds owe statutory and general duties to the union. On the other hand, the officials deploy their energy and sometimes their employer's resources for the benefit of the fund. This gives rise to actual or potential conflicts of interest. Often these funds have no or no adequate record keeping. Management decisions are made informally or without due process. Directors' or shareholders' meetings are not held. If they are held, minutes are not kept. Transactions are often effected by cash. When records are maintained, they are often maintained in a haphazard fashion. [42]

A specific type of slush fund is a "fighting fund" or an "election fund" which union officials use for their own reelection. This practice is problematic for democratic outcomes within labor unions where "members contributions are not truly voluntary" because it is designed to entrench control by the incumbent officials. [43] As highlighted above, this can be facilitated by parties not keeping proper records. Worse, in other cases the Commission uncovered conduct masked by the creation of false invoices, or where records that did exist had been destroyed. This is a democratic problem within labor unions because members are unable to make decisions based on the true state of affairs.

A related issue uncovered by the Royal Commission in Australia was the practice of falsely reporting union membership numbers. These records are obviously important for the integrity of internal union elections. But they are also important for representation with peak union bodies and in political parties that have formal links to labor unions such as the Labour Party in the United Kingdom and the Australian Labor Party.

Of course, none of the above examples should be interpreted that employers are always innocent parties. The Royal Commission uncovered a number of examples where it was in the employer's interest to contribute to slush funds to buy industrial peace. These "sweetheart deals" saw secret payments allegedly made to union officials in exchange for trading away workers' entitlement. For example, one union and a cleaning company agreed to extend a collective agreement that saved the company an estimated $2 million in wages ". . . in exchange for paying [the union] $25,000 per year and provided lists of 100 bogus 'members.'" [44] One aspect of the coercive "club" relationship with unions is that it may be convenient for employers to deal with a single union and have a single set of employment obligations for all workers within the business, lowering the transaction costs of hiring new workers. But these actions compromise internal democratic outcomes of labor unions by increasing agency costs.

In summarizing his findings, Commissioner Heydon commented that "These aberrations cannot be regarded as isolated. They are not the work of a few rogue unions, or a few rogue officials. The misconduct exhibits great variety. It is widespread. It is deep-seated."[45] Again, this conduct occurs in the shadows provided by coercion.

At this point we find ourselves at an important fork in the road. A collective voice lowers decision costs in the employment contracts choice. A representative model of union representation makes it possible that a greater number of preferences are taken into account in making collective decisions about working conditions. The collective voice provides workers with a less costly mechanism for exercising their individual property rights in their labor. However, positive externalities mean that coercion is required to force free riders to contribute to the collective benefit. The long-run pressures of coercion and a declining membership density have ultimately undermined the collective voice of workers and have led to a number of observable agency costs. Those that are sensitive to these agency costs will be tempted to lobby for legislative interventions to increase the relative costs of organizing and collective bargaining. While this legislation might be aimed at making labor unions more democratic, it is arguable that imposing constitutional rules and additional regulations could actually take decision-making power away from union members. On the other hand, those more sensitive to decision costs are will be tempted to change the law to increase the relative cost of engaging individual contactors. For example, in the face of the sharing economy there has been an effort in a number of jurisdictions from unions to classify ride-sharing (e.g., Uber, Lyft, etc.) drivers as employees rather than independent contracts—among other calls for a hybrid category of "dependent worker" with mandatory minimum conditions.[46] While these actions might be well intentioned, if successful, the law takes away choice and individual autonomy over working conditions and will centralize employment decision making.

There is a third alternative. Our DIPF model is dynamic and predicts that technological change has an impact on the governance of traditional institutions including labor unions. What new possibilities does blockchain open up that could strengthen collective action without relying on coercion? In the following section we outline three new institutional possibilities in the cryptodemocratic labor union.

HOW COULD LABOR UNIONS UTILIZE BLOCKCHAIN?

A recent discussion paper from the United Kingdom's Trades Union Congress is generally positive about taking up new technology to deliver greater benefits to workers.[47] Blockchain technology, however, is not canvassed in the paper. It is at this point that we can move to detailing a number of applications for blockchain technology that have relevance for the way that labor unions are governed. In this section we focus on applications of blockchain within the tasks of unions as they currently exist, before exploring how blockchain fundamentally changes union governance in latter sections. Our prediction is that the application of blockchain limits the worst of the agency costs within labor unions while also allowing new solutions for worker protection inside labor markets including recording membership information, processing financial transactions, and building new human resource or payroll systems.

The first possible application of blockchain is to transform the way that membership records are kept. Institutional cryptoeconomics recognizes the central role that ledgers have played in society throughout history. For the labor union the most basic ledger is membership. The membership list is a record of all those people that have been accepted and met the conditions of membership. This is analogous to decisions around forming the franchise in the political environment. These conditions might include paying their union dues. Other relevant ledgers concern those listing those people with rights within the organization, a record of those people that are entitled to run for and hold official positions, and a record of those that have a stake in the collective employment agreements in a workplace or industry.

Union membership records are currently kept and maintained on a centralized union database. Privacy concerns require that only certain officials have permission to access the stored information and make any necessary amendments. The union secretariat functions as a trusted intermediary; members trust that the records will be accurately recorded, not improperly manipulated, or otherwise used for improper purposes. Our brief review of the Australian Royal Commission highlighted that misconduct such as stacking or otherwise falsifying membership records is an actual rather than hypothetical risk. There are other reasons why trust in a central database may be low. For instance, organized workers in a remote online working environment may not be able to foster the same personal connections with union representatives as those on a building site or factory floor. So instead of storing membership records on a centralized database, labor unions could implement a decentralized blockchain-based membership system. Such a system could work on a permissioned network, where unions could maintain privacy and control.

The immediate advantage of a decentralized membership record will be that it guards against manipulation because any changes would be append-only, auditable, and require consensus of the network according to an established protocol. As a practical note, many labor unions currently operate with a centralized secretariat but have a distributed branch or divisional structure. Here, the nodes of the distributed union network could be maintained by

existing branches of a union without needing to maintain a separate centralized register of members.

A second possible application of blockchain is for handling financial
transactions. The main agency cost observed here is the misuse of union
funds for private and other unauthorized purposes. This could be ameliorated
through smart contracts (agreements or parts of agreements that are written
into code and can be executed when specific conditions are validated). The
concept of smart contracting dates several decades.[48] However, blockchain-
enabled networks function as a new architecture for contracting to take place.
For instance, in August 2018, global law firm Herbert Smith Freehills, along
with Data61 and IBM, announced that they are in the process of jointly
developing a trusted platform for blockchain-based smart contracts for Australian businesses.[49] Labor unions could leverage off these developments
rather than needing to build their own platforms. Smart contracting could
function as a way for union members to achieve tighter financial control over
officials. For instance, in some cases spending could be completely automat-
ed. Other discretionary spending measures could be paid subject to the approval of a majority of members. The record of the transactions would be
recorded, providing real-time transparency.

A third possibility is that unions could become a voice for implementing
technology within businesses and governments to achieve better outcomes
for workers. For example, collective employment agreements, or other mandated centralized wage awards, could be stored on a blockchain and coded to
standardized smart contracts to transform payroll systems, thereby ensuring
employees are paid their full entitlements. Unions are pejoratively labeling
this "wage theft," although in truth it is a basic issue of ex-post contract
enforceability. In this system, courts or tribunals could act as "oracles" in the
event of a dispute. There are also problems in enforcing ethical employment
practices in the international supply chain. Two of us, along with colleagues
at RMIT University, have previously written about the potential of blockchain for supply chains.[50] In this application, the union acts as a voice to
drive down decision costs—whereas the first two possibilities reshape
governance from the agency cost perspective. The adoption of this technology within labor unions could see a new type of collective action emerge. In
the final section of the chapter, we examine how blockchain technology can
be applied to the governance of labor unions in a new institutional possibility
we call cryptodemocratic labor unions.

TOWARD A CRYPTODEMOCRATIC LABOR UNION

In previous chapters we have argued that collective decision making is constrained by prevailing technologies. This means that the way that collective

decisions are made within organizations will change when technology changes. If unions take advantage of blockchain technology, collective bargaining may become a more attractive institutional possibility for a greater number of workers. However, greater transparency and accountability shifts control over collective organization from union officials to union members and increases the scope for new forms of collective action to emerge. In this respect, there is an analogy between the potential adoption of blockchain and the adoption of other Information and Communication Technologies (ICT).

Over the last two decades, many unions have harnessed the power of the internet to provide information to workers on demand. It was predicted that ICT would enhance union democracy.[51] In our DIPF model, this can be explained by the use of web platforms and email communications driving down decision costs of collective bargaining.

For instance, union websites have assisted in recruiting new members and increasing member participation. Diamond and Freeman argued that ICT provided the capability of arming all members with relevant information "rather than just the few who attend a union meeting" and allowed members a greater ability to communicate their views to the union leadership.[52] But websites also provided a platform for new possibilities of organizing. For example, UNISON—a large union in the United Kingdom—used ICT to form several "virtual" union branches.[53] Participation is central to democratic outcomes, and it has been argued that ICT allows greater input from women and other minority workers that have barriers to trade union participation.[54] In other contexts, ICT provided the possibility of gaining access to new workplaces that did not have collective bargaining representation.[55]

Email databases provided another tool for unions to organize workers. Email is significantly cheaper than the traditional option of hardcopy print handouts or postal mail, therefore increasing the amount and frequency of union communication.[56] Email can provide targeted information directly to workers, without intermediaries, and in real time. Such functionality is important in the context of dynamic enterprise bargaining negotiations or industrial disputes. Another benefit of online organizing is bypassing the workplace; union activity can be shielded from the view of management.[57]

However, the effect of ICT on agency costs on unions is questionable because of the centralized nature of the union machine. For instance, Sandra Cockfield, in a case study on an Australian union, observed that the "most obvious problem with the web site, and one that limits its democratic possibilities the most, is the over-reliance on one person, to keep it up-to-date."[58] There is a similar integration problem with e-voting. Although the internet has reduced the cost of polling union members and has the potential to increase voter turnout (decision costs), the centralized representative hierarchies and record keeping have remained (agency costs). Likewise, while social media is another new web-based tool to provide information and organize members, it has been recognized that it is difficult to integrate these tools into centralized internal decision-making structures. [59]

At the beginning of the internet age, optimists saw the potential of "e-unions" or "cyber-unions" to emerge as new forms of collective action. [60] For instance, Diamond and Freeman predicted that in the future "unions will deal with free-rider problems by customizing services to members only, and will operate in a more decentralized, member-driven manner."[61] Similarly, Freeman and Joel Rogers foresaw "open-source" unionism based on

> . . . a common collaborative platform, language, and practice among workers and union activists—often operating at some distance from one another, or at different work sites, or moving across multiple sites over their working life-times—as part of a more unified labor movement defined by shared values more than by present employment. [62]

Those authors classified union democracy in a traditional union as being "'heavily bureaucratic,' 'top-down,' and 'unresponsive,'" as compared to an 'open-source union' which would provide 'stronger' democracy with 'members able to force greater accountability by leaders . . . and more decentralised political governance.'"[63]

This change has not occurred yet. As we have shown, unions remain centralized power structures with associated high agency costs. But at the beginning of the blockchain age there are reasons to remain optimistic that these visions may be realized. Membership lists and financial tracking, discussed in the previous section, are the basic infrastructure of a labor union. Blockchain could be used to make these things operate more efficiently. Alternatively, blockchain could open up entirely new forms of collective action to emerge a *cryptodemocratic labor union*.

Entrepreneurs are central to new ways of organizing emerging and disrupting traditional labor unions. One proposal for a decentralized union, *UnionD*, was pitched to the 2016 Consensus Hackathon in New York by Jonathan Hamel, Hugh O'Connor, Thomas Sarek, and Scott Morris. [64] The creation of a tokenized eco-system would continue to provide both the "voice" and "monopoly" aspects of unionism. That is, the platform could facilitate communications, claims and arbitrations (voice), negotiations (monopoly), and other value-added services such as insurance. [65] Under this model, people could be popularly elected by members for "special roles." In their example, a treasurer would be given authorization to spend union funds under a multi-signatory account. Another aspect of this proposal was delegated democracy. In our conception, the ability to decompose and delegate votes would be a defining feature of a cryptodemocratic labor union.

Cryptodemocratic labor unions would reshape employment decision making toward polycentric governance. For example, members could disaggregate employment agreements. Rather than collective agreements being presented on a take it or leave it basis after they have been substantively negotiated by union officials, members could have input on a clause-by-clause basis. Members could also choose to split their votes on a collective employment agreement—delegating wage and salary conditions to one delegate, working hours to a second, dispute resolution to a third, and so on.

A delegative democratic ecosystem furthers polycentricism inside the union movement too. For instance, each delegate could offer a different combination of representation, negotiation, or dispute resolution services. Alternatively, delegates could specialize in a particular area. Additionally, members could choose to associate based on skills and interests rather than workplaces or geographic areas (a point made by *UnionD* proponents).[66] A consequence of polycentric collective action is a much greater level of choice and competition for workers.

A stated feature of the *UnionD* pitch was that workers would have portability of their data and reputations. This may provide greater stability to those workers in online, freelance, and "gig economy" environments. Further, it has been argued that one consequence of the "fissuring" of the workplace is less bargaining power for workers and less collective action.[67] A cryptodemocratic labor union could push back against this and lead to greater levels of collective action along fragmented vertical supply chains.

It is important to note that *UnionD* provides us with just one example. There is no single type of cryptodemocratic labor union. Constitutional rules and incentive design—protocols—will be important. Of course, there are also legislative barriers in that these new employment arrangements need to be legally recognized and enforceable.[68] But it sharpens our understanding of how new institutional possibilities will emerge. Union officials are reimagined as entrepreneurs—actively seeking out opportunities for discourse, coordination, and mutually beneficial exchange between workers and businesses. In one sense, cryptodemocratic labor unions may take on a form similar to labor hire firms. In another sense, ordinary workers may have access to a service akin to the professional agents that only professional athletes or Hollywood stars can afford. In any case, we can move to making a number of general observations comparing traditional labor unions with new possibilities.

In a traditional labor union, coercion solves the free-rider problem at the expense of agency problems. As we have detailed earlier in this chapter, there are positive externalities requiring legal or social coercion to make collective bargaining work. That is, the increased pay and conditions that unions exact from negotiation with employers are not captured exclusively by trade union members. Historically, it is difficult to exclude non-members from enjoying these benefits. The solution to that is to force workers to collectively organize; the externality is coerced onto them. Workers are forced to join or support labor unions, but they have limited or no choice about which labor union to join, are prevented from strike-breaking, or are required to pay fees to a union because they are covered by an employment agreement negotiated by the union. In a traditional union, warring factions and contested elections provide a check on the power of officials. However, an inherent lack of inter-union competition means workers do not have a choice about their bargaining representatives. As we have seen in the corporate setting, unhappy shareholders can sell their shares. Unhappy union members are limited in their ability to join another union. Throughout history, the coercive power of the state has been used to counter the coercive practices of unions. The major problem with both types of coercive action is that it does not respect individual liberty—the individual property right in labor.

In a cryptodemocratic labor union, the ability to decompose membership rights, delegate, and bargain enables collective decision making by way of compensation instead of coercion. That is, by tokenizing membership, the incentive structure changes. For example, bargaining can occur between those passive members that receive the benefits from collective action and those members that actively contribute and wear greater costs. Although we do not discount the possibility that organizers might provide incentives for other workers to join the union. In any case, it means that members can decide how much of the union services that they want to consume. It also means that membership of the organization would have its own tangible value, capable of being exchanged. A greater depth of interaction allows an opportunity for greater discovery of preferences. Importantly, a blockchain mechanism enables this bargaining to occur on a delegated peer-to-peer basis rather than an aggregative or representative manner. This allows union members to choose their own trade-off between decision costs and agency costs. Practically, it would be possible for a cryptodemocratic labor union to be integrated into human resource systems and online work platforms. This would further limit spill-over effects and greater enable collective action to be more exclusive to union members.

Finally, in a cryptodemocratic labor union there is the ability to exit and form new decentralized organizations. Forking is an inherent feature of the blockchain ecosystem.[69] This is where the protocol splits and changes in some way; a shared transaction history remains intact but there is no ability to exchange between the new strands. Applied in this setting, entrepreneurs could "cryptosecede" and develop a distinct protocol to govern a new decentralized organization.[70] Of course, there would be high transaction costs involved in this process—and those forked decentralized organizations may well be short lived, or exist only for a specific purpose. For example, entrepreneurial union organizers may see an opportunity to collectively organize workers in an emerging market—a "Greenfields" agreement. This implies that cryptodemocratic labor unions will be smaller, polycentric, and more direct.

There is no certainty about what forms cryptodemocratic labor unions will ultimately take. However, by way of summary, we can predict a number of defining features. First, cryptodemocratic labor unions for collective bargaining will emerge through entrepreneurial action. Second, blockchain enables delegation, bargaining, and exchange to occur, incentivising collective action and keeping union organizers accountable in real time. Third, these dynamic organizations will foster polycentric governance, better tailored to the preferences of workers in new economic environments.

CONCLUSION

In this chapter we have examined the case of employment contracts and labor union governance as a second case study in applying cryptodemocratic principles to lower-level collective decision making. This chapter moves beyond strictly voting to consider the trade-offs involved in decision making within other democratic organizations. Our starting point was that each individual worker faces a choice about how to exchange his or her labor and many will opt for some type of employment contract. But how the terms and conditions of the employment contract are determined will also be a matter of institutional choice. Employees and employers may not be completely free to determine these institutional arrangements for themselves as workplace and industrial relations are often a highly regulated space. Nevertheless, in this chapter we applied the DIPF to employment bargaining to show a spectrum of institutional possibilities including individual contracts, collective bargaining at the enterprise level, and centralized wage fixing. Our principal focus was on collective bargaining, where we observed having union (or other employee representatives) negotiate wages and conditions lowers the decision costs of forming and enforcing employment agreements for both employees and employers. However, collective bargaining through union officials presents an increase in agency costs, as compared to individual contracting. The "free rider" problem means that unions rely on coercive practices to drive and maintain collective action. Employees are forced to become union members or are otherwise locked into union deals—and are unable to exit to another union. We have proposed that the long-run result of these coercive practices (combined with technological change) has been a decline in union membership figures and heightened agency costs, as evidenced by case study data from the recent Australian Royal Commission into Trade Union Governance and Corruption.

There are many challenges facing workers in the modern economy. Rather than resort to coercive practices, we proposed two possibilities that blockchain could improve governance and spur greater levels of collective action. First, existing labor unions could implement blockchain for membership records, financial transactions, and negotiated employment agreements. Second, a new type of collective decision making—a cryptodemocratic labor union—could emerge echoing previous calls for "e-unions" and "open source unions." This new collective bargaining will be dynamic and foster the formation of polycentric governance structures. Having considered two practical examples, in this chapter and the previous chapter, our next chapter will provide a summary and wider reflection of cryptodemocracy and its institutional possibilities.

NOTES

1. Sidney Webb and Beatrice Webb, *The History of Trade Unionism*, revised edition, extended to 1920 ed. (Longmans, Green and Co., 1920), 8.
2. John Locke, "Two Treatises of Government," (London: A. Millar et al., 1764).
3. Pope Leo XII, "Rerum Novarum," (1891), n. 5.
4. This point is classically illustrated by Leonard E. Reed, "I, Pencil."
5. Oliver E. Williamson, "The Economics of Organization: The Transaction Cost Approach," *American Journal of Sociology* 87, no. 3 (1981).
6. This builds on Oliver Williamson's *The Economic Institutions of Capitalism*.
7. For a broader discussion of this point, see David H. Autor, "Wiring the Labor Market," *Journal of Economic Perspectives* 15, no. 1 (2001).
8. Xin Wang et al., "Human Resource Information Management Model Based on Blockchain Technology" (paper presented at the Service-Oriented System Engineering [SOSE], 2017 IEEE Symposium on, 2017).
9. This decision is known as an "award."
10. See Hayek, "The Use of Knowledge in Society."
11. Richard B. Freeman and James L. Medoff, "The Two Faces of Unionism," *The Public Interest* (1979).
12. Ibid., 71.
13. Margaret Levi et al., "Union Democracy Reexamined," *Politics and Society* 37, no. 2 (2009): 204.
14. Ibid.
15. Ibid., 72.
16. Mancur Olson, *The Logic of Collective Action*, vol. 124 (Harvard University Press, 2009), 66.
17. Freeman and Medoff, "The Two Faces of Unionism," 71.
18. Ibid.
19. Ibid.
20. See Jon Messenger et al., *Working Anytime, Anywhere: The Effects on the World of Work* (Publications Office of the European Union, 2017).
21. Olson, *The Logic of Collective Action*, 124, 15.
22. Ibid., 76.
23. Ibid.
24. Friedrich A. Hayek, *The Constitution of Liberty* (London: Routledge and Kegan Paul, 1960), 267.
25. For this discussion, see ibid., 279–83.
26. Ibid., 282.
27. "Trade Union Act 1984," (UK1984).

28. For a good explainer, see Anthony Forsyth and Carolyn Holbrook, "Australian Politics Explainer: The Prices and Incomes Accord," (2017), https://theconversation.com/australian-politics-explainer-the-prices-and-incomes-accord-75622.

29. Hayek, *The Constitution of Liberty*, 282–83. See also "The Use of Knowledge in Society."

30. *The Constitution of Liberty*, 283.

31. Gerard Henderson, "The Industrial Relations Club," *Quadrant* 27, no. 9 (1983). See also *The Return of the Industrial Relations Club*, podcast audio, Forest: Minerals Council of Australia, accessed September 10, 2018, http://podcast.thesydneyinstitute.com.au/podcasts/Other/MCA_The%20return%20of%20the%20Industrial%20Relations%20Club_WEB.pdf.

32. Australian Bureau of Statistics, "Characteristics of Employment (Cat. No. 6333)," (2017); "Trade Union Members in Australia (Cat. No. 6325)"; "Employee Earnings, Benefits and Trade Union Membership Australia (Cat. No. 6310)."

33. Statistics Canada, "Description for Chart 1: Unionization Rates of Employed Individuals Aged 17 to 64, 1981 to 2012," https://www150.statcan.gc.ca/n1/pub/75-006-x/2013001/article/11878/c-g/desc/desc01-eng.htm.

34. Bob Mason and Peter Bain, "The Determinants of Trade Union Membership in Britain: A Survey of the Literature," *Industrial and Labor Relations Review* 46, no. 2 (1993); Department for Business, Energy, and Industrial Strategy, "Trade Union Membership 2017: Statistical Bulletin," (2018).

35. Bureau of Labor Statistics, "Union Members—2017," news release, January 19, 2018, https://www.bls.gov/news.release/pdf/union2.pdf; Megan Dunn and James Walker, "Union Membership in the United States," (US Bureau of Labor Statistics, 2016).

36. For example of the academic literature, see the edited volumes compiled by British Industrial Relations Professor Gregor Gall: Gregor Gall, ed., *Union Recognition: Organising and Bargaining Outcomes* (Routledge, 2006); *Union Revitalisation in Advanced Economies: Assessing the Contribution of Union Organising* (Palgrave, 2009); *The Future of Union Organising: Building for Tomorrow* (Palgrave, 2009).

37. Gary N. Chaison, "A Note on Union Merger Trends, 1900–1978," *Industrial and Labor Relations Review* 34, no. 1 (1980): 116.

38. Mark Wooden, "Union Amalgamations and the Decline in Union Density," *Journal of Industrial Relations* 41, no. 1 (1999): 36.

39. Ibid.

40. The Australian Workers Union; the Construction Forestry Mining and Energy Union; the Communications Electrical, Electronic, Energy, Information, Postal, Plumbing, and Allied Services Union of Australia; the Health Services Union, the Transport Workers Union of Australia; and the National Union of Workers.

41. Commonwealth of Australia, "Royal Commission into Trade Union Governance and Corruption, Final Report," (2015); "Royal Commission into Trade Union Governance and Corruption, Interim Report," (2014).

42. "Royal Commission into Trade Union Governance and Corruption, Interim Report," 22.

43. "Royal Commission into Trade Union Governance and Corruption, Final Report," 37.

44. Ibid., 26.

45. Ibid., 12.

46. For example, see Miriam A. Cherry and Antonio Aloisi, "Dependent Contractors in the Gig Economy: A Comparative Approach," *American University Law Review* 66, no. 3 (2016).

47. Trade Union Congress, "Shaping Our Digital Future," (2017).

48. See Szabo, "The Idea of Smart Contracts."

49. Herbert Smith Freehills, "Herbert Smith Freehills, 'Data61 and Ibm Create Consortium to Deliver Smart Legal Contracts on Blockchain to Australian Businesses," (2018), https://www.herbertsmithfreehills.com/latest-thinking/herbert-smith-freehills-data61-and-ibm-create-consortium-to-deliver-smart-legal.

50. Allen et al., "Blockchain Tradetech."

51. See Wayne J. Diamond and Richard B. Freeman, "Will Unionism Prosper in Cyberspace? The Promise of the Internet for Employee Organization," *British Journal of Industrial Relations* 40, no. 3 (2002).

52. Ibid., 583.

53. Allan Kerr and Jeremy Waddington, "E-Communications: An Aspect of Union Renewal or Merely Doing Things Electronically?" *British Journal of Industrial Relations*, 52, no. 4 (2014).

54. Anne-Marie Greene and Gill Kirton, "Possibilities for Remote Participation in Trade Unions: Mobilising Women Activists," *Industrial Relations Journal* 34, no. 4 (2003).

55. Richard B. Freeman and Joel Rogers, "Open Source Unionism: Beyond Exclusive Collective Bargaining," *WorkingUSA* 5, no. 4 (2002).

56. Diamond and Freeman, "Will Unionism Prosper in Cyberspace? The Promise of the Internet for Employee Organization."

57. Freeman and Rogers, "Open Source Unionism: Beyond Exclusive Collective Bargaining."

58. Sandra Cockfield, "Union Renewal, Union Strategy and Technology," *Critical Perspectives on International Business* 1, no. 2–3 (2005): 104.

59. See, for example, Martin Upchurch and Rickard Grassman, "Striking with Social Media: The Contested (Online) Terrain of Workplace Conflict," *Organization* 23, no. 5 (2016).

60. These are reviewed in Cockfield, "Union Renewal, Union Strategy and Technology."

61. Diamond and Freeman, "Will Unionism Prosper in Cyberspace? The Promise of the Internet for Employee Organization," 592.

62. Freeman and Rogers, "Open Source Unionism: Beyond Exclusive Collective Bargaining," 13.

63. Ibid., 16.

64. UnionD Project, "Uniond—Consensus 2016 Hackathon Nyc Final Pitch," https://www.youtube.com/watch?v=bFC6H6urtvw.

65. Another example, not considered in the UnionD pitch, could be implementing a "universal basic income" for union members.

66. UnionD, "#Uniond," GitHub, https://github.com/btalabs/uniond.

67. David Weil, *The Fissured Workplace: Why Work Became So Bad for So Many and What Can Be Done to Improve It* (Cambridge: Harvard University Press, 2017).

68. A point made in relation to e-voting. See Diamond and Freeman, "Will Unionism Prosper in Cyberspace? The Promise of the Internet for Employee Organization."

69. Although the concept of forking can be seen in other societal contexts. For a discussion see Berg and Berg, "Exit, Voice, and Forking."

70. See Allen, "Entrepreneurial Exit: Developing the Cryptoeconomy."

Chapter Eight

The Future of a Cryptodemocracy

WHAT IS A CRYPTODEMOCRACY?

This chapter summarizes the cryptodemocratic framework we have proposed in this book before exploring the ways in which democratic governance might evolve. A cryptodemocracy ordered through blockchain technology lays the foundations for more emergent, evolutionary, and polycentric democratic orderings. We focus on the emergent properties of a cryptodemocracy as propelled through political entrepreneurship, as well as the potential use of other new technologies in a cryptodemocracy. We begin by summarizing our definition of a cryptodemocracy. Then in the second section we examine how a cryptodemocracy might evolve through a process of political entrepreneurship, both from the perspective of delegates and from voters. The final section provides future directions and concludes.

The economic problem of democracy is to coordinate dispersed subjective preferences to make collective choices. Because of positive transaction costs societies implement democratic institutions. Over time the institutional structure that democracies take has been constrained by technologies available. New technologies open up new institutional possibilities within the Democratic Institutional Possibility Frontier (DIPF) space, enabling more effective democratic coordination and cooperation. In this book we have proposed that blockchain technology—as a technology for governing distributed ledgers of information—could be used to open up a new institutional possibility for collective action: a cryptodemocracy. A cryptodemocracy is a collective choice infrastructure on which individuals coordinate their voting property rights. In a cryptodemocracy voting property rights are governed through blockchain technology. In a cryptodemocracy votes are conceived as property rights that may be used to express political preferences. Blockchain technology enables voters to both delegate and conditionally decompose votes in a secure way. For instance, a voter may delegate certain decision-making powers to others while reserving his or her right to vote on particular issues and verify whether those conditions are fulfilled. Blockchains enable such agreements to be enforced more effectively by reducing the potential for *ex post* opportunistic behavior through smart contracts and facilitated by oracles. Rather than incorporating more people into the franchise, a cryptodemocracy deepens the franchise by extending the bundle of rights that may be exercised. A cryptodemocracy is a bespoke space of political and collective action. Voters hold a presumption of liberty in their voting rights and they may contract those rights as they wish. The structure of a democracy will evolve in a dynamic and polycentric way, conducive to knowledge coordination and discovery. We explore these characteristics below.

Votes Are Bundles Property Rights

In modern democracies voting rights are often highly constrained. Voting rights are connected to residence in particular geographical electorates, and are directed toward pre-selected representatives. There is rarely freedom to buy and sell votes, despite the centralized processes of logrolling and lobbying that occurs through representatives. Voters are constrained to voting at particular times and under particular institutional conditions, such as the secret ballot. In stark contrast a cryptodemocracy begins from the presumption that votes are allocated equally among the franchise, and the bundle of rights include the right to decompose, delegate, and bargain for compensation with others. There is a presumption of voter liberty over voter rights. To be sure, a society may choose to constrain those rights—either directly such as banning compensation, or indirectly through constitutional changes such as decision rules—but the latter is a collective choice.

Votes Are Governed through Blockchain Technology

The understanding that votes are property rights suggests that democracy becomes a process of contracting between voters. Following the basic understandings of institutional economics—that economic organization is required to economize on transaction costs and facilitate mutually beneficial exchange—in a cryptodemocracy blockchain technology is used to govern this contracting process. The immutability, transparency, and verifiability that blockchain technology provides lower transaction costs. Acting as a new collective choice infrastructure, blockchain lowers agency and decision costs for individuals to engage in collective choice, opening up the new institutional possibilities to structure decision making. Individuals cast, delegate, and receive compensation over voting rights through verifiable records on a blockchain, including by using smart contracts and oracles. That is, individuals are free to develop delegative smart contracts with conditions attached such that, if the delegate fails to fulfill his or her role based on information provided by some oracle, will revert the property rights back to the original rights holder.

The Structure of Collective Choice Will Be Emergent and Eynamic

The cryptodemocratic framework enables new polycentric orders of decision making to emerge through individual contracts between voters and delegates. A cryptodemocracy is analyzed through a contract-theoretic rather than a choice-theoretic lens of analysis. We do not focus on an optimal allocation of votes across the franchise, or on the grounds of Pareto efficiency. Rather, we approach cryptodemocracy as an institution for collective choice with the primary unit of analysis being delegates who transact voluntarily. This means that whatever structures exist within a cryptodemocracy are emergent orders stemming from the underlying subjective choices of individuals over how to best express and engage in collective choice. At a first approximation this decision will be the result of individual calculations attempting to minimize the dual costs of agency and decision costs of various courses of action. Indeed, individuals can decide whether to delegate their vote and to whom, to compensate a representative to act in a particular way, decomposing their voting rights and contracting them to different parties, or to simply cast a vote themselves. What this suggests, as we will see in the following section, is an emergent polycentric ordering of collective choice—with holdings of voting property rights as the basis of a constellation of contracts between voters.

A Cryptodemocracy Incentivizes Knowledge Coordination and Creation

Nobel Laureate Friedrich Hayek argued that the constraints and limits of democracy must be made based on an understanding of its purpose. Hayek argued that a primary benefit of democracy is in the formation of opinions. Put another way, preferences and the intensity of those preferences are not given; they emerge as a process of coordinating dispersed contextual knowledge with others. Preferences will evolve through time. When delegating and bargaining with others, individuals in a cryptodemocracy must engage in the process of negotiation and discourse. They must discuss and articulate the opportunity costs of the various paths of collective action. In particular, if a vote is delegated in return for compensation, this suggests that individuals have engaged with others who have different political views to their own—that is, an out-group. How this process will occur, we suspect, will be driven through the actions of a new form of political entrepreneur: the delegate. In efforts to make gains from exchange, delegates will seek to discover and persuade voters to engage in mutually beneficial exchange. For this reason a cryptodemocracy is more likely to have desirable epistemic properties from a Hayekian perspective.

In this book we not only developed the Democratic Institutional Possibility Frontier (DIPF) and theoretically examined a cryptodemocracy, we also applied these principles and understandings to the grounded examples of corporate governance and the governance of wage negotiation. In the corporate setting this showed that there are relatively high decision costs involved in corporate decision making that can be economized through delegation and exchange of voting rights. But shareholder voting rights could be strengthened by adopting cryptodemocratic corporate governance made possible by upcoming changes to share exchange settlement systems. We propose that this will lead to greater shareholder decision making—disrupting the historical power-sharing settlement of between shareholders and directors. In the labor context, we showed that individual workers are subject to coercive practices that economize decision costs but exacerbate agency costs. We propose a new type of polycentric collective action through cryptodemocratic labor unions where collective bargaining can occur without coercion—strengthening individual property rights over labor. Combined, these case examples show the potential for mutually beneficial exchange based on cryptodemocratic principles for collective decision making beyond the political environment. Indeed, we think that is probable that experimentation will first occur at lower levels of collective action such as these.

In the following section we outline some conjectures over how the cryptodemocratic process might progress, with a focus on entrepreneurial discovery—both by delegates seeking votes and by voters applying complementary technologies.

DISCOVERING DEMOCRACY

A cryptodemocracy is the collective choice infrastructure within which individuals may delegate voting property rights and bargain for compensation. We suggest that a cryptodemocracy is institutionally possible because of how blockchain lowers the transaction costs of exchange. But how would such a cryptodemocratic process work in practice? At what boundaries, and under what conditions, would people delegate their vote? How will voters develop and deploy smart contracts? Will new polycentric decision-making structures emerge, or would standard political parties retain their place in the political process?

The structure of collective action decision making is emergent within the cryptodemocratic institutional framework. A cryptodemocracy acts as collective choice infrastructure—the institutional rules of the game—within which voters exchange their property rights. What would emerge from the individual interactions of people through time is shrouded under uncertainty.[1] The way the democratic process will play out within these constraints will be evolutionary. Nevertheless, future analyses of a cryptodemocracy must always stem from a methodologically individualist perspective: only individual voters choose to delegate, compensate, and exchange votes with others, including the process of the decomposition of those voting rights. The structure of voting rights with a cryptodemocracy is organic and comes from a process of bargaining between voters and delegates. The institutions and structures that emerge within a cryptodemocracy will primarily be the result of efforts to entrepreneurially engage in mutually beneficial exchange.

The decentralized process of a cryptodemocracy suggests a new form of political entrepreneurship. In modern democracies political entrepreneurship is regularly associated with the process of lobbying. The political entrepreneur is tightly associated with rent seeking. Political entrepreneurs engage with policymakers through the demand and supply of regulation. But a cryptodemocracy incentivizes a new type of political entrepreneurship that is not focused solely on extracting rent from government, but from seeking mutually beneficial trades with peers. In a cryptodemocracy political entrepreneurship is both decentralized and voluntary. Political entrepreneurship within a cryptodemocracy includes any efforts to increase mutually beneficial exchange. In response to voters experiencing decision costs, for instance, delegates may be incentivized to create standardized open source delegative contracts. That is, delegates could write the code for various standardized contracts that assist voters in decomposing their vote in various ways. Secondary markets for votes might also emerge where votes are bundled together and where entrepreneurs can seek to act on arbitrage opportunities. If secondary markets emerge then votes may begin to incorporate some commission or compensation that is sent back to them for further delegates of their vote. In this way political entrepreneurs are incentivized to create private orderings that minimize the cost of delegation. What's important, however, is how the incentive structure of a cryptodemocracy pushes voters and delegates to create deeper information about preferences. That is, delegates themselves are incentivized to create private orderings that will minimize the costs of exchanging votes and therefore expand the number of mutually beneficial trades. Delegates effectively act as political entrepreneurs with the DIPF space, searching for more institutional possibilities.

The type of delegative political entrepreneurship we focus on here, however, begins with the provision of goods and services in return for votes. In effect this is analogous to the emergence of nation states. For instance, imagine a delegate signs a contract with a number of voters, perhaps collectively, to provide some goods or services. What is interesting about these polycentric organizational forms that might exist within a cryptodemocracy is that individuals maintain the potential for exit. They are emergent voluntary states. These delegates could also provide governing services, such as dispute resolution or insurance, as part of the deal. This suggests the potential for emergent state-like governing clubs within the democratic process. Political entrepreneurs undertake a more entrepreneurial process of discovering potentially valuable trades with others voters. What institutional economics teaches us is that delegates are a new form of political entrepreneur who will themselves develop institutions to overcome the frictions and decision costs between them and mutually beneficial delegation contracts.

We can also hypothesize over the actions of voters in a cryptodemocracy from an entrepreneurial perspective. In particular we expect that votes will employ new technologies, such as artificial intelligence (AI), to engage in mutually beneficial exchange. Just like delegates, voters are incentivized to reap the gains from exchange for their property rights. Voters may employ new technologies to bargain on their behalf. Indeed, a cryptodemocratic structure ordered by blockchain provides the foundational infrastructure on which other technologies may be applied. A voter could use AI to analyze their preferences over time, observe the preferences of others, and propose potential trades. AI could be used for cryptodemocracy in a number of ways. For instance, entrepreneurs could create decentralized markets for votes for cryptocurrency. Second, there may be a process of high-frequency bartering where AI agents suggest along what dimensions votes may be conditionally decomposed, and conduct searches for possibly vote trades. Of course voters could restrict this by only seeking trades where they are happy to sell their vote. On the other hand, too, delegates could use AI to better analyze voter preferences to bundle voting rights in particular ways. We would also expect some matching services to emerge to overcome the search costs of discovering mutually beneficial trades. We expect that blockchain will act as the foundations on which other new technologies will be powered up to create a more fluid and dynamic cryptodemocratic system.

CONCLUSION

This book has moved us toward a deeper understanding of the relationship between technology, governance, and institutional choice. A cryptodemocracy draws on the decentralization and cryptographic security of blockchains to establish and govern a system of property rights over votes. Once property rights over votes are allocated and enforceable, individuals are able to contract, exchange, and utilize their votes in a decentralized and evolutionary way. Cryptodemocracy provides for a democratic, polycentric, spontaneously ordered system of collective choice that has not yet been possible under the existing institutional and technological framework. It is a new institutional possibility to solve the age old problem of discovering and coordinating diverse preferences into a collective choice.

NOTE

1. George Lennox Sharman Shackle, *Epistemics and Economics* (Transaction Publishers, 1992); Shackle, "The Bounds of Unknowledge," in *Beyond Positive Economics*, ed. J. Wiseman (London: Macmillan, 1983).

Bibliography

Acemoglu, Daron. "Why Not a Political Coase Theorem? Social Conflict, Commitment, and Politics." *Journal of Comparative Economics* 31, no. 4 (2003): 620–52.

Achen, Christopher H., and Larry M. Bartels. *Democracy for Realists: Why Elections Do Not Produce Responsive Government.* Vol. 4: Princeton University Press, 2017.

Alger, Dan. "Voting by Proxy." *Public Choice* 126, no. 1–2 (2006): 1–26.

Allen, Darcy W.E. "Entrepreneurial Exit: Developing the Cryptoeconomy." In *Blockchain Economics*, edited by Melanie Swan, Jason Potts, S. Takagi, P. Tasco and F. Witte: World Scientific, 2019.

———. "The Private Governance of Entrepreneurship: An Institutional Approach to Entrepreneurial Discovery." RMIT University, 2017.

Allen, Darcy W.E, Alastair Berg, and Brendan Markey-Towler. "Blockchain and Supply Chains: V-Form Organisations, Value Redistributions, De-Commoditisation and Quality Proxies." *The Journal of the British Blockchain Association* 2, no. 1 (2018): 1–8.

Allen, Darcy W.E, and Chris Berg. "Subjective Political Economy." *New Perspectives on Political Economy* 13, no. 1–2 (2017): 19–40.

Allen, Darcy W.E, Chris Berg, Sinclair Davidson, Mikayla Novak, and Jason Potts. "Blockchain Tradetech." In *APEC Study Centres Consortium Conference (ASCCC)*. Port Moresby, Papua New Guinea 2018.

Allen, Darcy W.E, Chris Berg, Aaron M. Lane, and Jason Potts. "Cryptodemocracy and Its Institutional Possibilities." *The Review of Austrian Economics* (2018): 1–12.

Allen, Darcy W.E, Aaron M. Lane, and Marta Poblet. "The Governance of Blockchain Dispute Resolution." In *The Australasian Law and Economics Conference.* Brisbane, Australia, 2018.

Anderson, Gary M., and Robert D. Tollison. "Democracy in the Marketplace." *V in Pre* (1990).

Andresen, Julie Tetel. *Linguistics and Evolution: A Developmental Approach.* Cambridge University Press, 2013.

Aronstein, Martin J. "The Decline and Fall of the Stock Certificate in America." *Journal of Comparative Corporate Law and Securities Regulation* 1, no. 3 (1978): 273–84.

Arrow, Kenneth J. "A Difficulty in the Concept of Social Welfare." *Journal of Political Economy* 58, no. 4 (1950): 328–46.

Attanasi, Alessandro, Andrea Cavagna, Lorenzo Del Castello, Irene Giardina, Asja Jelic, Stefania Melillo, Leonardo Parisi, et al. "Emergence of Collective Changes in Travel Direction of Starling Flocks from Individual Birds' Fluctuations." *Journal of The Royal Society Interface* 12, no. 108 (2015): 20150319.

Australia, Commonwealth of. "Royal Commission into Trade Union Governance and Corruption, Final Report." 2015.

141

———. "Royal Commission into Trade Union Governance and Corruption, Interim Report." 2014.

Autor, David H. "Wiring the Labor Market." *Journal of Economic Perspectives* 15, no. 1 (2001): 25–40.

Axe, Leonard H. "Corporate Proxies." *Michigan Law Review* 41, no. 1 (1942): 38–65.

Barnard, Alan. *Language in Prehistory.* Cambridge University Press, 2016.

Bazazi, Sepideh, Jerome Buhl, Joseph J Hale, Michael L Anstey, Gregory A Sword, Stephen J Simpson, and Iain D Couzin. "Collective Motion and Cannibalism in Locust Migratory Bands." *Current Biology* 18, no. 10 (2008): 735–39.

Bebchuk, Lucian A. "The Myth of the Shareholder Franchise." *Virginia Law Review* 93, no. 3 (2007): 675–732.

Bebchuk, Lucian A., Alon Brav, and Wei Jiang. "The Long-Term Effects of Hedge Fund Activism." *Columbia Law Review* 115 (2015): 1085.

Beitz, Charles R. *Political Equality: An Essay in Democratic Theory.* Princeton University Press, 1989.

Benčić, Federico Matteo, and Ivana Podnar Žarko. "Distributed Ledger Technology: Blockchain Compared to Directed Acyclic Graph." *arXiv preprint arXiv:1804.10013* (2018).

Beniger, James. *The Control Revolution: Technological and Economic Origins of the Information Society.* Harvard University Press, 2009.

Bentham, Jeremy. "Rights, Representation, and Reform: Nonsense Upon Stilts and Other Writings on the French Revolution by Jeremy Bentham." (2002).

Berg, Alastair, and Chris Berg. "Exit, Voice, and Forking." *RMIT University Working Paper* (2017).

Berg, Chris. "Adam Smith and Jeremy Bentham in the Australian Colonies." *History of Economics Review* 68, no. 1 (2017): 2–16.

———. "The Biggest Vested Interest of All: How Government Lobbies to Restrict Individual Rights and Freedom." Melbourne: Institute of Public Affairs, 2013.

———. *The Growth of Australia's Regulatory State: Ideology, Accountability and the Mega-Regulators.* Melbourne, Australia: Institute of Public Affairs, 2008.

———. "An Institutional Theory of Free Speech." In *RMIT Blockchain Innovation Hub Working Paper Series,* 2017.

———. *Liberty, Equality and Democracy.* Connor Court Publishing Pty Ltd., 2015.

———. "Safety and Soundness: An Economic History of Prudential Bank Regulation in Australia, 1893–2008." RMIT University, 2016.

———. "What Diplomacy in the Ancient Near East Can Tell Us About Blockchain Technology." *Ledger* 2 (2017): 55–64.

Berg, Chris, and Sinclair Davidson. *Against Public Broadcasting: Why and How We Should Privatise the ABC.* Queensland, Australia: Connor Court Publishing Pty Ltd., 2018.

———. "Media Regulation: A Critique of Finkelstein and Tiffen." *Available at SSRN 2669271* (2015).

———. "Section 18c, Human Rights, and Media Reform: An Institutional Analysis of the 2011–13 Australian Free Speech Debate." *Agenda: A Journal of Policy Analysis and Reform* 23, no. 1 (2016): 5–30.

Berg, Chris, Sinclair Davidson, and Jason Potts. "The Blockchain Economy: A Beginner's Guide to Institutional Cryptoeconomics." In *Cryptoeconomics Australia,* 2017.

———. "Blockchains Industrialise Trust." *SSRN https://www.ssrn.com/abstract=3074070* (2017).

———. *How to Understand the Blockchain Economy: An Introduction to Institutional Cryptoeconomics.* Edward Elgar, 2019.

———. "Ledgers." *Available at SSRN 3157421* (2018).

Berle, Adolf A., and Gardiner C. Means. "The Modern Corporation and Private Property." Harcourt, Brace, Jovanovich; Commerce Clearing House, 1968 [1933].

Bialek, William, Andrea Cavagna, Irene Giardina, Thierry Mora, Edmondo Silvestri, Massimiliano Viale, and Aleksandra M. Walczak. "Statistical Mechanics for Natural Flocks of Birds." *Proceedings of the National Academy of Sciences* (2012).

Bishop, J. David. "The Cleroterium." *The Journal of Hellenic Studies* 90 (1970): 1–14.

Blackstone, William. *Commentaries on the Laws of England in Four Books.* Indianapolis: Liberty Fund, 1973 [2011].

Blackwell, Christopher W. *Dēmos: Classical Athenian Democracy.* Stoa: A Consortium for Electronic Publication in the Humanities, 2003.

Blanton, Richard E., and Lane F. Fargher. *How Humans Cooperate: Confronting the Challenges of Collective Action.* University Press of Colorado, 2016.

Block, Walter. "Alienability: Rejoinder to Kuflik." *Humanomics* 23, no. 3 (2007): 117–36.

Boegehold, Alan L., Margaret Crosby, Mabel Lang, David R. Jordan, and Rhys F. Townsend. "The Lawcourts at Athens Sites, Buildings, Equipment, Procedure, and Testimonia." *The Athenian Agora* 28 (2009).

Boettke, Peter J. "Liberty vs. Power in Economic Policy in the 20th and 21st Centuries." *The Journal of Private Enterprise* 22, no. 2 (2007): 7–36.

Boettke, Peter J., and Matthew Mitchell. *Applied Mainline Economics: Bridging the Gap between Theory and Public Policy.* Arlington, VA: Mercatus Center at George Mason University, 2017.

Boettke, Peter J., Vlad Tarko, and Paul Aligica. "Why Hayek Matters: The Epistemic Dimension of Comparative Institutional Analysis." In *Revisiting Hayek's Political Economy*, 163–85: Emerald Group Publishing Limited, 2016.

Boldi, Paolo, Francesco Bonchi, Carlos Castillo, and Sebastiano Vigna. "Viscous Democracy for Social Networks." *Communications of the ACM* 54, no. 6 (2011): 129–37.

———. "Voting in Social Networks." Paper presented at the Proceedings of the 18th ACM Conference on Information and Knowledge Management, 2009.

Bonsón, Enrique, Lourdes Torres, Sonia Royo, and Francisco Flores. "Local E-Government 2.0: Social Media and Corporate Transparency in Municipalities." *Government Information Quarterly* 29, no. 2 (2012): 123–32.

Braithwaite, John. "Accountability and Governance under the New Regulatory State." *Australian Journal of Public Administration* 58, no. 1 (1999): 90–94.

Brennan, Geoffrey. "Politics-as-Exchange and the Calculus of Consent." *Public Choice* 152, no. 3–4 (2012): 351–58.

Brennan, Geoffrey, and Philip Pettit. *The Economy of Esteem: An Essay on Civil and Political Society.* Oxford University Press, 2004.

Brennan, Jason. *Against Democracy.* Princeton University Press, 2016.

———. *The Ethics of Voting.* Princeton University Press, 2012.

Brent, Peter. "The Australian Ballot: Not the Secret Ballot." *Australian Journal of Political Science* 41, no. 1 (2006): 39–50.

Buchanan, Allen. "Political Legitimacy and Democracy." *Ethics* 112, no. 4 (2002): 689–719.

Buchanan, James M. *Cost and Choice: An Inquiry in Economic Theory.* University of Chicago Press, 1979.

———. "Rights, Efficiency, and Exchange: The Irrelevance of Transaction Costs." *Berlin: Duncker and Humblot* (1984): 9–24.

Buchanan, James M., and Gordon Tullock. *The Calculus of Consent.* Ann Arbor: University of Michigan Press, 1962.

———. *The Calculus of Consent.* Vol. 3. Ann Arbor: University of Michigan Press, 1962.

Burke, Edmund. *Select Works of Edmund Burke, Vol. 1 (Thoughts on the Cause of the Present Discontents; Two Speeches on America).* Indianapolis: Liberty Fund, 1770.

Canada, Statistics. "Description for Chart 1: Unionization Rates of Employed Individuals Aged 17 to 64, 1981 to 2012." https://www150.statcan.gc.ca/n1/pub/75-006-x/2013001/article/11878/c-g/desc/desc01-eng.htm.

Caplan, Bryan. *The Myth of the Rational Voter: Why Democracies Choose Bad Policies.* Princeton University Press, 2011.

Catalini, Christian, and Joshua S. Gans. "Some Simple Economics of the Blockchain." National Bureau of Economic Research, 2016.

Cavagna, Andrea, Irene Giardina, Thierry Mora, and Aleksandra M. Walczak. "Physical Constraints in Biological Collective Behaviour." *Current Opinion in Systems Biology* 9 (2018): 49–54.

Cavale, Siddharth. "P&G Appoints Peltz to Board Despite Losing Proxy Battle." *Reuters,* December 16, 2017.

Chaison, Gary N. "A Note on Union Merger Trends, 1900–1978." *Industrial and Labor Relations Review* 34, no. 1 (1980): 114–20.

Cherry, Miriam A., and Antonio Aloisi. "Dependent Contractors in the Gig Economy: A Comparative Approach." *American University Law Review* 66, no. 3 (2016): 635–89.

Chomsky, Noam. *On Nature and Language.* Cambridge University Press, 2002.

———. "Three Factors in Language Design." *Linguistic inquiry* 36, no. 1 (2005): 1–22.

Christoff, Zoé, and Davide Grossi. "Liquid Democracy: An Analysis in Binary Aggregation and Diffusion." *arXiv preprint arXiv:1612.08048* (2016).

Cicero, Marcus Tullius. *The Political Works of Marcus Tullius Cicero, Vol. 2 (Treatise on the Laws) [-51].* London: Edmund Spettigue, 1842.

Clark, Robert Charles. "Vote Buying and Corporate Law." *Case Western Reserve Law Review* 29 (1979): 776–807.

Clarkson, Chris, Zenobia Jacobs, Ben Marwick, Richard Fullagar, Lynley Wallis, Mike Smith, Richard G. Roberts, et al. "Human Occupation of Northern Australia by 65,000 Years Ago." *Nature* 547, no. 7663 (2017): 306.

Coase, Ronald H. "Industrial Organization: A Proposal for Research." In *Economic Research: Retrospect and Prospect, Volume 3, Policy Issues and Research Opportunities in Industrial Organization,* 59–73, NBER, 1972.

———. "The Nature of the Firm." *Economica* 4, no. 16 (1937): 386–405.

———. "The Problem of Social Cost." *Journal of Law and Economics* 3 (1960): 1.

Cockfield, Sandra. "Union Renewal, Union Strategy and Technology." *Critical Perspectives on International Business* 1, no. 2–3 (2005): 93–108.

Cohen, Marty, David Karol, Hans Noel, and John Zaller. *The Party Decides: Presidential Nominations Before and After Reform.* University of Chicago Press, 2009.

———. "Party Versus Faction in the Reformed Presidential Nominating System." *Political Science and Politics* 49, no. 4 (2016): 701–8.

Cohensius, Gal, Shie Mannor, Reshef Meir, Eli Meirom, and Ariel Orda. "Proxy Voting for Better Outcomes." Paper presented at the Proceedings of the 16th Conference on Autonomous Agents and MultiAgent Systems, 2017.

Coleman, James S. "The Possibility of a Social Welfare Function." *The American Economic Review* 56, no. 5 (1966): 1105–22.

Coleman, William. "Australia's Electoral Idiosyncracies." In *Only in Australia: The History, Politics, and Economics of Australian Exceptionalism,* edited by William Coleman. Oxford University Press, 2016.

Collins, Hugh. "Political Ideology in Australia: The Distinctiveness of a Benthamite Society." *Daedalus* (1985): 147–69.

Congleton, Roger D. *Perfecting Parliament: Constitutional Reform, Liberalism, and the Rise of Western Democracy.* Cambridge University Press, 2010.

Congress, Trade Union. "Shaping Our Digital Future." 2017.

Cortada, James W. *Before the Computer: IBM, NCR, Burroughs, and Remington Rand and the Industry They Created, 1865–1956.* Princeton University Press, 2000.

Couzin, Iain D., and Jens Krause. "Self-Organization and Collective Behavior in Vertebrates." (2003).

Couzin, Iain D., Jens Krause, Nigel R Franks, and Simon A Levin. "Effective Leadership and Decision-Making in Animal Groups on the Move." *Nature* 433, no. 7025 (2005): 513.

Croman, Kyle, Christian Decker, Ittay Eyal, Adem Efe Gencer, Ari Juels, Ahmed Kosba, Andrew Miller, et al. "On Scaling Decentralized Blockchains." Paper presented at the International Conference on Financial Cryptography and Data Security, 2016.

Crook, Malcolm, and Tom Crook. "The Advent of the Secret Ballot in Britain and France, 1789–1914: From Public Assembly to Private Compartment." *History* 92, no. 308 (2007): 449–71.

Dahl, Robert Alan. *Polyarchy: Participation and Opposition.* Yale University Press, 1973.

Davidson, Iain, and William Noble. "Why the First Colonisation of the Australian Region Is the Earliest Evidence of Modern Human Behaviour." *Archaeology in Oceania* 27, no. 3 (1992): 135–42.

Davidson, S. "Environmental Protest: An Economics of Regulation Approach." *Australian Environment Review* 29, no. 10 (2014): 283–86.

Davidson, Sinclair. "Productivity Enhancing Regulatory Reform." *Australia Adjusting: Optimising National Prosperity* (2013): 66.

———. "Submission to Parliamentary Joint Committee on Law Enforcement Inquiry into Illicit Tobacco." (2016).

Davidson, Sinclair, Primavera De Filippi, and Jason Potts. "Blockchains and the Economic Institutions of Capitalism." *Journal of Institutional Economics* (2018): 1–20.

Davidson, Sinclair, and Jason Potts. "A New Institutional Approach to Innovation Policy." *Australian Economic Review Policy Forum: Research and Innovation* 49, no. 2 (2016): 200–207.

———. "Social Costs and the Institutions of Innovation Policy." *Available at SSRN 2565574* (2015).

Davis, Otto A., Melvin J. Hinich, and Peter C. Ordeshook. "An Expository Development of a Mathematical Model of the Electoral Process." *American Political Science Review* 64, no. 2 (1970): 426–48.

de Tocqueville, Alexis. *Democracy in America* 2003 [1835].

de Vries, Alex. "Bitcoin's Growing Energy Problem." *Joule* 2, no. 5 (2018): 801–5.

Demsetz, Harold. "Toward a Theory of Property Rights." *The American Economic Review* 57, no. 2 (1967): 347–59.

Dent Jr., George W. "A Defense of Proxy Advisors." *Michigan State Law Review* (2014): 1287–330.

Department for Business, Energy, and Industrial Strategy. "Trade Union Membership 2017: Statistical Bulletin." 2018.

Diamond, Wayne J., and Richard B. Freeman. "Will Unionism Prosper in Cyberspace? The Promise of the Internet for Employee Organization." *British Journal of Industrial Relations* 40, no. 3 (2002): 569–96.

Djankov, Simeon, Edward Glaeser, Rafael La Porta, Florencio Lopez-de-Silanes, and Andrei Shleifer. "The New Comparative Economics." *Journal of Comparative Economics* 31, no. 4 (2003): 595–619.

Dodgson, Charles Lutwidge. *The Principles of Parliamentary Representation*. Harrison and Sons, 1884.

Dow, Sterling. "Aristotle, the Kleroteria, and the Courts." *Harvard Studies in Classical Philology* 50 (1939): 1–34.

Downs, Anthony. "An Economic Theory of Political Action in a Democracy." *Journal of Political Economy* 65, no. 2 (1957): 135–50.

Dunn, Megan, and James Walker. "Union Membership in the United States." US Bureau of Labor Statistics, 2016.

Easterbrook, Frank H., and Daniel R Fischel. "Voting in Corporate Law." *The Journal of Law and Economics* 26, no. 2 (1983): 395–427.

Edelman, Paul H, and Robert B Thompson. "Corporate Voting." *Vanderbilt Law Review* 62 (2009).

Edgerton, William F. "The Government and the Governed in the Egyptian Empire." *Journal of Near Eastern Studies* 6, no. 3 (1947): 152–60.

Elgie, Robert. "The President of Ireland in Comparative Perspective." *Irish Political Studies* 27, no. 4 (2012): 502–21.

Ellison, Nick, and Michael Hardey. "Social Media and Local Government: Citizenship, Consumption and Democracy." *Local Government Studies* 40, no. 1 (2014): 21–40.

Engelstad, Fredrik. "The Assignment of Political Office by Lot." *Information (International Social Science Council)* 28, no. 1 (1989): 23–50.

Epstein, Richard A. "Why Restrain Alienation?" *Columbia Law Review* 85, no. 5 (1985): 970–90.

Errington, Wayne, and Peter Van Onselen. *Battleground: Why the Liberal Party Shirtfronted Tony Abbott.* Parkville, Victoria: Melbourne University Publishing, 2015.

Ervin, Eric. "Blockchain Technology Set to Revolutionize Global Stock Trading." *Forbes,* August 16, 2018.

Essinger, James. *Jacquard's Web: How a Hand-Loom Led to the Birth of the Information Age.* Oxford University Press on Demand, 2007.

Fagan, Edward James. "Marching Orders? US Party Platforms and Legislative Agenda Setting 1948–2014." *Political Research Quarterly* (2018): 1–11.

Fisch, Jill E. "Standing Voting Instructions: Empowering the Excluded Retail Investor." *Minnesota Law Review* 102 (2017): 11.

Fischer, Julia, and Dietmar Zinner. "Communication and Cognition in Primate Group Movement." *International Journal of Primatology* 32, no. 6 (2011): 1279–95.

Fleming, Daniel E. *Democracy's Ancient Ancestors: Mari and Early Collective Governance.* Cambridge University Press, 2004.

Ford, Bryan. "Delegative Democracy." *Manuscript.* (2002).

Forsyth, Anthony, and Carolyn Holbrook. "Australian Politics Explainer: The Prices and Incomes Accord." (2017). https://theconversation.com/australian-politics-explainer-the-prices-and-incomes-accord-75622.

Franklin, Mark N. "Too Much Democracy? How Elections to the European Parliament Depress Turnout at National Elections in Europe." Paper presented at the Congress of the European Consortium of Political Research, Marburg, Germany, 2003.

Fredman, L. E. "The Introduction of the Australian Ballot in the United States." *Australian Journal of Politics and History* 13, no. 2 (1967): 204–20.

Freehills, Herbert Smith. "Herbert Smith Freehills, 'Data61 and IBM Create Consortium to Deliver Smart Legal Contracts on Blockchain to Australian Businesses." (2018). Published electronically August 28, 2018. https://www.herbertsmithfreehills.com/latest-thinking/herbert-smith-freehills-data61-and-ibm-create-consortium-to-deliver-smart-legal.

Freeman, Richard B., and James L. Medoff. "The Two Faces of Unionism." *The Public Interest* (1979): 69–93.

Freeman, Richard B., and Joel Rogers. "Open Source Unionism: Beyond Exclusive Collective Bargaining." *WorkingUSA* 5, no. 4 (2002): 8–40.

Freiman, Christopher. "Vote Markets." *Australasian Journal of Philosophy* 92, no. 4 (2014): 759–74.

Gall, Gregor. *The Future of Union Organising: Building for Tomorrow.* Palgrave, 2009.

———, ed. *Union Recognition: Organising and Bargaining Outcomes*: Routledge, 2006.

———. *Union Revitalisation in Advanced Economies: Assessing the Contribution of Union Organising.* Palgrave, 2009.

Geis, George S. "Traceable Shares and Corporate Law." *Northwestern University Law Review* 113, no. 2 (2018): 227–77.

Glaeser, Edward L., and Andrei Shleifer. "The Rise of the Regulatory State." *Journal of Economic Literature* 41, no. 2 (2003): 401–25.

Glassman, James K., and J. W. Verret. "How to Fix Our Broken Proxy Advisory System." In *Mercatus Research*, 2013.

Green-Armytage, James. "Direct Democracy by Delegable Proxy." *DOI= http://fc. antioch. edu/~ james_greenarmytage/vm/proxy. htm* (2005).

———. "Direct Voting and Proxy Voting." *Constitutional Political Economy* 26, no. 2 (2015): 190–220.

Greene, Anne-Marie, and Gill Kirton. "Possibilities for Remote Participation in Trade Unions: Mobilising Women Activists." *Industrial Relations Journal* 34, no. 4 (2003): 319–33.

Gross, Charles. "The Early History of the Ballot in England." *The American Historical Review* 3, no. 3 (1898): 456–63.

Gueron, Shay, Simon A. Levin, and Daniel I. Rubenstein. "The Dynamics of Herds: From Individuals to Aggregations." *Journal of Theoretical Biology* 182, no. 1 (1996): 85–98.

Hadley, Elaine. *Living Liberalism: Practical Citizenship in Mid-Victorian Britain.* University of Chicago Press, 2010.

Haeberlin, Barbara. "The Industrialization of Democracy." In *Computing for Science, Engineering and Production—Mathematical Tools for the Second Industrial Revolution*, edited by Karl Kleine. Norderstedt: Books on Demand, 2013.

Hanham, Harold John. *Elections and Party Management: Politics in the Time of Disraeli and Gladstone*. Shoe String Pr Inc., 1959.

Hanrahan, Pamela, and Geof Stapledon. *Commercial Applications of Company Law*. 17th edition. South Melbourne: Oxford University Press, 2016.

Hansen, Mogens Herman. *The Athenian Democracy in the Age of Demosthenes: Structure, Principles, and Ideology*. University of Oklahoma Press, 1999.

———. *The Athenian Ecclesia II: A Collection of Articles, 1983–1989*. Vol. 2. Museum Tusculanum Press, 1989.

Hardt, Steve, and Lia C. R. Lopes. "Google Votes: A Liquid Democracy Experiment on a Corporate Social Network." In *Technical Disclosure Commons*, 2015.

Hasen, Richard L. "Vote Buying." *California Law Review* 88, no. 5 (2000): 1323–72.

Hayek, Friedrich A. *The Constitution of Liberty*. London: Routledge and Kegan Paul, 1960.

———. *The Constitution of Liberty: The Definitive Edition*. United Kingdom: Routledge, 2013.

———. *Law, Legislation and Liberty: A New Statement of the Liberal Principles of Justice and Political Economy*. United Kingdom: Routledge, 2012.

———. "The Use of Knowledge in Society." *The American Economic Review* 35, no. 4 (1945): 519–30.

Headlam, James Wycliffe. *Election by Lot at Athens*. The University Press, 1891.

Heckelman, Jac C. "The Effect of the Secret Ballot on Voter Turnout Rates." *Public Choice* 82, no. 1–2 (1995): 107–24.

Heinlein, Robert. *The Moon Is a Harsh Mistress*. Tom Doherty Associates Inc.,: New York, 1966.

Henderson, Gerard. "The Industrial Relations Club." *Quadrant* 27, no. 9 (1983): 21.

———. *The Return of the Industrial Relations Club*. Podcast audio. Forest: Minerals Council of Australia. Accessed September 10, 2018. http://podcast.thesydneyinstitute.com.au/podcasts/Other/MCA_The%20return%20of%20the%20Industrial%20Relations%20Club_WEB.pdf.

Hirst, Derek. *The Representative of the People? Voters and Voting in England under the Early Stuarts*. Cambridge University Press, 2005.

Hirst, John. *Making Voting Secret*. Victorian Electoral Commission, 2006.

Hitz, Joerg-Markus, and Nico Lehmann. "Empirical Evidence on the Role of Proxy Advisors in European Capital Markets." *European Accounting Review* 27, no. 4 (2018): 713–45.

Hu, Henry T. C., and Bernard Black. "Empty Voting and Hidden (Morphable) Ownership: Taxonomy, Implications, and Reforms." *The Business Lawyer* (2006): 1011–70.

———. "Equity and Debt Decoupling and Empty Voting II: Importance and Extensions." *University of Pennsylvania Law Review* 156 (2007): 625–740.

———. "Hedge Funds, Insiders, and the Decoupling of Economic and Voting Ownership: Empty Voting and Hidden (Morphable) Ownership." *Journal of Corporate Finance* 13, no. 2–3 (2007): 343–67.

———. "The New Vote Buying: Empty Voting and Hidden (Morphable) Ownership." *Southern California Law Review* 79 (2006): 811–908.

Iliev, Peter, Karl V. Lins, Darius P. Miller, and Lukas Roth. "Shareholder Voting and Corporate Governance around the World." *The Review of Financial Studies* 28, no. 8 (2015): 2167–202.

Issacharoff, Samuel, and Richard H. Pildes. "Politics as Markets: Partisan Lockups of the Democratic Process." *Stanford Law Review* 50, no. 3 (1998): 643–717.

Jacobsen, Thorkild. "Primitive Democracy in Ancient Mesopotamia." *Journal of Near Eastern Studies* 2, no. 3 (1943): 159–72.

Jenkins, Jeffery A., and Nathan W. Monroe. "On Measuring Legislative Agenda-Setting Power." *American Journal of Political Science* 60, no. 1 (2016): 158–74.

Jones, Douglas W. "A Brief Illustrated History of Voting." http://homepage.cs.uiowa.edu/~jones/voting/pictures/#lever.

———. "Early Requirements for Mechanical Voting Systems." Paper presented at the Requirements Engineering for e-Voting Systems (RE-VOTE), 2009 First International Workshop on, 2010.

Kahan, Marcel, and Edward Rock. "The Hanging Chads of Corporate Voting." *Georgetown Law Journal* 96 (2007): 1227–81.

Kam, Christopher. "The Secret Ballot and the Market for Votes at 19th-Century British Elections." *Comparative Political Studies* 50, no. 5 (2017): 594–635.

Karlan, Pamela S. "Not by Money but by Virtue Won? Vote Trafficking and the Voting Rights System." *Virginia Law Review* (1994): 1455–75.

———. "Politics by Other Means." *Virginia Law Review* 85 (1999): 1697–724.

Katz, Richard S., and Peter Mair. "The Cartel Party Thesis: A Restatement." *Perspectives on Politics* 7, no. 4 (2009): 753–66.

———. "Changing Models of Party Organization and Party Democracy: The Emergence of the Cartel Party." *Party Politics* 1, no. 1 (1995): 5–28.

Keane, John. *The Life and Death of Democracy.* Simon and Schuster, 2009.

———. "The Origins of Monitory Democracy." *The Conversation*, September 24, 2012.

Kelly, Paul. *Triumph and Demise: The Broken Promise of a Labor Generation.* Parkville, Victoria: Melbourne University Publishing, 2014.

Kerr, Allan, and Jeremy Waddington. "E-Communications: An Aspect of Union Renewal or Merely Doing Things Electronically?" *British Journal of Industrial Relations* 52, no. 4 (2014): 658–81.

Kinzer, Bruce L. *The Ballot Question in Nineteenth Century English Politics.* Vol. 9: New York: Garland Pub., 1982.

Kishlansky, Mark A. *Parliamentary Selection: Social and Political Choice in Early Modern England.* Cambridge University Press, 1986.

Kochin, Michael S., and Levis A. Kochin. "When Is Buying Votes Wrong?" *Public Choice* 97, no. 4 (1998): 645–62.

Koppl, Roger. *Expert Failure.* Cambridge: Cambridge University Press, 2018.

Kordana, Kevin A., and Eric A. Posner. "A Positive Theory of Chapter 11." *New York University Law Review* 74 (1999): 161.

Kramer, Gerald H. "On a Class of Equilibrium Conditions for Majority Rule." *Econometrica: Journal of the Econometric Society* 41, no. 2 (1973): 285–97.

Kriesi, Hanspeter. *Direct Democratic Choice: The Swiss Experience.* Lanham, MD: Lexington Books, 2005.

Krimmer, Robert. "The Evolution of E-Voting: Why Voting Technology Is Used and How It Affects Democracy." *Tallinn University of Technology Doctoral Theses Series I: Social Sciences* 19 (2012).

Kroll, John H. *Athenian Bronze Allotment Plates.* Harvard University Press, 1972.

Kuhn, Steven L., and Mary C. Stiner. "What's a Mother to Do?: The Division of Labor among Neandertals and Modern Humans in Eurasia." *Current Anthropology* 47, no. 6 (2006): 953–81.

Kuran, Timur. *Private Truths, Public Lies: The Social Consequences of Preference Falsification.* Harvard University Press, 1997.

Lalley, Steven P., and E. Glen Weyl. "Quadratic Voting: How Mechanism Design Can Radicalize Democracy." Paper presented at the AEA Papers and Proceedings, 2018.

Lambert, Wilfred G., Alan Ralph Millard, and Miguel Civil. *Atra-Ḥasīs: The Babylonian Story of the Flood.* Eisenbrauns, 1999.

Lan, Luh Luh, and Loizos Heracleous. "Negotiating the Minefields of Corporate Vote-Buying." *Corporate Governance: An International Review* 15, no. 5 (2007): 969–78.

Laster, J. Travis. "The Block Chain Plunger: Using Technology to Clean up Proxy Plumbing and Take Back the Vote." Address to Council of Institutional Investors, Chicago, September 29, 2016.

Latcham, Franklin C., and Frank D. Emerson. "Proxy Contest Expenses and Shareholder Democracy." *Western Reserve Law Review* 4 (1952): 5–18.

Lawrence, Jon. *Electing Our Masters: The Hustings in British Politics from Hogarth to Blair.* Oxford University Press, 2009.

Lee, Larissa. "New Kids on the Blockchain: How Bitcoin's Technology Could Reinvent the Stock Market." *Hastings Business Law Journal* 12 (2016): 81.

Leifman, Yefim I. "Secret and Verifiable Delegated Voting for Wide Representation." *IACR Cryptology ePrint Archive* (2014): 1–17.

Lesh, Matthew. "A Regulatory Culture?" In *Australia's Red Tape Crisis: The Causes and Costs of Over-Regulation*, edited by Darcy W.E. Allen and Chris Berg, 97–113. Australia: Connor Court, 2018.

Levi, Margaret, David Olson, Jon Agnone, and Devin Kelly. "Union Democracy Reexamined." *Politics and Society* 37, no. 2 (2009): 203–28.

Levmore, Saul. "Voting with Intensity." *Stanford Law Review* 53 (2000): 111–61.

Levy, David M, and Sandra J Peart. *Escape from Democracy: The Role of Experts and the Public in Economic Policy.* New York: Cambridge University Press, 2016.

Llewellyn, David Geoffrey Matthew. "Australia Felix: Jeremy Bentham and Australian Colonial Democracy." University of Melbourne, 2016.

Lockard, Alan A. "Decision by Sortition: A Means to Reduce Rent-Seeking." *Public Choice* 116, no. 3–4 (2003): 435–51.

Locke, John. "Two Treatises of Government." London: A. Millar et al., 1764.

Logsdon, Jeanne M., and Harry J. Van Buren. "Beyond the Proxy Vote: Dialogues between Shareholder Activists and Corporations." *Journal of Business Ethics* 87, no. 1 (2009): 353–65.

MacDonald, Trent J. "Theory of Non-Territorial Internal Exit." *Available at SSRN 2661226* (2015).

———. "Theory of Unbundled and Non-Territorial Governance." RMIT University, 2015.

MacDonald, Trent J., Darcy W.E. Allen, and Jason Potts. "Blockchains and the Boundaries of Self-Organized Economies: Predictions for the Future of Banking." In *Banking Beyond Banks and Money: A Guide to Banking Services in the Twenty-First Century*, edited by Paolo Tasca, Tomaso Aste, Loriana Pelizzon, and Nicolas Perony, 279–96. Cham: Springer International Publishing, 2016.

Maddicott, John Robert. *The Origins of the English Parliament, 924–1327.* Oxford University Press, 2010.

Madison, James. "Federalist No. 10." *November* 22 (1787).

Maggetti, Martino. "Legitimacy and Accountability of Independent Regulatory Agencies: A Critical Review." *Living Reviews in Democracy* 2, no. 1 (2010): 1–9.

Majone, Giandomenico. "Nonmajoritarian Institutions and the Limits of Democratic Governance: A Political Transaction-Cost Approach." *Journal of Institutional and Theoretical Economics* 157, no. 1 (2001): 57–78.

———. "The Rise of the Regulatory State in Europe." *West European Politics* 17, no. 3 (1994): 77–101.

Malenko, Andrey, and Nadya Malenko. "The Economics of Selling Information to Voters." *Journal of Finance* (forthcoming).

Manne, Henry G. "Some Theoretical Aspects of Share Voting. An Essay in Honor of Adolf A. Berle." *Columbia Law Review* 64, no. 8 (1964): 1427–45.

Manry, David, and David Stangeland. "Greenmail: A Brief History." *Stanford Journal of Law, Business and Finance* 6 (2000): 217.

Mason, Bob, and Peter Bain. "The Determinants of Trade Union Membership in Britain: A Survey of the Literature." *Industrial and Labor Relations Review* 46, no. 2 (1993): 332–51.

Mayer, Jane. *Dark Money: The Hidden History of the Billionaires Behind the Rise of the Radical Right.* Anchor Books, 2016.

McKelvey, Richard D. "General Conditions for Global Intransitivities in Formal Voting Models." *Econometrica: Journal of the Econometric Society* (1979): 1085–112.

———. "Intransitivities in Multidimensional Voting Models and Some Implications for Agenda Control." *Journal of Economic Theory* 12, no. 3 (1976): 472–82.

McKenna, Mark. "Building 'A Closet of Prayer' in the New World: The Story of the Australian Ballot." In *Elections: Full, Free and Fair*, edited by Marian Sawer, 256. Federation Press, 2001.

McLean, Iain S., Alistair McMillan, and Burt L .Monroe. *A Mathematical Approach to Proportional Representation: Duncan Black on Lewis Carroll.* Springer Science and Business Media, 2012.

Messenger, Jon, Oscar Llave Vargas, Lutz Gschwind, Simon Böhmer, Greet Vermeylen, and Mathijn Wilkens. *Working Anytime, Anywhere: The Effects on the World of Work.* Publications Office of the European Union, 2017.

Mill, John Stuart. *The Collected Works of John Stuart Mill, Volume XIX—Essays on Politics and Society Part 2 (Considerations on Rep. Govt.).* Toronto: University of Toronto Press, 1977.

———. *On Liberty.* London: J. W. Parker and Son, 1859.

Miller, James C. "A Program for Direct and Proxy Voting in the Legislative Process." *Public Choice* 7, no. 1 (1969): 107–13.

Millon, David. "Radical Shareholder Primacy." *University of St. Thomas Law Journal* 10 (2013): 1013.

Mudde, Cas, and Cristóbal Rovira Kaltwasser. *Populism: A Very Short Introduction.* Oxford University Press, 2017.

Mueller, Dennis C. "The Possibility of a Social Welfare Function: Comment." *The American Economic Review* 57, no. 5 (1967): 1304–11.

Muhlberger, Steven. "Republics and Quasi-Democratic Institutions in Ancient India." In *The Secret History of Democracy*, edited by Benjamin Isakhan and Stephen Stockwell, 49–59: Springer, 2011.

Müller, Jan-Werner. *What Is Populism?* Penguin UK, 2017.

Müller, Julian F. "Epistemic Democracy: Beyond Knowledge Exploitation." *Philosophical Studies* (2018): 1–22.

Nakamoto, Satoshi. "Bitcoin: A Peer-to-Peer Electronic Cash System." 2008.

"New Laws: Elections Regulation Act." *The Argus*, April 15, 1856, 4.

North, Douglass C. *Institutions, Institutional Change and Economic Performance.* Cambridge University Press, 1990.

Novak, Mikayla, Sinclair Davidson, and Jason Potts. "The Cost of Trust: A Pilot Study." *Journal of the British Blockchain Association* 1, no. 2 (forthcoming).

O'Gorman, Frank. "Campaign Rituals and Ceremonies: The Social Meaning of Elections in England 1780–1860." *Past & Present*, no. 135 (1992): 79–115.

———. "The Culture of Elections in England: From the Glorious Revolution to the First World War, 1688–1914." In *Elections before Democracy: The History of Elections in Europe and Latin America*, edited by Eduardo Posada-Carbó, 17–31. Palgrave, 1996.

O'Leary, Cornelius. "The Elimination of Corrupt Practices in British Elections, 1868–1911." (1962).

Ober, Josiah. *The Athenian Revolution: Essays on Ancient Greek Democracy and Political Theory.* Princeton University Press, 1996.

Office, US Government Accountability. "Proxy Advisory Firms' Role in Voting and Corporate Governance Practices." In *Highlights of GAO-17-47, a report to the Chairman, Subcommittee on Economic Policy, Committee on Banking, Housing, and Urban Affairs, U.S. Senate,* 2016.

Olson, Mancur. *The Logic of Collective Action.* Vol. 124. Harvard University Press, 2009.

Orlandini, Alessandro. "Kleroterion: Simulation of the Allotment of Dikastai." Academia.edu.

Ostrom, Elinor. *Governing the Commons: The Evolution of Institutions for Collective Action.* Cambridge University Press, 1990.

Parisi, Francesco. "The Market for Votes: Coasian Bargaining in an Arrovian Setting." *George Mason Law Review* 6 (1997): 745–66.

———. "Political Coase Theorem." *Public Choice* 115, no. 1–2 (2003): 1–36.

Patriquin, Larry. *Economic Equality and Direct Democracy in Ancient Athens.* Springer, 2015.

Peltzman, Sam. "Toward a More General Theory of Regulation." In *National Bureau of Economic Research Working Paper 133*: National Bureau of Economic Research, Cambridge, MA, USA, 1976.

Piazza, Fiammetta S. "Bitcoin and the Blockchain as Possible Corporate Governance Tools: Strengths and Weaknesses." *Bocconi Legal Papers* 9 (2017): 125.

Pinker, Steven. *The Language Instinct: How the Mind Creates Language.* Penguin UK, 2003.

Plott, Charles R. "Axiomatic Social Choice Theory: An Overview and Interpretation." *American Journal of Political Science* 20, no. 3 (1976): 511–96.

———. "A Notion of Equilibrium and Its Possibility under Majority Rule." *The American Economic Review* 57, no. 4 (1967): 787–806.

Posner, Eric A., and E. Glen Weyl. "Voting Squared: Quadratic Voting in Democratic Politics." *Vanderbilt Law Review* 68 (2015): 441–500.

Posner, Richard A. "Quadratic Voting." 2016.

Powell, G. Bingham, and G. Bingham Powell Jr. *Elections as Instruments of Democracy: Majoritarian and Proportional Visions.* Yale University Press, 2000.

Project, UnionD. "Uniond—Consensus 2016 Hackathon Nyc Final Pitch." https://www.youtube.com/watch?v=bFC6H6urtvw.

Quintyn, Marc. "Independent Agencies: More Than a Cheap Copy of Independent Central Banks?" *Constitutional Political Economy* 20, no. 3–4 (2009): 267.

Radin, Margaret Jane. "Market-Inalienability." *Harvard Law Review* 100, no. 8 (1987): 1849–937.

Rancière, Jacques. *Hatred of Democracy.* London: Verso Books, 2009.

Raval, Siraj. *Decentralized Applications: Harnessing Bitcoin's Blockchain Technology.* 1st edition. United States of America: O'Reilly, 2016.

Rehfeld, Andrew. *The Concept of Constituency: Political Representation, Democratic Legitimacy, and Institutional Design.* Cambridge University Press, 2005.

Responsibility, Interfaith Center on Corporate. "A Faithful Voice for Justice: Annual Report 2016–2017." 2017.

Reuland, Eric. "Language: Symbolization and Beyond." In *The Prehistory of Language*, edited by Rudolf Botha and Chris Knight, 201–24. Oxford University Press, 2009.

Riker, William H. "Implications from the Disequilibrium of Majority Rule for the Study of Institutions." *American Political Science Review* 74, no. 2 (1980): 432–46.

Riker, William H., and Steven J. Brams. "The Paradox of Vote Trading." *American Political Science Review* 67, no. 4 (1973): 1235–47.

Rix, Kathryn. "'The Elimination of Corrupt Practices in British Elections?': Reassessing the Impact of the 1883 Corrupt Practices Act." *The English Historical Review* 123, no. 500 (2008): 65–97.

Rowley, Charles K. "The Relevance of the Median Voter Theorem." *Journal of Institutional and Theoretical Economics*, no. H. 1 (1984): 104–26.

Rydgren, Jens. "Radical Right Populism in Sweden: Still a Failure, but for How Long?" *Scandinavian Political Studies* 25, no. 1 (2002): 27–56.

Rydgren, Jens, and Sara Van der Meiden. "Sweden, Now a Country Like All the Others? The Radical Right and the End of Swedish Exceptionalism." *SU Department of Sociology Working Paper Series* (2016).

Saltman, Roy. *The History and Politics of Voting Technology: In Quest of Integrity and Public Confidence.* Springer, 2006.

Sandel, Michael J. "What Money Can't Buy: The Moral Limits of Markets." *Tanner Lectures on Human Values* 21 (2000): 87–122.

Sartori, Giovanni. *Parties and Party Systems: A Framework for Analysis.* ECPR Press, 2005.

Savva, Niki. *The Road to Ruin: How Tony Abbott and Peta Credlin Destroyed Their Own Government.* Melbourne, Victoria: Scribe Publications 2016.

Saward, Michael. *The Representative Claim.* Oxford University Press, 2010.

Sawer, Marian. "Inventing the Nation through the Ballot Box." In *From Subjects to Citizens: A Hundred Years of Citizenship in Australia and Canada*: University of Ottawa Press, 2004.

Schaffer, Frederic Charles. "What Is Vote Buying? Empirical Evidence." *Vote Buying: Who, What, When and How* (2002).

Schemeil, Yves. "Democracy before Democracy?" *International Political Science Review* 21, no. 2 (2000): 99–120.

Schneier, Bruce. "The Problem with Electronic Voting Machines." In *Schneier on Security*, 2004.

Schwartzberg, Melissa. *Counting the Many: The Origins and Limits of Supermajority Rule.* Vol. 10. Cambridge: Cambridge University Press, 2013.

Sciarini, Pascal, Fabio Cappelletti, Andreas C Goldberg, and Simon Lanz. "The Underexplored Species: Selective Participation in Direct Democratic Votes." *Swiss Political Science Review* 22, no. 1 (2016): 75–94.

Shackle, George Lennox Sharman. "The Bounds of Unknowledge." In *Beyond Positive Economics*, edited by J Wiseman, 28–37. London: Macmillan, 1983.

———. *Epistemics and Economics.* Transaction Publishers, 1992.

Shankman, Paul. "Kent Flannery and Joyce Marcus, the Creation of Inequality: How Our Prehistoric Ancestors Set the Stage for Monarchy, Slavery, and Empire." *Asian Ethnology* 73 (2014): 293–96.

Shanton, Karen. "Most Recall Elections Are Politically Motivated." In *The Thicket at State Legislatures.* NCSL, 2013.

Shepsle, Kenneth A. "Institutional Arrangements and Equilibrium in Multidimensional Voting Models." *American Journal of Political Science* 23, no. 1 (1979): 27–59.

Shleifer, Andrei. *The Failure of Judges and the Rise of Regulators.* Cambridge, MA: MIT Press, 2012.

———. "Understanding Regulation." *European Financial Management* 11, no. 4 (2005): 439–51.

Shleifer, Andrei, and Robert W Vishny. "A Survey of Corporate Governance." *The Journal of Finance* 52, no. 2 (1997): 737–83.

Siegel, Zachary J. "Recall Me Maybe: The Corrosive Effect of Recall Elections on State Legislative Politics." *University of Colorado Law Review* 86 (2015): 307.

Simon, Herbert A. "Rationality as Process and as Product of Thought." *The American Economic Review* 68, no. 2 (1978): 1–16.

Sinclair, Robert K. *Democracy and Participation in Athens.* Cambridge University Press, 1991.

Snowdon, Christopher. "Sock Puppets: How the Government Lobbies Itself and Why." London, United Kingdom: Institute of Economic Affairs, 2012.

Statistics, Australian Bureau of. "Characteristics of Employment (Cat. No. 6333)." 2017.

———. "Employee Earnings, Benefits and Trade Union Membership Australia (Cat. No. 6310)." 2013.

———. "Trade Union Members in Australia (Cat. No. 6325)." 1996.

Statistics, Bureau of Labor. "Union Members—2017." News release, January 19, 2018, https://www.bls.gov/news.release/pdf/union2.pdf.

Stigler, George J. "The Theory of Economic Regulation." *The Bell Journal of Economics and Management Science* (1971): 3–21.

Stockemer, Daniel, and Patricia Calca. "Presidentialism and Voter Turnout in Legislative Elections." *Parliamentary Affairs* 67, no. 3 (2012): 561–83.

Stone, Peter. *The Luck of the Draw: The Role of Lotteries in Decision Making.* Oxford University Press, 2011.

Strine Jr., Leo E. "Can We Do Better by Ordinary Investors: A Pragmatic Reation to the Dueling Ideological Mythologists of Corporate Law." *Columbia Law Review* 114 (2014): 449.

Strøm, Kaare, Wolfgang Müller, Torbjörn Bergman, and Wolfgang C Müller. *Delegation and Accountability in Parliamentary Democracies.* Oxford University Press, 2003.

Stueckle, Sabine, and Dietmar Zinner. "To Follow or Not to Follow: Decision Making and Leadership During the Morning Departure in Chacma Baboons." *Animal Behaviour* 75, no. 6 (2008): 1995–2004.

Sueur, Cédric, and Jean-Louis Deneubourg. "Self-Organization in Primates: Understanding the Rules Underlying Collective Movements." *International Journal of Primatology* 32, no. 6 (2011): 1413–32.

Sunstein, Cass R. "Incommensurability and Valuation in Law." *Michigan Law Review* 92, no. 4 (1994): 779–861.

Swan, Melanie. *Blockchain: Blueprint for a New Economy.* O'Reilly Media, Inc., 2015.

Szabo, Nick. "The Idea of Smart Contracts." *Nick Szabo's Papers and Concise Tutorials* (1997).

Tavits, Margit. "Direct Presidential Elections and Turnout in Parliamentary Contests." *Political Research Quarterly* 62, no. 1 (2009): 42–54.

Thorley, John. *Athenian Democracy.* London: Routledge, 1996.

Thrasher, John. "The Ethics of Legislative Vote Trading." *Political Studies* 64, no. 3 (2016): 614–29.

Thrasher, John, and Gerald Gaus. "James Buchanan and Gordon Tullock, the Calculus of Consent." In *The Oxford Handbook of Classics in Contemporary Political Theory*, edited by Jacob T. Levy. Oxford University Press, 2015.

Tirole, Jean. "Cognition and Incomplete Contracts." *American Economic Review* 99, no. 1 (2009): 265–94.

Tobin, James. "On Limiting the Domain of Inequality." *The Journal of Law and Economics* 13, no. 2 (1970): 263–77.

"Trade Union Act 1984." UK, 1984.

Tridimas, George. "Constitutional Choice in Ancient Athens: The Rationality of Selection to Office by Lot." *Constitutional Political Economy* 23, no. 1 (2012): 1–21.

Trollope, Anthony. *An Autobiography. 1883.* Oxford University Press, 1999.

Troxler, Howard. *Electoral Abuse in the Late Roman Republic.* University of South Florida, 2008.

Tullock, Gordon. *Toward a Mathematics of Politics.* University of Michigan Press, 1967.

UnionD. "#Uniond." GitHub, https://github.com/btalabs/uniond.

Upchurch, Martin, and Rickard Grassman. "Striking with Social Media: The Contested (Online) Terrain of Workplace Conflict." *Organization* 23, no. 5 (2016): 639–56.

Vermeule, Adrian. "Open-Secret Voting." *Secrecy and Publicity in Votes and Debates* (2015): 215.

Visa. "Visa Acceptance for Retailers." https://usa.visa.com/run-your-business/small-business-tools/retail.html.

Wang, Xin, Libo Feng, Hui Zhang, Chan Lyu, Li Wang, and Yue You. "Human Resource Information Management Model Based on Blockchain Technology." Paper presented at the Service-Oriented System Engineering (SOSE), 2017 IEEE Symposium on, 2017.

Webb, Sidney, and Beatrice Webb. *The History of Trade Unionism.* Revised edition, extended to 1920 ed. Longmans, Green and Co., 1920.

Weil, David. *The Fissured Workplace: Why Work Became So Bad for So Many and What Can Be Done to Improve It.* Cambridge: Harvard University Press, 2017.

Weyl, Glen E. "The Robustness of Quadratic Voting." *Public Choice* 172, no. 1–2 (2017): 75–107.

Wicksell, Knut. "A New Principle of Just Taxation." In *Classics in the Theory of Public Finance*, 72–118. Springer, 1958.

Wieting Jr., Hardy Lee. "Philosophical Problems in Majority Rule and the Logrolling Solution." *Ethics* 76, no. 2 (1966): 85–101.

Williamson, Oliver E. *The Economic Institutions of Capitalism.* New York: Free Press, 1985.

———. "The Economics of Organization: The Transaction Cost Approach." *American Journal of Sociology* 87, no. 3 (1981): 548–77.

Wohlgemuth, Michael. "Democracy and Opinion Falsification: Towards a New Austrian Political Economy." *Constitutional Political Economy* 13, no. 3 (2002): 223–46.

Wooden, Mark. "Union Amalgamations and the Decline in Union Density." *Journal of Industrial Relations* 41, no. 1 (1999): 35–52.

Wright, Aaron, and Primavera De Filippi. *Blockchain and the Law: The Rule of Code.* Harvard University Press, 2018.

———. "Decentralized Blockchain Technology and the Rise of Lex Cryptographia." *Available at SSRN 2580664* (2015).

XII, Pope Leo. "Rerum Novarum." 1891.

Yermack, David. "Corporate Governance and Blockchains." *Review of Finance* 21, no. 1 (2017): 7–31.

———. "Shareholder Voting and Corporate Governance." *Annual Review of Financial Economics* 2, no. 1 (2010): 103–25.

Yoffee, Norman. *Myths of the Archaic State: Evolution of the Earliest Cities, States, and Civilizations.* Cambridge University Press, 2005.

Zuberbühler, Klaus, and Alban Lemasson. "Primate Communication: Meaning from Strings of Calls." In *Language and Recursion*, edited by Francis Lowenthal and Laurent Lefebvre, 115–25. New York: Springer, 2014.

Index

agency costs: delegation and, 41, 41–42, 59, 60; labor unions and, 112–113, 113, 115, 119, 121, 122, 122–123, 124, 125; in voting markets, 77–79

AI. *See* artificial intelligence

anti-commodifiable democracy, 75–76

Aristotle, 23

artificial intelligence (AI), 14

Assembly of the People, 22–23, 42

Athenian Constitution (Aristotle), 23

Athenian democracy, 22–24, 24, 31n17, 50; DIPF and, 41, 42–43

Athenian technology, 19

Athens: Assembly of the People in, 22–23, 42; collective choice in, 22–24; Council of the 500 in, 22, 23, 50; democracy in, 22–24, 24, 31n17; People's Court in, 22, 23; voting ballots in, 22–23, 24; voting in, 22–24

Australia, 37; labor unions in, 118, 119, 119–121; Royal Commission in, 119–121; voting ballots in, 26, 27. *See also* Westminster system

Australian Centre for Corporate Responsibility, 98–99

autocracy, 21

Babylonian creation story, 21

bargaining, 12–13; collective, 116, 117, 121; cryptodemocratic, 78–79, 83, 113

Beitz, Charles, 9–10

Bentham, Jeremy, 33n49

Bitcoin, 5, 6, 7

Bitcoin White Paper (Nakamoto), 5

Blanton, Richard, 20–21

blockchain: collective choice and, 29–30; corporate voting and, 103–105; cryptodemocracy and, 133–139; cryptodemocratic labor unions and, 114, 121–123; DIPF and, 38; electricity consumption for, 7; forking and, 127; as governance technology, 5–8; invention of, 2; limitations of, 7; property rights and, 77–78; record keeping in, 103; share register and, 103–105; voting and, 134; voting markets and, 77–79

boule. *See* Council of the 500

Brexit, 3

British Chartist movement, 27

brokerage firms, 101

Buchanan, James, 10, 72–73

Burke, Edmund, 4

byzantine fault tolerant, 6

campaign finance, 73

campaign promises, 73

Caplan, Bryan, 41

Carol, David, 3

cartel party thesis, 4–5

censorship, 6

chose-in-action, 91

Cicero, 25

Coase, Ronald, 8, 78–79, 95
Cockfield, Sandra, 124
coercion, 126–127; examples of, 118; in
    labor unions, 115–121
Cohen, Marty, 3
collective bargaining, 116, 117, 121
collective choice, 19; in Athens, 22–24;
    blockchain and, 29–30; in corporate
    governance, 89; costs in, 40–42; in
    cryptodemocracy, 71–72, 82–83, 83,
    133–137, 138–139; decision-making
    and, 20, 20–21, 29; DIPF and, 38–45;
    economics and, 29–30; information
    technology of democracy and, 27–30;
    language and, 20; localized
    coordination rules and, 20; political
    organisation and, 20–21; in populism,
    44–45; pre-democratic collective
    organisation and, 20–21; QV and,
    80–81; voices, voting ballots, and,
    24–27; in voting markets, 71–72;
    voting rights and, 38–39, 49. *See also*
    cryptodemocratic labor unions
communication technology, 53, 124–125
community, of digital citizens, 64–65
constituency, 50, 50–55
conventional cryptoeconomics, 8
corporate cryptodemocracy, 13–14,
    104–106, 136
corporate governance: collective choice in,
    89; corporate cryptodemocratic
    governance, 106, 136; decision costs in,
    92, 98; decision-making and, 92–93; in
    joint-stock companies, 90–91;
    legislation on, 90–91; in limited
    liability, 90–91; in public companies,
    91; stock exchange and, 91
corporate responsibility, 98–99
corporate share register, 101, 103–105
corporate vote buying, 99–100
corporate voting, 89–90; blockchain and,
    103–105; empty voting, 104; greenmail
    and, 100; law and, 90–92, 101;
    pathologies of, 100–105; shareholder
    voting and, 13, 89, 90–93, 106; share
    register and, 101, 103–105; share
    settlement and, 13, 101–103, 104–105,
    106

corporate voting markets, 93; corporate
    vote buying and, 99–100; proxy
    advisors as, 94–95; proxy voting as,
    95–98; shareholder organizations as,
    98–99
Corrupt Practices Act (1883), 27
costs: in collective choice, 40–42;
    delegation and, 59, 60–61; quadratic
    pricing rule and, 80, 81; in voting
    markets, 77–79. *See also* agency costs;
    decision costs
Council of the 500 (*boule*), 22, 23, 50
counterfeiting, 6
cryptocurrency: Bitcoin, 5, 6, 7;
    counterfeiting of, 6; development of,
    5–6; Ethereum, 6, 7; knowledge
    incentivized by, 135–136;
    representation in, 50
cryptodemocracy: analytic structure and
    approach to, 11–14; blockchain and,
    133–139; collective choice in, 71–72,
    82–83, 83, 133–137, 138–139;
    corporate, 13–14, 104–106, 136;
    decision-making in, 71–72; defining,
    1–2; delegation in, 49, 58–66, 59, 137;
    democratic nature of, 8–11; framework,
    10–11, 133–136; future of, 14, 83–84,
    85; predicting exchange in, 85; QV
    compared to, 80, 81–84; representative
    democracy compared to, 58–59, 59;
    structure of, 2, 82–84; voter preferences
    in, 83–84; voting in, 1–2, 12, 45–46;
    voting rights in, 83–84; Westminster
    system compared to, 58–59, 59; *See
    also specific topics*
cryptodemocratic bargaining, 78–79, 83,
    113
cryptodemocratic labor unions, 14,
    111–112, 136; blockchain and, 114,
    121–123; forking in, 127; labor union
    membership, 119, 121, 122, 127;
    legislation on, 126; smart contracts and,
    122–123; *UnionD*, 126; workers on
    demand and, 124; working toward,
    123–127
cryptoeconomics, 8

Dahl, Robert, 37

DAOs. *See* distributed autonomous organisations
DApps. *See* distributed applications
Darwinian natural selection, 20
decentralized ledger, 7
decentralized voting, 103–104, 105
decision costs: in corporate governance, 92, 98; DIPF and, 40–42, 41, 60; drivers, 40–41; labor unions and, 112–115, 113, 116, 117, 119, 121, 124
decision-making: collective choice and, 20, 20–21, 29; corporate governance and, 92–93; in cryptodemocracy, 71–72; delegation and, 36–37; in labor unions, 118–119; in representative democracy, 44
decision rules, supermajority, 70
delegation: agency costs and, 41, 41–42, 59, 60; community and, 64–65; costs and, 59, 60–61; in cryptodemocracy, 49, 58–66, 59, 137; decision-making and, 36–37; DIPF and, 41, 41–45; governance and, 36–38; group votes and, 50–55; law and, 36–37, 46n3; political engagement and, 60–61; in representative democracy, 50–51; in voting markets, 70–72, 74; voting rights and, 36
delegative democracy: contract terms, 62–63; governance in, 63–64; idea of, 55–58; parliament in, 63–64; political instability in, 63; representation in, 55–56, 58–59, 59; technology and, 56–57; voting in, 58–59, 59, 61–65; Westminster system compared to, 63–64
democracy: as anti-commodifiable, 75–76; defining, 9; discovering, 136–138; information technology of, 27–30; majority rule in, 10; political equality and, 9–10; procedural account of, 36–38; *See also specific topics*
democratic catallaxy, 2
democratic crisis, 3
democratic features, 8–9
democratic governance, 12
Democratic Institutional Possibility Frontier (DIPF), 12, 35–36, 133, 136; Athenian democracy and, 41, 42–43;

blockchain and, 38; collective choice and, 38–45; decision costs and, 40–42, 41, 60; delegation and, 41, 41–45; labor, 113, 114, 121, 124; Swiss democracy and, 41, 43; Westminster system and, 41, 42, 43–44
democratic participation, 71
democratic theory, 8–9
Dent, George, 94
Diamond, Wayne J., 125
dictatorship costs, 39–40
digital citizens, 64
DIPF. *See* Democratic Institutional Possibility Frontier
direct-recording electronic (DRE) voting machines, 29
distributed applications (DApps), 7
distributed autonomous organisations (DAOs), 7
document-based systems, 28
Dodgson, Charles, 55–56
Downs, Anthony, 4
DRE voting machines. *See* direct-recording electronic voting machines

Easterbrook, Frank, 92
economics: collective choice and, 29–30; cryptoeconomics, 8; IPF and, 39–40; voting markets and, 73–74
Edison, Thomas, 28–29, 29
efficiency arguments, on vote buying, 75
electricity consumption, 7
electronic voting machines, 28–29
Elgie, Robert, 51
empty voting, 104
England, 27, 90; parliaments of, 24, 51
Epstein, Richard, 76
equality: political, 9–10; voting markets and, 70, 74, 75
Ethereum, 6, 7
Exit, Voice, and Loyalty (Hirschman), 115

factionalism, 52
Fargher, Lane, 20–21
Federalists, 52
Fisch, Jill, 96–97
Fischel, Daniel, 92
Fleming, Daniel, 21
forgery, 19

forking, 127
Freeman, Richard B., 115–117, 125

game-theoretic economic incentives, 5
Geis, George, 101, 103
gerrymandering, 53
Glass Lewis (GL), 95, 97
governance: delegation and, 36–38; in
    delegative democracy, 63–64; IPF and,
    39–40; labor rights and, 112–113; labor
    unions and, 119–121; legislation and,
    36–37, 46n3; technology, 5–8; voting
    and, 134; Westminster system of, 35,
    36, 38, 42. *See also* corporate
    governance
Green-Armytage, James, 57
greenmail, 100
group votes, 50–55

Hamilton, Alexander, 52
Hansen, Richard, 89
Hawke, Bob, 118
Hayek, Friedrich, 2, 8, 71, 84, 117–118,
    135
Herbert Smith Freehills, 122
Hirschman, Albert, 115
Hirst, John, 33n48, 33n49
Hogarth, William, 25
Hollerith, Herman, 28
human institutions, 40
The Humours of an Election (Hogarth), 25

ICCR. *See* Interfaith Center on Corporate
    Responsibility
Iceland, 44
ICT. *See* Information and Communication
    Technologies
inalienability arguments, on vote buying,
    75–76
India, 24–25, 44
inequality, 70, 74, 75
Information and Communication
    Technologies (ICT), 123–124
information technology, 27–30
institutional choice, 12
institutional cryptoeconomics, 8
Institutional Possibilities Frontier (IPF),
    39–40

Institutional Shareholder Services (ISS),
    95, 97
Interfaith Center on Corporate
    Responsibility (ICCR), 98
IPF. *See* Institutional Possibilities Frontier
ISS. *See* Institutional Shareholder Services

joint-stock companies, 90–91
Jones, Douglas, 27

Kam, Christopher, 27
Karlan, Pamela, 75–76
kleroterion, 19, 23–24, 29
knowledge, incentivized by
    cryptodemocracy, 135–136

labor: contracts, 112–114; DIPF, 113, 114,
    121, 124; as property rights, 112–115;
    rights, 112–113
labor unions: agency costs and, 112–113,
    113, 115, 119, 121, 122, 122–123, 124,
    125; in Australia, 118, 119, 119–121;
    collective bargaining and, 116, 117,
    121; decision costs and, 112–115, 113,
    116, 117, 119, 121, 124; decision-
    making in, 118–119; governance and,
    119–121; labor, as property right,
    112–115; membership to, 119, 121,
    122, 127; monopoly, voice, and
    coercion in, 115–121; wage-fixing by,
    114–115, 118. *See also*
    cryptodemocratic labor unions
language, 6–7, 20
law: on corporate vote buying, 99;
    corporate voting and, 90–92, 101; on
    corporate voting and share register,
    101; delegation and, 36–37, 46n3; on
    proxy voting, 95–98
legislation: on corporate governance,
    90–91; on cryptodemocratic labor
    unions, 126; governance and, 36–37,
    46n3
limited liability, 90–91
localized coordination rules, 20
The Logic of Collective Action (Olson),
    117
logrolling, 73

majority rule, 10

Mari, Syria, 21
Marx, Karl, 31n8
median voter model, 54–55
Medoff, James L., 115–117
Mesopotamia, 21
migration, 20
Mill, John Stuart, 25
Miller, James C., III, 56
miners, of Bitcoin, 5, 6
minorities, 70
monitory democracy, 61
monopoly, 115–121
Müller, Jan-Werner, 3
Muller, Julian, 83
Muste, A.J., 115–116
mythology, 21

Nakamoto, Satoshi, 5
natural selection, 20
New Zealand, 30
Noel, Hans, 3
non-document-based systems, 28
North, Douglass, 8

Olson, Mancur, 116, 117
one-person, one-vote (1p1v) rule, 10, 13, 81
Ostrom, Elinor, 8

parliament, 24, 51, 63–64
The Party Decides (Cohen, Carol, Noel, and Zaller), 3
PCT. *See* Political Coase Theorem
People's Charter, 1838, 27
People's Court, 22, 23
perpetual succession, 90
Piazza, Fiammetta, 104
Pinker, Stephen, 20
Plott, Charles R., 5
Plutarch, 25
Political Coase Theorem (PCT), 88n45
political engagement, 60–61
political equality, 9–10
political instability, 63
political organization, 20–24
political parties: party structure, 3, 4; Republican Party, 3; spatial models of, 4; technology and, 5
populism, 3–4, 44–45

pre-democratic technology, 19, 20–21
pre-modern political organization, 20–24
Principles of Parliamentary Representation (Dodgson), 55–56
printing, 19, 26, 33n54
property rights: blockchain and, 77–78; labor as, 112–115; transfer of, 58, 60; voting as, 35, 38–39, 50, 133–134
proportional representation, 55–56
proxy advisors, 94–95, 103, 104
proxy contest, 97–98
proxy voting, 95–98
public companies, 91
public key cryptography, 5
punch cards, 28

quadratic pricing rule, 80, 81
quadratic voting (QV), 69–70; collective choice and, 80–81; cryptodemocracy compared to, 80, 81–84; drawbacks of, 81; voter preferences and, 80–81, 82; voting markets and, 79–82

random constituencies, 52–55
rational irrationality, 41
record keeping, 103
Rehfeld, Andrew, 44, 50, 52–54, 64
representation: in cryptocurrency, 50; in delegative democracy, 55–56, 58–59, 59; proportional, 55–56
representative claims, 50
representative democracy: cryptodemocracy compared to, 58–59, 59; decision-making in, 44; delegation in, 50–51; voting in, 1, 30
Republican Party, 3
Rogers, Joel, 125
Royal Commission, Australia, 119–121

Sandel, Michael, 76
Sartori, Giovanni, 4
Schemeil, Yves, 21
Schneier, Bruce, 29
scripting languages, 6–7
secret ballots, 25–27, 27, 27–28, 33n49
security, of DRE voting, 29
shareholder organizations, 98–99
shareholder primacy, 91
shareholder solicitation, 97–98

shareholder voting, 13, 89; rights, 90–93, 106. *See also* corporate voting
share register, 101, 103–105
share settlement, 13, 101–103, 104–105, 106
sharing economy, 121
Shleifer, Andrei, 39–40
Simon, Herbert, 40
smart contracts, 6–7, 12, 78, 122–123
social choice, 2–5
social media, 124–125
Socrates, 32n25
sortition, 22, 23, 32n25
spatial models, 4
standing proxy, 96–97
stock exchange, 91, 104. *See also* corporate governance
supermajority decision rules, 70
Swiss democracy: DIPF and, 41, 43; voting in, 43, 61–62

Tasmania, 30
technology: Athenian, 19; collective choice and, 19; communication, 53, 124–125; delegative democracy and, 56–57; governance, 5–8; information, 27–30; political parties and, 5; pre-democratic, 19, 20–21
territorial voting, 50
Thatcher, Margaret, 118
Toqueville, Alexis de, 43
transfer of property rights, 58, 60
transparency, 104
Trollope, Anthony, 25
Trump, Donald, 3
tyranny of majority, 70

UnionD, 126
unionism. *See* cryptodemocratic labor unions
United Kingdom, 3, 118, 122, 124. *See also* England

Victoria, Australia, 26, 27
voice: cryptodemocratic bargaining and, 116; monopoly, labor unions, and, 115–121; voting ballots and, 24–27
vote buying and selling, 87n36; arguments against, 75–76; corporate vote buying,

99–100; efficiency arguments on, 75; inalienability arguments on, 75–76; introduction to, 69–70; tyranny of majority relating to, 70; voting markets for, 70–76
voter intimidation, 25, 26–27
voter preferences, 77, 85n1; in cryptodemocracy, 83–84; QV and, 80–81, 82
voter registration, 27
voter restrictions, 76, 84
voting: 1p1v rule, 10, 13; in Athens, 22–24; blockchain and, 134; communication technology and, 53; in cryptodemocracy, 1–2, 12, 45–46; decentralized, 103–104, 105; in delegative democracy, 58–59, 59, 61–65; governance and, 134; group votes, 50–55; median voter model of, 54–55; political equality and, 10; as property rights, 35, 38–39, 50, 133–134; in representative democracy, 1, 30; in Swiss democracy, 43, 61–62; systems of, 9–10; territorial, 50; in Westminster system, 43. *See also* corporate voting; delegation; quadratic voting
voting ballots: in Athens, 22–23, 24; in Australia, 26, 27; in English parliaments, 24; printing and, 26, 33n54; secret ballots, 25–27, 27, 33n49, 77; voice and, 24–27
voting contracts, 76–79
voting machines: document-based systems, 28; DRE, 29; electronic, 28–29; engineering requirements for, 27; information technology and, 27–29; *kleroterion*, 19, 23–24, 29; non-document-based systems, 28; punch cards, 28
voting markets, 13; agency costs in, 77–79; blockchain and, 77–79; campaign finance in, 73; campaign promises and, 73; collective choice in, 71–72; corporate, 93–100; costs in, 77–79; delegation in, 70–72, 74; democratic participation and, 71; economics and, 73–74; equality, inequality, and, 70, 74, 75; logrolling in, 73; minorities and, 70;

objections to, 74–76; QV and, 79–82; secret ballots in, 77; supermajority decision rules in, 70; for vote buying and selling, 70–76; voter restrictions and, 76; voting contract enforcement in, 76–79

voting rights: collective choice and, 38–39, 49; in cryptodemocracy, 83–84; delegation and, 36; shareholder, 90–93

Votomatic, 28

wage-fixing, 114–115, 118

Wall Street (film), 100

Wall Street rule, 94

Westminster system, 35, 36, 38; cryptodemocracy compared to, 58–59, 59; delegative democracy compared to, 63–64; DIPF and, 41, 42, 43–44; voting in, 43

Wicksell, Knut, 10

Williamson, Oliver, 8

workers on demand, 124

Yermack, David, 98, 103, 105

Zaller, John, 3

·

About the Authors

Darcy W.E. Allen is an institutional economist and writer focusing on the economics of new technologies. Dr. Allen is a Postdoctoral Research Fellow at the RMIT Blockchain Innovation Hub, an Adjunct Fellow with the Institute of Public Affairs, and an Academic Fellow with the Australian Taxpayers' Alliance. His research focuses on the economics and political economy of blockchain technology as a form of new economic infrastructure. Dr. Allen's scholarly contributions have appeared in a wide range of journals and books including the *Review of Austrian Economics, International Journal of the Commons*, and the *Journal of Public Finance and Public Choice*. Dr. Allen is a regular media commentator, sits on several editorial boards, and is the editor of *Australia's Red Tape Crisis: The Causes and Costs of Over-Regulation*. His PhD dissertation in economics was passed outright at RMIT University in 2017 and won the university-wide prize for research excellence.

Chris Berg is an economist and historian of technological change and institutional choice. He is a Senior Research Fellow at the RMIT Blockchain Innovation Hub, a Founding Board Member of the Worldwide Blockchain Innovation Association, a Senior Fellow with the Institute of Public Affairs, and an Academic Fellow with the Australian Taxpayers' Alliance. Dr. Berg is the author of seven books. His most recent is *The Classical Liberal Case for Privacy in a World of Surveillance and Technological Change* (Palgrave Macmillan, 2018). He holds a PhD in economics from RMIT University, which was awarded in 2017, and a bachelor's degree in history and political science from the University of Melbourne. His scholarly contributions on areas such as Australian history, economic methodology, regulation, and technological change civil liberties have appeared in journals such as *Austra-*

lian Journal of Political Science, Econ Journal Watch, History of Economics Review, Ledger, and *Trends in Anaesthesia and Critical Care.*

Aaron M. Lane is a Lecturer with RMIT University's Graduate School of Business and Law, an affiliated researcher at the RMIT Blockchain Innovation Hub, and an Adjunct Legal Fellow with the Institute of Public Affairs. He holds bachelor's degrees in commerce and law from Deakin University, a Graduate Diploma in Legal Practice from the College of Law, and a Graduate Diploma and Master of Arts from the University of Divinity—graduating as Vice-Chancellor's Scholar. Aaron's research sits at the intersection of innovation and regulation. His scholarly research has been published in a selection of academic journals and edited volumes and has been presented at international conferences. Aaron's public policy work has seen him give evidence before parliamentary inquires in Australia and assist in compiling a brief Amicus Curiae in the Supreme Court of the United States. Aaron was admitted as an Australian Lawyer in the Supreme Court of Victoria in 2012.

www.ingramcontent.com/pod-product-compliance
Lightning Source LLC
Chambersburg PA
CBHW050608280326
41932CB00016B/2963